OUT OF TIME

The Pleasures and the
Perils of Ageing

OUT OF
TIME

LYNNE SEGAL

With an Introduction by Elaine Showalter

VERSO
London • New York

First published by Verso 2013
© Lynne Segal 2013
Introduction © Elaine Showalter 2013

All rights reserved

The moral rights of the authors have been asserted

1 3 5 7 9 10 8 6 4 2

Verso
UK: 6 Meard Street, London W1F 0EG
US: 20 Jay Street, Suite 1010, Brooklyn, NY 11201
www.versobooks.com

Verso is the imprint of New Left Books

ISBN-13: 978-1-78168-139-8

British Library Cataloguing in Publication Data
A catalogue record for this book is available from the British Library

Library of Congress Cataloging-in-Publication Data

Segal, Lynne.
 Out of time : the pleasures and perils of ageing / Lynne Segal ; with an
introduction by Elaine Showalter.
    pages cm
Includes index.
 ISBN 978-1-78168-139-8 (hardback)
1. Old age. 2. Aging. 3. Intergenerational relations. I. Title.
HQ1061.S418 2013
305.26 – dc23
                          2013019104

Typeset in Fournier by MJ & N Gavan, Truro, Cornwall
Printed and bound by CPI Group (UK) Ltd, Croydon, CR0 4YY

For Agnes, Éamonn and Zim

Contents

Acknowledgements

Since this book is about affirming life, whatever our age, acknowledging the necessity and significance of the love, friendship and support of those around me is part of its purpose. I am grateful to Verso for publishing my reflections on old age, when I feared that my topic might frighten everyone away. In particular I have benefited from the editing skills of Leo Hollis, determined to keep the writing as precise and succinct as possible, as well as from the wise advice of my own personal editor and friend, Sarah Benton. I am also thankful for the support of my agent, Rachel Calder, for stepping in just when I needed her. Above all, I want to express my love and gratitude to all those who have given me confidence or in other ways assisted me in my writing. One way and another, up close or from a distance, these include Agnes Bolsø, Éamonn McKeown, João Manuel de Oliveira, Stine Svensen, Mirjam Hadar Meerschwam, Ross Poole, Paddy Maynes, Kjetil Berge, Nick Davidson, Mandy Merck, Catherine Hall, Stuart Hall, Judith Butler, Wendy Brown, Nel Druce, Bill Schwarz, Cora Caplan, Sally Alexander, Barbara Taylor, Stephen Frosh, Peter Osborne, Lisa Baraitser, Wencke Muhleisen, Mehmet Ali Dikerdem, Leonore Tiefer, Sheila Rowbotham, Maria Aristedemou, Amber Jacobs,

Mustafa Gur, Daniel Monk, Matt Cook, Uri Hadar and Misha Hadar, Marina Warner, Mark Martin, and Zimri, Graeme and Barbara Segal.

Introduction
by Elaine Showalter

It's not easy to come out as an old person, especially as an old woman. While the coming-out process is usually seen as the public acknowledgment of an attribute that might otherwise stay invisible, such as being gay, and promises acceptance into a welcoming community, identifying yourself as old is to admit something everyone can see, and is thus somehow more shaming, carrying more of a stigma. We're supposed to deny being old; it is seen as an insulting, or at least unwelcome, self-description, unless jocular and well padded with euphemisms: senior citizen, oldie. Ageing is a process, a matter of degree rather than a fixed identity.

Like being fat, being old also has its own kind of secret closet. The late literary critic and gay theorist Eve Sedgwick gave a famous conference talk in which she came out as fat, and described her fat dream of entering a closet full of luscious clothes, all in her size, and then seeing that their label was a pink triangle. Old people have age dreams as well. In her study *La Vieillesse* (*The Coming of Age*, 1970), written when she was only fifty-four, Simone de Beauvoir confessed that 'often in my sleep I dream that I'm fifty-four, I awake, and find I'm only thirty. "What a terrible nightmare I had," says the woman who thinks she's awake.' 'In a dream you are never eighty,' wrote Anne Sexton.

Beauvoir quickly discovered that old age was a forbidden subject. 'What a furious outcry I raised when I offended against this taboo ... great numbers of people, particularly old people, told me kindly or angrily, but always at great length ... that old age simply does not exist.' There are a hundred ways to deny, defy, or avoid the fact of ageing, from strenuous exercise and cosmetic surgery to relentless workaholism and maniacal activity. For some, there's the philosophy of agelessness, which Catherine Mayer calls 'amortality' or 'living agelessly'. Recent polls find that most adults over fifty feel at least ten years younger, while those over sixty-five feel twenty years younger. 'How can a seventeen-year-old like me suddenly be eighty-one?' the scientist Lewis Wolpert asks ruefully in his book *You're Looking Very Well*.

Since the second wave of the women's movement began in the late 1960s and 1970s, feminists have re-examined the myths and stereotypes, the stigmas and truisms of every phase of the life cycle. Our generation did not grow up with feminism, but came to it when we were already in our twenties and thirties, and our first bulletins were about issues facing young women – menstruation, sexuality, the body, lifestyles. Germaine Greer famously challenged the ancient taboo about menstruation by asking women if they had tasted their own menstrual blood. If not, baby, she taunted, you haven't come a very long way. Kate Millett raised consciousness about the sexual politics of literature and life. The poet Adrienne Rich placed motherhood, with all its ambivalence and conflict, in a feminist context. Books about maternity and infants were followed by books about parenting teenagers, then about living with empty nests. Books about marriage were followed by books about divorce, changes in sexual identity, or living alone. Many of our icons died young, and did not or would not face the problem of time. Sylvia Plath died at thirty, Anne Sexton at forty-six, Angela Carter at fifty-two. As a young woman in 1972, Susan Sontag maintained that 'growing old is mainly an ordeal of the imagination'.

But those who lived longer moved on to darker subjects. There were feminist studies of the experience of menopause; and, inexorably, memoirs of caretaking, loss, and death. The feminist bookshelf has expanded to hold books on feminists getting older by Betty Friedan, Gloria Steinem, Germaine Greer, Carolyn Heilbrun, Jane Miller, May Sarton, and Irma Kurtz; poems of mourning in old age by Elaine Feinstein and Ruth Fainlight; grief and widowhood memoirs by Joan Didion and Joyce Carol Oates. We even have records and meditations on feminism and dying from Eve Sedgwick and Ruth Picardie; rages against the night from Susan Sontag; and graceful good-byes from Wendy Wasserstein and Nora Ephron.

Lynne Segal has lived through every phase, literary and political, of the women's movement as an activist, a scholar, a teacher, and a writer. In 2007, in her autobiography *Making Trouble* (2007), Segal described herself as 'a reluctantly ageing woman', and mused about the need for 'a feminist sexual politics of ageing'. But the timing was wrong. She was cautioned by some of her friends 'to avoid thinking, let alone writing, of my generation ... as "old." ' Now in *Out of Time*, she has written the big book we have been waiting for on the psychology and politics of ageing, for both women and men. The subjects that used to be unmentionable are now urgent and essential to discuss, and 'we can be fairly certain that old taboos are already collapsing, often indeed that the floodgates are opening.' In Segal's philosophical take on old age, 'the self never ages', although the body changes and the culture evolves. Ageing is also timeless, 'not simply linear, nor ... any simple discrete process when, in our minds we race around, moving seamlessly between childhood, old age, and back again.' What really matters, she argues, is 'neither the sociology nor the biology of ageing', but the narrative of the self, 'the stories we tell ourselves' of how to '*be* our age as we age'. Ultimately, as we age, the central question is still 'How are we to live our lives?'

Segal brings to her book a lifetime of personal, intellectual, and political experience of the changing roles of men and women. An Australian by birth, she received her Ph.D. in psychology at the University of Sydney in the late '60s at the height of the radical arts movement called 'The Push'. When she came to London in 1970, Segal immediately became involved in leftwing politics in Islington, and helped set up the Islington Women's Centre. Living in a communal household, raising a child along with other mothers and children, she experienced the feminist axiom that 'the personal is political'. During that decade of idealistic and exhilarating action, she now observes, what was most needed was 'courage – at times little more than bravado'. In 1979, along with Sheila Rowbotham and Hilary Wainwright, Segal wrote *Beyond the Fragments*, calling for alliances between leftwing groups, feminists, and trade unions.

Indeed, Segal's work has continued to advocate inclusion, negotiation, and alliances, rather than separation and rigid ideological boundaries between the sexes, the classes, or the generations. From the beginning she has courageously questioned easy assumptions or sloganeering stereotypes of gender, whether of violent men or benign motherly women, and has emphasized the possibilities for change and progress in domestic and political life. In 1984, she joined the Advisory Board of Virago Press, and wrote her first speculative book, *Is the Future Female? Troubled Thoughts on Contemporary Feminism* (1987), questioning the myths of female superiority then being offered in feminist circles. In 1990, she followed up with *Slow Motion: Changing Masculinities, Changing Men*. In *Making Trouble*, Segal recalls how the 'newly born feminist', despite her bravado, was 'frequently unsure and insecure', while 'men were entangled with feminism from the start'. Within feminism, as well as between women and men, there were skirmishes over housework, childcare, monogamy, sexual freedom, sexual orientation. The newly born feminists of the 1970s lived through love affairs, long-term relationships that ended painfully, the stresses of parenting, alongside bruising encounters with the enormous difficulties of effecting political change.

In her position as professor of psychology and gender studies at Birkbeck College, Segal examined the changing and complex roles of both women and men, emphasizing always the 'contradictions at the heart of desire', whether in pornography or the social experiments of collective living. In *Out of Time*, although she writes from a socialist–feminist position, she never writes only about socialism or about women, but about the range of lifestyles and commitments that have informed the contemporary experience of aging. There are as many stories about men in the book – including Jacques Derrida, John Updike, Philip Roth, and John Berger – as there are about women. But consistently Segal looks at ageing with the vision derived from her politics, her feminism, her personal life, her lifelong love of literature and art, and her sense of humour. In her professional role, she turns also to psychoanalysis to find 'possibilities for affirming old age'. Freud had little to say about the unconscious in old age. Dreading age himself, he bleakly declared that people over fifty were poor candidates for psychoanalysis – 'old people are no longer educable'. But, Segal inquires, could we interpret the terrifying Freudian images of the uncanny, the double haunting us in the mirror, as protective and comforting rather than threatening? Are there transitional objects for ageing as well as for childhood?

The old are both outside of time and running out of time, seeking meaning through eternal categories of anger, activism, attachment, and art. Segal begins with the contemporary increase in anger between generations, as the young are encouraged to resent the old for monopolizing increasingly scarce resources. Neil Boorman catches the contemporary mood in *It's All Their Fault*: the Baby Boomers were responsible for driving younger generations into unemployment and debt. Second-wave feminists have long experienced generation-bashing from younger women, and 'mother-blaming' from their feminist daughters, as well as having to endure the culture's mythology, which has always demonized old women as hags, crones, or witches.

But rather than hitting back with anger, bitterness, and condemnation, Segal recommends protesting against ageism, in the model of such pioneers of Age Studies as Margaret Morganroth Gullette, Kathleen Woodward, Anne Wyatt-Brown, Barbara Frey Waxman, Sylvia Hennenberg, and Cynthia Rich, the estranged younger sister of poet Adrienne Rich (who knew?). While the popular image of political commitment among the old is a move to the right, many people 'sustain their radical outlook to the very end', continuing to campaign for peace, women's liberation, socialism, and progressive change, and finding that politics still gives 'meaning to their lives'. Despite disappointment in the slowness of change, Grace Paley, Rosalind Baxandall, and Adrienne Rich, among many others, speak for the enduring satisfactions of continued activism. In his late seventies, Trevor Huddleston affirmed his ongoing dedication to anti-Apartheid and anti-racism: 'I've become more revolutionary every year I've lived.' For Segal, continuing to affirm the moral and political beliefs of our lifetimes keeps us attached to the world, along with our attachments to old friends, grandchildren, and new relationships. Old age is a time, Segal suggest, to acknowledge 'the value of our lifelong mutual dependence', as well as to defend our independence.

Above all, Segal values art and takes comfort in the flaming, exuberant creativity of Paula Rego, Louise Bourgeois, Yayoi Kusama, Lucian Freud, Barbara Hepworth, Frank Auerbach, and David Hockney. She directs our attention to the work of writers and poets who have told the stories of age, including May Sarton, 'America's poet laureate of ageing', who explained, 'We have to make myths out of our lives in order to sustain them and I think this partly how one handles the monster.' For Sarton, age was 'magnificent', but the point is not cheerfulness and consolation, but a fearless confrontation with the fearful ageing self, in writers as varied as Martin Amis and Penelope Lively, Roland Barthes and Doris Lessing. Segal scrutinizes at the relationship between grief and memoir, in which the book becomes a 'form of public mourning', an act of writing and performance which is itself a 'guide to survival', at the same time that it hints at the perverse glamour of bereavement and tragedy, 'with its vividness and intensity compared to normal life'.

As Angela Carter observed, 'Comedy is tragedy that happens to other people.' Finally, Segal's meditations on grief, loneliness, and loss are balanced by her understanding that attitude and humour are the strongest weapons in the armaments of ageing. Laughter, rather than another documentary on Alzheimer's or a nice night out to see Michael Haneke's film *Amour*, is among the truest pleasures and consolations of ageing. Segal wisely includes comic writers and performers in her pantheon of the artists of age – Virginia Ironside and her granny lit; Jo Brand's brilliant TV series *Getting On*, set in an NHS geriatric ward, where one newly discharged old lady tells the doctor she is off for a well-earned holiday to Zurich; and the searing black comedy of Philip Roth.

It's about time for a book like *Out of Time*, compassionate, seasoned, honest, and wise, which asks questions about age but aims to enlighten, rather than frighten us. Read on!

1

How Old Am I?

How old am I? Don't ask; don't tell. The question frightens me. It is maddening, all the more so for those like me, feminists on the left, approaching our sixth or seventh decade, who like to feel we have spent much of our time trying to combat prejudices on all sides. Yet fears of revealing our age when the years start to race by, speeding up as they mount, are hard to smother. Why write about ageing, when this troubling topic is so daunting, so complicated? My very hesitation, of course, tells me just how much needs to change before we can start to face up to the fearful disparagement of old age, including our own prejudices. I have to keep at bay so much anxiety around the subject, all that I project onto putative readers, my own abiding ambivalence.

It is when we are young that we are most obviously busy with the project of trying to construct a self we hope the world will appreciate, monitoring and re-arranging the impressions we make upon others. Yet as we age, most of us are still trying to hold on to some sense of who and what we are, however hard this may become for those who start to feel increasingly invisible. Everywhere I look nowadays I see older people busily engaged with the world and eager, just as I am, to relate to others, while also struggling to shore up favoured ways of seeing ourselves. However, the world in general is rarely sympathetic to these attempts, as though the time had come, or were long overdue, for the elderly to withdraw altogether from worrying about how they appear to others. In my view, such a time never comes, which means finding much better ways of affirming old age than those currently available.

The need to think again, to think more imaginatively, about ageing should be obvious once we confront the rapid increase in life expectancy around the globe. Despite deep disparities locally and globally, ever more people are living into old age, often very old age. In Britain, ten million people are currently over sixty-five years old, around a sixth of the population, with that number likely to double over the next few decades.[1] The figures in the USA are equally arresting, where around forty million people are currently over sixty-five, some 13 per cent of the total population, with that number also predicted to double by 2030, accounting for nearly twenty per cent of the population.[2] Yet this greying of society has not only been largely either disregarded or deplored, it has also amplified rather than diminished social antipathy towards the elderly. Tellingly, in his parting statement to the British House of Lords as Archbishop of Canterbury at the close of 2012, Rowan Williams suggested that negative stereotypes of the ageing population are fostering attitudes of contempt and leaving them vulnerable to verbal and physical abuse.[3] There is thus aversion towards the very topic of ageing, although this is just one of the issues I will be struggling to change in tackling the varied and often paradoxical issues of old age.

Ageing encompasses so much, and yet most people's thoughts about it embrace so little. Against the dominant fixation, for instance, this book is not primarily about ageing bodies, with their rising demands, frequent embarrassments, and endless diversities – except that of course our bodies are there, in every move we make, or sometimes fail to complete. It will have little to say, either, about the corrosions of dementia, although it does look at the surprisingly interesting thoughts of some of those who have cared for, or continue to tend, loved ones affected by cognitive deterioration. It is telling nowadays how often those who address the topic of ageing alight on dementia – often, paradoxically, in criticism of others who simply equate ageing with decline, while doing just this themselves. For the faint-hearted, I need to point out that although the incidence of dementia will indeed accelerate in the age group now headed towards their nineties, even amongst the very oldest it will not predominate – though this information hardly eliminates our fear of such indisputable decline.[4]

Conversely, this book is not, or not in quite the usual way, an exploration of those many narratives of resilience, which suggest that with care of the self, diligent monitoring, and attention to spiritual concerns we can postpone ageing itself, at least until those final moments of very old age. On this view, we can stay healthy, fit and 'young' – or youngish – performing our yoga, practising Pilates, eating our greens, avoiding hazards and spurning envy and resentment. It is true, we may indeed remain healthy, but we will not stay young. 'You are only as old as you feel', though routinely offered as a jolly form of reassurance, carries its own disavowal of old age.

Ageing faces, ageing bodies, as we should know, are endlessly diverse. Many of them are beautifully expressive, once we choose to look – those eyes rarely lose their lustre, when engrossed. However, in this book I plan to skim lightly over both the many depredations of the flesh as well as its potential renewals, to look more closely at the psychology and politics of ageing. I am primarily concerned with the possibilities for and impediments to staying alive to life itself, whatever our age. This takes me first of all to the temporal paradoxes of ageing, and to the enduring ways of remaining open and attached to the world.

As we age, changing year on year, we also retain, in one manifestation or another, traces of all the selves we have been, creating a type of temporal vertigo and rendering us psychically, in one sense, all ages and no age. 'All ages and no age' is an expression once used by the psychoanalyst Donald Winnicott to describe the wayward temporality of psychic life, writing of his sense of the multiple ages he could detect in those patients once arriving to lie on the couch at his clinic in Hampstead in London.[5] Thus the older we are the more we encounter the world through complex layerings of identity, attempting to negotiate the shifting present while grappling with the disconcerting images of the old thrust so intrusively upon us. 'Live in the layers, / not on the litter', the North American poet Stanley Kunitz wrote in one of his beautiful poems penned in his seventies.[6]

Many people are likely to mourn the passionate pleasures and perils of their younger life, fearing that never again can they recapture what they have lost. Yet, one way or another, for better and for worse, there are devious means by which we always live with those passions of the past in the strange mutations of mental life in the present, whatever our age. We do not have to be Marcel Proust to recapture traces of them without even trying, though it will surely be harder to find just the right words, or perhaps any language at all, to express our own everyday time-travelling.

Thus, on the one hand it can seem as though the self never ages; on the other we are forced to register our bodies and minds in constant transformation, especially by the impact we make upon others. As Virginia Woolf, always so concerned with issues of time, memory and sexual difference, wrote in her diary in 1931, just before reaching fifty: 'I sometimes feel that I have lived 250 years already, and sometimes that I am still the youngest person on the omnibus.'[7] This is exactly how I feel.

'I don't feel old,' elderly informants repeatedly told the oral historian Paul Thompson. Their voices echo the words he'd read in his forays into published autobiography and archived interviews.[8] Similarly, in the oral histories collected by the writer, Ronald Blythe, an eighty-four-year-old ex-schoolmaster reflects: 'I tend to look upon other old men as *old* men – and not include myself ... My boyhood stays imperishable and is such a great part of me now. I feel it very strongly – more than ever before.'[9]

'How can a seventeen-year-old, like me, suddenly be eighty-one?' the exactingly scientific developmental biologist Lewis Wolpert asks in the opening sentences of his book on the surprising nature of old age, wryly entitled *You're Looking Very Well*.[10] Once again, this keen attachment to youth tells us a great deal about the stigma attending old age: 'you're looking old' would never be said, except to insult. On the one hand there can be a sense of continuous fluidity, as we travel through time; on the other, it is hard to ignore those distinct positions we find ourselves in as we age, whatever the temptation. I have been finding, however, that it becomes easier to face up to my own anxieties about ageing after surveying the radical ambiguities in the speech or writing of others thinking about the topic, especially when they do so neither to lament nor to celebrate old age, but simply to affirm it as a significant part of life. This is the trigger for the pages that follow, as I assemble different witnesses to help guide me through the thoughts that once kept me awake at night, pondering all the things that have mattered to me and wondering what difference ageing makes to my continuing ties to them.

Beauvoir's Blues

'I don't feel old' may for differing reasons be one of the chief messages we hear from the old, often familiar to us in the words of ageing relatives, friends, or perhaps an insistent voice arising from within. Yet sometimes, of course, now at the very close of my sixties writing this, I do feel old. But then my manner of displaying confidence, strength and independence has from the beginning often been accompanied by an awareness of also feeling somewhat weak, fragile and dependent – characteristics always attributed to the elderly and, not coincidentally, seen as prototypically 'feminine'. Despite a rather paradoxical official eagerness nowadays to present an encouraging view of 'successful' ageing, I know that there are always competing voices, seemingly coming from within and without, conflicting with any sense of satisfaction that I might have in later life. For however we may feel 'on the inside', this has little impact on the abiding fears of ageing that usually begin assaulting us from mid-life, seemingly from the outside.

Turning to my first guide into the territory of old age, no one depicted the contradictions of ageing more sharply than that intrepid feminist avatar, Simone de Beauvoir. Entering middle age, she felt she could not recover from the shock of realizing she was no longer young: 'How is it that time, which has no form nor substance, can crush me with so huge a weight that I can no longer breathe?'[11] Beauvoir was, of course, the pre-eminent inspiration for so many of my very particular 'post-war' generation in our youth, rousing us to confront and resist the situation of women's symbolic and social marginalization in, and as, *The Second Sex*. Fifteen years after publishing that rallying call, however, Beauvoir was unable to resist the searing sorrow she felt confronting her own ageing when concluding her third autobiographical book recording her life and times, *Force of Circumstance*, first published in 1963.

Beauvoir was just fifty-five when expressing her words of anguish in that book: we learn that she loathed observing her own face in the mirror, lamented finding herself without any lover, perhaps all the more so as she watched the oversupply of beautiful, desiring women flocking around the man she claimed as her own lifetime companion, the by then physically frail and fast deteriorating Jean-Paul Sartre. Most of all, she despaired that she would never again be able, never again be allowed, to experience any new desires, or to display her yearnings publicly. 'Never again!' she laments, naming the passing of all the things now slipping away from her grasp. Listing her former joys, plans and projects, she wrote: 'It is not I who am saying goodbye to all those things I once enjoyed, it is they who are leaving me.'[12]

I've read that same sentiment so many times from women, sometimes expressed piteously, other times more flippantly, as in the words of the north American novelist, Alison Lurie: 'Soon after I reached sixty I was abandoned by *Vogue* magazine and all its clones ... Without intending it I had permanently alienated them, simply by becoming old. From their point of view, I was now a hopeless case.'[13] Beauvoir's thoughts are much heavier when she closes her book with the cry: 'Memories grow thin, myths crack and peel, projects rot in the bud; I am here, and around me circumstances. If this silence is to last, how long it seems, my short future!'[14]

'Never again', Beauvoir mourned, seemingly inconsolable, in her mid-fifties. Never again would she be in control of her life, able to realize or allowed to express desire, whereas once she had been 'drawn into the future by all [her] new plans'. And yet, it turned out that Beauvoir would afterwards shift many times in relation to what, if anything, she was again able to do and to say. Indeed, her 'never again' was a sentiment never again repeated in the same bleak way in any of her subsequent writing. Just under ten years later, writing *All Said and Done* (first published in 1974), we find that things were neither all said nor, even less so, all done. Beauvoir was busy taking control and making changes after all.

Thus, in another assertive contradiction of her title, we find that much had shifted in her life, along with changing political contexts and new personal attachments, among other things. Indeed, now in her sixties, Beauvoir had no new man, apparently, but interestingly she had found new joy, a new love, even a new sense of unity. This time it was not simply with Sartre (she never moved very far away from her attachment to him) but with a woman, Sylvie Le Bon, who was thirty-three years her junior. Furthermore, she was committed to new projects and even had a new political identification, with feminism. 'Today I've changed,' she said around this time, 'I've really become a feminist.'[15]

However, what is especially significant was that while Beauvoir herself had managed to make another turn in her life, by at least partly bonding and identifying herself with a much younger partner, she was nevertheless determined to document the plight of the old in her later writing (if no longer exactly her own plight). Beauvoir's thoughts on ageing provide one of the threads that will weave throughout this book, surveying how she explored the ways in which the old are positioned as culture's subordinated and negated other; just as twenty years earlier she had once described women as symbolically always in a secondary position to men and masculinity.

The need to tackle her own very deep fear and horror of ageing launched Beauvoir's second major piece of theoretical research, *La Vieillesse*, published in 1970.[16] She used her now familiar formula, once again contrasting the marginalized Other (the old) with the norm (the young and male). Here again, she insisted that the disparaged meanings attached to this abject or demeaned Other are not fixed in the body, but contingent upon a comprehensive cultural situation of neglect and disparagement: 'man never lives in a state of nature', she wrote. Nor women either. Moreover, despite her own dread of ageing, Beauvoir was not simply in denial, as we might say, when she set out to reclaim old age, and to speak on its behalf. Her point was that whatever our age we must also see the 'old' within ourselves, even though – frighteningly – the face of the 'old' we must be prepared to recognize ourselves in was, in her description, almost always a somewhat pitiable thing. It belonged to a creature whose situation, economically, socially and psychically, had mostly been, and remained, deplorable. Thus, on the one hand, Beauvoir insisted: 'We must stop cheating: the whole meaning of our life is in question ... let us recognize ourselves in this old man or that old woman.'[17] On the other, she loathed the ageing body, particularly her own. As we shall see, in her novels, she had portrayed the older, abandoned woman, with little sympathy.

So, Beauvoir recognized her ageing self, and yet, simultaneously, she repudiated it. She dreamed, in her case quite literally, of escaping old age: 'often in my sleep I dream that in a dream I'm fifty-four [which at the time she is], I awake and find I'm only thirty. "What a terrible nightmare I had," says the woman who thinks she's awake.' And then she finally wakes up. Sometimes, she added, 'just before I come back to reality, a giant beast settles on my breast: "It's true! It's my nightmare of being more than fifty that's come true!" '[18] Beauvoir's earlier analysis of the situation of women as men's culturally disdained female Other had not led her, as it would later lead some feminists, to repudiate men or masculinity, but instead to insist on women's possible unity with them as 'free and autonomous beings'.[19] Similarly, Beauvoir's analysis of the privileging of the young against the old did not lead her to criticize youth, but rather to work to establish forms of unity with a younger generation (both with a particular young woman, Sylvie, and with a new political movement, feminism), making her, she felt, young as well as old: 'The better I knew Sylvie, the more akin I felt to her … There is such an interchange between us that I lose the sense of my age: she draws me forwards into her future, and there are times when the present recovers a dimension that it had lost.'[20]

Yet however extreme her ambivalence about accepting her own age, what was critical about Beauvoir's writing was her repeated insistence that 'old age' is an Other which lives within everyone, whatever our age. Short of premature death, no one can escape it, no matter how much we may try to distance ourselves from it. Moreover, and crucially, Beauvoir wondered whether recognizing the inevitability of ageing could help us all to re-conceptualize our responsibilities towards those we are so often inclined to reject.

There seem, however, to be certain inevitabilities around generational conflict as youth enters adulthood, often in distinctly different historical conjunctures. Forging their own pathways, the young have always eyed with suspicion the generation preceding them. Nowadays, this suspicion may well be of the privileges or status acquired mid-life by professional men and women, or perhaps it is a hostility to what is seen as older people's attachment to yesterday's orthodoxies, or simply, and emphatically, a suspicion of the old as Other, and all that might suggest about the losses and difficulties of ageing. Meanwhile, as we shall see illustrated in later chapters, the old have often expressed resentment, even fear, of the young, perhaps seeing in them not just the threat of redundancy, but also the source of feelings of shame, embarrassment and more, in a world that nowadays begins to eject them from its continuous recycling of the new early on.

Feminist Constraints

Nevertheless, we might expect feminists to be the very first to cultivate Beauvoir's hopes for cross-generational recognition, at least between women. Feminism not only hoped to reach out to all women, but also strongly rejected the ways in which women are surveyed and defined in relation to their bodies, while often deploring the many hours of a day, of a lifetime, women spent trying, and sooner or later failing, to prove themselves desirable creatures in the world at large, the world of men. 'Stay young and beautiful if you want to be loved', was sung with glorious irony by the overwhelmingly young women at the very first national march of the Women's Liberation Movement in Britain, on International Women's Day in 1971.[21] I was on that march, but few if any of us joyously singing along then could appreciate what some of us later came to experience as the bitter gravity of our words. On that day, many of us had our boyfriends or girlfriends, alongside many other friends, marching with us. Yet the fading of our youthful confidence and togetherness left us no more prepared than anyone else to deal with the dilemmas of ageing. As she grew older, Sue O'Sullivan – a feminist on that march who has remained an activist for more than forty years, from day one of women's liberation in Britain – expressed her dismay that 'feminists, so confident in their youthful twenties and thirties about the ephemeral nature of "attractiveness", and its male-defined meanings, began to waver and lose confidence in their forties and fifties'.[22]

As feminists we had consciously disdained the dictates of the youthful beauty culture. It was easier to do when we were young ourselves, and hence less vulnerable to being ignored as intrinsically outside its radar. Yet we still remained largely unprepared for the dismay, fears, anxiety, even for many the sudden horror, which the ageing woman can experience on looking into the mirror and seeing a face she cannot accept, yet one uncannily familiar. It is frequently the face of her own ageing mother, from whom she had often struggled to distance herself. It was, for example, another very committed feminist in the USA, the cultural studies scholar Vivian Sobchack, who proclaimed in her book *Carnal Thoughts*: 'I despair of ever being able to reconcile my overall sense of well-being, self-confidence, achievement, and pleasure in the richness of the present with the image I see in the mirror.'[23]

Ageing affects us all, and affects us all differently, but it is women who have often reported a very specific horror of ageing. It is associated, of course, with the place of the body, and fertility, in women's lives; above all, with what is seen as beauty, attractiveness, good looks, in defining the quintessentially 'feminine', however fleeting, however unattainable, this will prove. 'Beauty is always doomed', as William Burroughs declared (even if only a tiny minority of men actually kill their young 'wives', as he did, accidentally).[24] Nothing, in my view, quite prepares us to deal easily with this. We live in an atmosphere where youth, fitness, speed, glamour are so prized that somehow, even as we age, we must still try to remain forever young, but women, in particular, must struggle vainly to retain their youthful allure. This is what has triggered that cry of women's despair, echoing down through the ages, especially when older women have tried to embark on new love affairs. Colette, for example, was busy recording this in her novels written in the early twentieth century, as she charted all the activity required 'to disguise that monster, an old woman'.[25]

'That monster', which Beauvoir, Colette and Sobchack recognized, has something to do with the distinct horror attached to the image of the ageing female. Fears of ageing are fed almost from birth by terrifying images in myth and folktale – the hag, harridan, gorgon, witch or Medusa. Such frightening figures are not incidentally female, they are quintessentially female, seen as monstrous because of the combination of age and gender. No such symbolic resonance trails through time from the male Gods of old – despite Cronus, for instance, being depicted mythically as an old man with a sickle, who had castrated his father and would later eat five of his own children. As will be evident in later chapters, men's fears of ageing, their yearning for the potency and the pleasures of their youth, are certainly on record, sometimes indeed issuing in howls of rage and ongoing fears of powerlessness and death. But there are far fewer texts from men that express quite the same level of repulsion, the same degree of dread and disgust, that we hear from, and far more often about, older women, evident from their early middle age. It is still apparent everywhere that our cultures of ageing are gendered. 'Growing old is mainly an ordeal of the imagination – a moral disease, a social pathology – intrinsic to which is that it affects women much more than men', protested the well-known writer and cultural critic Susan Sontag, in 1972, in an early piece addressing 'The Double Standard of Aging'.[26]

Younger feminists were slower to register the full extent of this social pathology. It is now clear that despite a few older women's memories of ageing in the exciting, and for them welcoming, arms of a shared 'sisterhood', many older feminists recall feeling marginalized in what was at first predominantly a movement of young women, determined to reject the lives of their mothers. The once prominent British sociologist, the late Meg Stacey, for instance, already in her late forties at the birth of second-wave feminism, wrote of all she gained from women's liberation, yet also of what she saw as the ageism of that movement:

> As well as finally leading me to this personal liberation, the WLM did cause a good deal of pain, then and later ... Not only was I, along with other women of my age, not invited to consciousness-raising groups ... it was made clear to me that I was one of the 'traitor generation' who had retreated after the Second World War to marriage and family ... how much one could have done with sisterly support in that male-dominated

world [of academia]! ... The sense of sisterhood, although I was personally excluded by the ageism of the movement, seemed to me a most important and valuable feature of the WLM.[27]

Stacey's sense of exclusion was expressed by many other older feminists from that period, suggesting that feminism had indeed failed to prevent younger women from distancing themselves from older women; at least, unless they had a very particular fiery clout, charisma or charm, such as that possessed by those two American poets, Grace Paley or Adrienne Rich, able to capture the admiration, even the love, of a younger generation.

However, the rise of what became known as 'identity politics' in the 1980s led some older feminists to begin to write about their specific invisibility within the women's movement. This began, as ever, in the USA, with all the recognizable rhetoric and passion of what were by then ongoing conflicts between the differing feminist identifications of the period – invoking class, race, ethnicity, sexual orientation, and more. Barbara MacDonald was just one of the older women's voices speaking out in 1985:

From the beginning of this wave of the women's movement, from the beginning of Women's Studies, the message has gone out to those of us over sixty that your 'Sisterhood' does not include us, that those of you who are younger see us as men see us – that is, as women who used to be women but aren't any more. You do not see us in our present lives, you do not identify with our issues, you exploit us, you patronize us, you stereotype us. Mainly you ignore us.[28]

It would be over a decade before things began to shift within mainstream feminist thought; indeed, it did so only after more feminist scholars reached middle age themselves. By the late 1990s, the impressive self-styled feminist ageist resister, Margaret Morganroth Gullette, called for a new research field of 'Age Studies' to explore all the ramifications of attitudes towards ageing, agreeing that they amounted to a form of social pathology. In book after book, beginning with her investigations of middle age for her opening text, *Declining to Decline: Cultural Combat and the Politics of Midlife* (1997), Gullette has continued to uncover the high costs of ageism present not just in society generally, but even within feminism and progressive academic forums, such as cultural studies.[29] 'How can we ever have thought we age by nature alone?' she asks rhetorically, in her book dedicated to answering just that question, *Aged by Culture*.[30] In all her writing, Gullette explores how relentlessly, if often surreptitiously, that work is done: 'We think we age by nature; we are insistently and precociously being aged by culture. But how we are aged by culture – that we need to know more about.'[31] Soon Gullette was joined by other feminist compatriots, such as Kathleen Woodward, eager to expand the field of Age Studies in the humanities and agreeing that 'ageism is entrenched within feminism itself'. Although, as Woodward adds, it is hardly surprising that women have also 'internalized our culture's prejudice against ageing and old age'.[32] This explains why, despite her unique influence on second-wave feminism, Beauvoir's own book on old age was itself ignored by feminists when it first appeared in the early 1970s.

Elaborating further on the need for 'Age Studies', Gullette notes that although critical theory has been busy making trouble for and attempting to subvert so many of the old binaries producing and marking identity, highlighting the role of culture and language in securing hierarchies of gender, race, ethnicity, class, sexual orientation and more, it has rarely turned its attention to age. Age seemed to remain a 'different difference' that many people were keen to avoid as some personal dilemma: 'Many think "age" always refers to people older than they are and is thus of no present interest', Gullette suggests.[33] Age is everywhere, but the complex practices registering it are far from obvious, making it perplexing and frightening for the many haunted by its presence.

Psychoanalytic Framings

Trying to find my bearings for writing this book, at first I hardly knew which way to turn or what tools to use for confronting my own trepidations. I have already suggested that culturally we find two narratives of ageing, expressing the standard binary logic: stories of progress and stories of decline; of ageing well and ageing badly. Officially sanctioned discourses of ageing well have become the dominant themes of gerontology, the science of ageing. They are nowadays promoted by Western governments around the world, ever more anxious about the welfare resources that will be needed to deal with the demographic changes caused by the unprecedented increase in human longevity. It is currently estimated that over the twentieth century a whole extra thirty years was added to life expectancy, thus vastly swelling the percentage of people post-retirement compared with the numbers in paid work.[34] 'Ageing well' means people taking responsibility for their own wellbeing, encouraged via the promotion of healthy lifestyles to follow practices that can hopefully activate and empower them all the way through old age right up to the doors of death itself.

Yet this narrative of ageing well, ageing healthily, can itself be problematic, even contradictory. In many of the chapters ahead we will see instances of uncritical promotion of positive active ageing, as if we could all live into old age unburdened by actual signs of ageing. This scenario is thus itself partially complicit with the disparagement of old age, refusing to accept much that ageing entails, including facing up to greater dependence, fragility and loss, as well as the sadness, resentment or anger that accrue along with life itself. As other prominent voices note, again most often in the USA, there is a barely concealed politics in this particular notion of positive ageing. Stephen Katz, for instance, argues that this new official line ties in with the anti-welfare agenda of what is usually described as neo-liberalism, with its refusal to acknowledge many older people's need to accept and live with dependency, and even less to provide adequate resources to enable them to live well.[35] It is conversely those who cannot conceal their need for care, assistance and support who are seen as ageing badly, reinforcing notions of actual signs of ageing as indicative of seamless decline.

I have said, however, that it is not so much the ageing body, and how to keep it spruce, that is my main concern, but rather the complexities of mental life within ageing bodies. I am most interested in the less familiar cultural narratives that we might draw upon to provide more nuanced thoughts on ageing. These stories are distinct from exhortations to stay enduringly fit and young, on the one hand, or from the blatant dread or blinkered denial of the whole situation of the frequent unmet needs, isolation and neglect of the elderly, on the other. Without these alternative stories, it is hard to see how we can ever begin to beat back the abiding stigma and menacing stereotypes of old age, to enable some affirmation of its own diverse distinctiveness and intricate, shifting particularities.

The most frightening of images are implanted early on, along with language itself and all the affect-laden symbolic apparatus of fantasies, metaphor, condensation, accompanying our encounters with those witches of folktales, ghouls of horror movies, and the countless other versions of crones or dementing oldies, both male and – far more savagely – female. We need to search hard to find, and then foster, possibilities for affirming old age. Once we start looking, however, the going gets easier. Drawing on my own experience and that of others, watching out and listening for richer versions of ageing, I explore some of those differing accounts, beginning with the diverse psychic and political possibilities and challenges that accrue with ageing. As I've already mentioned, they come from the understanding that the more we age, the more access we have to all the 'baggage' of our past, to all the selves we have been, or imagine ourselves to have been. Ageing is neither simply linear, nor is it any single discrete process when, in our minds, we race around, moving seamlessly between childhood, old age and back again. There are ways in which we can, and we do, bridge different ages, psychically, all the time.

Oddly, despite its awareness of the timelessness of the unconscious, until very recently, and still only sporadically, the temporal instabilities of old age have been little theorized in Freudian thought, not even in the writing of those scholars and clinicians most eager to begin telling psychoanalytic stories differently. With just a few notable exceptions, up until very recently there has been sparse psychoanalytic reflection on ageing.[36] The neglect is usually traced back to Freud's own intense fears and phobias around ageing, which were evident from his middle age. At forty-nine, Freud decided older people were unsuitable for analysis because of their psychic inflexibility: 'near or above the age of fifty, the elasticity of mental processes on which treatment depends is, as a rule, lacking: old people are no longer educable'.[37]

Things could only get worse for this particular middle-aged man, although it was not his mental elasticity that deserted him, as he was still writing expressively twenty years later, at seventy-one: 'with me crabbed old age has arrived – a state of total disillusionment, whose sterility is comparable to a lunar landscape, an inner ice age'.[38] Clearly, creativity remained in profusion, accompanying his horror of ageing. For Freud, the abhorrence of old age was presented as a given, seemingly in little need of explanation: 'The trouble is – I am an old man – *you do not think it worth your while to love me*', Freud had angrily announced to the surprise of his patient, the then middle-aged poet Hilda Doolittle (H. D.), when she lay on his couch in Vienna in 1933, with Freud by then seventy-seven. She said she was not aware of having said anything that might account for his outburst.[39]

However, almost despite himself, Freud presented other thoughts on the ways in which we may be haunted by encounters with old age, including our own. We find this especially in his reflections on those odd and alarming experiences we describe as 'uncanny', the peculiar anxiety that is aroused by images that seem both startling and strange, and yet in some sense also familiar. Such experiences, he said, were like ghostly hauntings, while noting the cultural ubiquity of ghost stories and haunted houses. Unsurprisingly, Freud suggested that these haunting or uncanny experiences might arise from places or experiences that triggered the arousal of repressed complexes from childhood. However, in this essay Freud also suggested that we can also be haunted by a sense of something familiar but somehow associated with archaic or primitive beliefs, such as ancient fears of the return of dead spirits: 'many people experience the [uncanny] feeling in the highest degree in relation to death and dead bodies, to the return of the dead, and to spirits and ghosts'.[40] Thus a living person can appear uncanny, and weirdly frightening, if they trigger thoughts of extinction, reminding us of our mortality, when thoughts of death always hover somewhere in the presence of life.

In the final autobiographical footnote to his influential essay, 'The "Uncanny"', published in 1919, when he was sixty-three, Freud provided a memorable example of himself being frightened by just such a figure, when he feels he encountered his own 'double' while travelling in a train by night, after it suddenly lurched violently. At that moment he thought he saw the door to his carriage flung open and the arrival of 'an elderly gentleman in a dressing gown and travelling cap'. This ageing figure, whose appearance Freud 'thoroughly disliked', turned out to his astonishment to be none other than his own reflection in the mirror on the connecting door. In his account, this image was not only experienced as that of a 'stranger', but came to serve him as an example of the 'uncanny', arousing a displeasure that led him to wonder whether what he experienced might best be seen as a 'vestigial trace of the archaic reaction which feels the "double" to be something uncanny'.[41] In an interesting reading of the essay, the British psychoanalytic scholar Stephen Frosh suggests that one way of understanding Freud's memory of his intense dislike of his 'double' would be to see it as a type of haunting not from the past, but rather from the future: 'What sends shivers down *his* spine, it seems, is not the return of the infantile repressed, but the beckoning from the *future*; that is, it is the *future* that haunts the present, and not the past. This future is one in which Freud is an old man, in which he will regret what he comes to be; in which death calls him, and daily reminds him of its threat.'[42]

Fears of death almost certainly do feed the familiar dread of old age, a fear that Freud suggested in this essay had hardly changed 'since the very earliest times', including 'the old belief that the dead man becomes the enemy of his survivor and seeks to carry him off to share his new life with him'.[43] And certainly, the ageing face that looks back at us in the mirror in later life, usually resembling that of a parent, can indeed make our elderly reflections a trifle uncanny. Personally, nowadays, I continually find it strange (yet oddly, also interesting, sometimes even reassuring) to watch my mother staring back at me from the mirror; or to hear, not my own laugh, but *hers*, when I am trying to please others.

Yet that ageing 'double' in the mirror may be a much-loved parent, perhaps a protective parent right up until their death, which one might think could just perhaps make old age, and even the inevitability of death, easier – rather than harder – to come to terms with. This means that there is more to say about these hauntings, whether from the past or the future. In her book *Ghostly Matters*, for instance, the psychoanalytically versed American sociologist Avery Gordon sees Freud's encounter with his 'double' in the train more in terms of a 'clawing narcissism', aroused when viewing that 'shabby' figure, which he misattributes to a type of archaic ghostly haunting, with its intimations of mortality.[44] What is interesting to me about Gordon's account of haunting is that she views it as a social as much as a personal phenomenon, introducing the notion of a 'social unconscious', which enables her to look at the impact that enduring social stigma, dispossession, repression and exploitation have on people and society.

I don't want to choose between these two interpretations, personal fears and social denigration, since I think both contribute to any aversion towards those ageing faces that look back at us in old age. However, I do think that adding in Gordon's account of how images are culturally implanted, knowing that horror and old age are always already mythically twinned, would help explain Freud's instant dislike of that 'elderly gentleman' – himself. Whether or not we find the notion of a 'social unconscious' useful for describing the process, I am sure that attending to the imprint of the social on the personal unconscious can at least assist us in trying to be more hospitable to those figures who haunt our imaginations, especially when old and shabby. In Gordon's account: 'Freud gets so close to dealing with the social reality of haunting only to give up the ghost and everything social that comes in its wake.'[45] As I will suggest much later in this book, those hauntings from the dead are not always frightening; indeed, sometimes they are welcome. The American poet Mark Doty, for instance, wrote of finding his dead lover in a dream: 'Bless you. You came back, so I could see you / once more, plainly, so I could rest against you/ without thinking this happiness lessened anything, / without thinking you were alive again'.[46]

Yet if Freud could offer nothing but gloom around old age, as a sterile and frightening condition inevitably triggering thoughts of death, it seems to me there are more interesting uses that could be made of psychoanalytic reflection. Nowadays there are some analysts, most notably Pearl King in the UK, and several others in the USA, beginning with Kurt Eissler, who have attempted this. They suggest, for instance, that you could reverse Freud's views on the difficulties presented by older patients in analysis. Thus they propose that the well-known reluctance of analysts to work with the elderly could be largely a projection of their own anxieties and prejudices, especially in the analyst's personal fears around illness, loss and mortality likely to be triggered in forms of counter-transference when dealing with older patients.[47] Moreover, by prioritizing the past over the future, as well as stressing the wayward temporality of psychic life, psychoanalysis has at least the potential to help us think more imaginatively about ageing and old age. Practising in Britain, Christopher Bollas is one psychoanalyst who writes evocatively of all psychic life as 'a kind of haunting', populated by the residue of others who leave the traces of our encounters with them over a lifetime, but in ways that are 'not intelligible, or even clearly knowable: just intense ghosts … who inhabit the human mind'. No wonder, Bollas continues, that as we age 'we come to believe more and more in life's mystery and in the strangeness of being human'.[48]

As the writer Eva Hoffman points out in her book on the nature of 'time', the French psychoanalyst André Green also tries to capture the strange recurring residues of the past in the present, and of the present in our recollections of the past, when he refers to the 'heterochrony' of psychic temporalities.[49] Highlighting the many affinities between literature and psycho-analysis, as well as the way in which scholars in the humanities have helped keep psychoanalytic thought alive, an anthology by Kathleen Woodward and Murray Schwartz, entitled *Memory and Desire*, contains many impressive essays addressing the complexities and paradoxes of ageing and old age. Some writers here, also turning to Winnicott, make use of his notion of 'space of illusion', space of play, in which what he called 'transitional objects' enable both the renunciation *and* the recuperation of early relationships. It is a process, surely, which does not end with childhood; few do. Introducing this collection, Murray Schwartz, an American cross-disciplinary scholar who has taught in both the humanities and psychiatry, uses Winnicott to argue that 'varieties of playing, uses of illusion, can thus be seen as the threads of continuity that enable us to differentiate and recapitulate past experiences as we negotiate the crises of middle age and old age.' Of course, as he quickly adds, the possibilities for creative repetitions are always precarious, dependent upon our physical, economic and cultural situation, which may either encourage or, almost, foreclose them.[50]

Others, including Schwartz, have also turned to the thoughts of Jacques Lacan to ponder the peculiarities of self-perceptions and ageing. For Lacan the images we have of ourselves are always flawed, whatever our age. From the beginning we only gain any form of self-recognition and wholeness from the outside, mediated by the reflected desire of another and masking inner turbulence, fragmentation and division.[51] This initial mis-recognition, or false sense of self-coherence and identity is furthered through language, as we are slotted into pre-assigned positions in its symbolic order.[52] Hence, we can say that there is never any true self but only a multiplicity of continuities over time which means, as Schwartz sums up: 'everything depends upon our ability to make use of the self as an object of memory and fantasy that simultaneously is and is not equivalent to its present manifestations'.[53] Another American literary scholar, Herbert Blau, also draws upon Lacan to point out that 'the voids of memory, with age, are an opening into imagination, so long as the aged are not made to feel that a failing memory is a felony of sorts'.[54] So long as, indeed! In fact, of course, felony or not, huge social concern, if not censure, is precisely what memory lapses do tend to evoke.

Shifting Voices

'Keep young and beautiful, if you want to be loved', we sang mockingly when young; we do not sing it any more. It is certainly challenging for an older woman to know how to talk about and deal with desire, when we are all too aware of our growing erotic invisibility and perhaps also confronting disabilities, loss, mortality and other difficulties. Indeed, women seem early on to acquire a special affinity with ageing, when many of the experiences and emotions of old age have been associated with the feminine all along: from its apparent fragilities and frequent humiliations to the laborious work of caring for those in need, starting with birth all the way through to dealing with death and dying. It is women as a group who live longer than men in all developed countries and a majority of less developed ones, often by as much as ten years. The gender discrepancy is greatest among the very old, with women centenarians worldwide outnumbering men nine to one.[55] Moreover, although I remain somewhat sceptical of the claim, we often hear women themselves affirm that it is they who can accept ageing more easily, less bitterly, than men.

It is over fifty years since that energetic and ambitious anthropologist Margaret Mead, then in her late fifties, first spoke of women's prolonged 'post-menopausal zest', in an interview with *Life* magazine in 1959. She continued to shock audiences with this thought for another two decades, most memorably when she silenced her interviewer, David Frost, by mentioning the menopause on television in 1970. According to her biographer it was a topic that had never before been broached on screen, let alone with such glee.[56] Yet it turns out she was not alone. In different ways a minority of women have tried to dismiss the frightening spectre of the ageing female that haunts so many women from early middle age as they head towards what is seen as the definitive turning point of the menopause. Recently Jane Miller, at seventy-eight, opened her book *Crazy Age* with the reflection: 'I like being old at least as much as I liked being middle-aged and a good deal more than I liked being young.'[57]

Yet whatever women's distinct affinities or difficulties with ageing might be, their accounts of it could hardly be more varied and inconsistent, even coming from the very same person. Untangling the twisted ties between women and old age thus takes us to a dissonant clash of emotions: ranging from horror and denial of old age to celebration and solace regarding its possibilities for reinvention and renewal; from mourning the losses of a long life to militant resistance against ageism; from introspective withdrawal to fierce struggles against the neglect of the needs of the elderly, sometimes expanding into active support for other battles against the brutalities and disorders of the world, near and far. Given such diversity, it seems unlikely that any generalization about which sex copes better with ageing could be useful.

However, what certainly is true is that the stories available about ageing often have a gendered tone. The Californian literary theorist Helene Moglen started exploring divergent experiences of women and ageing a few years ago in her essay 'Aging and Trans-aging'. She begins her reflections by informing us of her own horror when, at around forty, she saw in the mirror not her own, but her mother's face. It made her realize at once, she continued, that she had suddenly caught the mortal disease of ageing.[58] 'Late mid-life astonishment', is how Sarah Pearlman referred to the disruptions of identity and self-esteem that women can suddenly experience, usually nowadays between the ages of fifty and sixty – although, tellingly, the timeframe differs considerably across time and place.[59]

Moglen herself manages to come to terms with ageing as she reflects that in old age we have access to many different sub-jectivities, or self-states, through all the possible re-visitings of our younger selves. However, I wonder quite how conscious or comprehensible our ability to reclaim those former selves might be. We are not really in charge of the process: we are no longer those people we once were, there is real loss and usually something for us to mourn; and yet, when contexts allow it, the residues of those former selves may not only be expressed, but can sometimes be seen and affirmed by others. In our minds, the whole history of our attachments, the shifting sense we have of ourselves over a lifetime, accompanies the external losses of ageing. The past returns, never exactly as it was, but also never truly lost.

Looking back on old attachments is one thing, starting new ones is an altogether more challenging task. Nevertheless, a few years after writing her general reflections on ageing, Moglen wrote a brief autobiographical fragment in which she describes the re-emergence of desire and pleasure in her own old age, in ways that took her by surprise. At seventy-three, she describes falling in love again, and this time loving quite differently, indeed, with a new sort of passion, in her late life. Facing her husband's death in 2000, after forty-four years of marriage,

Moglen entered psychoanalytic therapy for the first time, finding herself unable to cope with the loss of the security that had been part of a life hitherto enmeshed with that of her late husband, 'like two roots that had twisted together'. Psychoanalysis was a perspective she had long been interested in and was now ready to explore directly. In therapy, she encountered what felt like strange yet oddly familiar aspects of herself that had become truncated or submerged over time, generating 'an uncanny self that had survived the losses by which it had irrevocably been stamped'. Not long after starting, however – feeling both newly empowered as well as frustrated in the complexities of the transference with a male therapist – Moglen decided to end her clinical treatment when, unexpectedly, she fell in love again. She felt she now wanted 'to replace self-obsession with self-expression' with her new lover: 'Gender, age, and sexuality lost their conventional references altogether, and in order to comprehend their current meanings, I had to disinter curtailed identifications, buried memories and transgressive desires.' Her new lover was twenty years younger, a woman in her fifties, who also happened to be a psychotherapist. Separately, her younger partner wrote of giving up her own clinical practice, now wishing to embrace fully this new love in her own middle age, and deciding she had listened to enough sad stories.[60]

It is by listening to such different stories of old people, looking out for less familiar images of the elderly, that we may begin to encompass the extensive densities of ageing, while also surveying the multifarious ways we feel about ourselves, whatever our age. One writer who is always eloquent in elucidating the persistence of the past throughout our lives, and the ease with which we summon up different versions of our youth, or any other age, at will, is the British author Penelope Lively. In one of her interviews she explains how in her writing she tries to capture that sense that there is nothing linear about personal time: 'all these snatches of other presents exist at once in your mind ... A very elusive and tricky concept, time.'[61] Whether in her novels or her more recent memoirs, the unwinding of these diverse temporalities always lies at the heart of Lively's vivid prose. In her award-winning novel *Moon Tiger* (1987), for instance, the sharp and acidic heroine, Claudia Hampton, a historian, lies in hospital recycling her memories from her deathbed, telling us, in a memorable opening sequence: 'Chronology irritates me. There is no chronology inside my head. I am composed of a myriad Claudias who spin and mix and part like sparks of sunlight on water. The pack of cards I carry around is forever shuffled and re-shuffled; there is no sequence, everything happens at once.'[62] Lively's writing is equally compelling on the historical embeddedness of personal memories in their particular time and place. Our life-stories inevitably draw upon the more general collective narratives around at the time, allowing us, selectively, to make sense of the jumble of our experiences and suggesting the way in which we are all, as she puts it, 'manipulated by history'.[63]

Similar reflections on the lively, unpredictable resources of memory, summoning up lifetimes of commitments and evasions, joys and losses, hopes and humiliations, have been increasingly evident of late in the memoirs of a small but growing number of older authors, accompanying the burgeoning interest in auto-biography, and related literary criticism. In her best-selling text, *Somewhere towards the End*, Diana Athill, at eighty-one, reported that for a variety of reasons, especially the success of her writing in old age, she had managed to enjoy the return of some of 'the comfortable warmth of early youth', when she could sometimes feel pleased with herself: 'If this is smugness it is a far more comfortable state to be in than its opposite.'[64] Old age and pleasure – this is not a combination that we often see, although their coupling will appear and disappear in a variety of ways in the pages ahead.

The idea of us all having multiple and internally divided selves is neither new, nor restricted to ageing. However, the psychic resources it can offer seem to me particularly important for refiguring our ageing selves. Even when we may want to be, we are never entirely removed from who or what we have been, when that demanding, self-centred, long-forgotten infant might reappear at any moment, whether in intimate relations, in our dreams or, more embarrassingly, in public life, where her manifestation is usually most unwelcome. At other times, the distant playfulness and pleasures of childhood can sneak out arousing far less suspicion, indeed at the very best of times producing mutual delight. As many have noticed, infantile pleasures can resurface, for instance, in the special affinity grandparents often exhibit playing with their grandchildren, perhaps in ways they never managed with their own children, when responsible adulthood was a status they were still struggling hard to achieve. At seventy-three, Doris Lessing summed up this feeling in an article for the *Sunday Times*: 'The great secret that all old people share is that you really haven't changed in seventy or eighty years. Your body changes, but you don't change at all. And that, of course, causes great confusion.'[65] This too is a simplification, but it suggests how much creative work there is to be done in thinking about the paradoxes of ageing.

Seeing Differently

Paying more attention to the radical ambiguities of old age, trying to glimpse the appearance and disappearances of the many buried, or half-buried selves, perhaps better seen simply as continuities and discontinuities over a lifetime, can help to subvert the most familiar typecasting of ageing. This is usually dismal, whatever the official talk of 'ageing well'. Though attitudes to old age vary considerably across time and place, they are rarely free from dread, disgust and other discriminatory perceptions. Classically, from the days of ancient Greece or Rome to the present, those who did write more positively of old age spoke of it as a time of potential serenity, all passion spent, acclaiming the greater tolerance, personal acceptance, surviving dignity of ageing men and women, although it was men, in the past, who were the main focus of such thoughts. Yet, especially recently, contrasting accounts of old age are more widely and vividly aired. These might echo Dylan Thomas' now classic poetic rage at the 'dying of the light', or, more intriguingly, engage with the posthumously published reflections on 'late style' penned by the eminent literary critic Edward Said in his final years, when he was already battling against the leukaemia from which he died, aged sixty-seven.

Said's writing explores not the quiet tolerance and self-acceptance of old age, but rather the intransigence, difficulties and contradictions evident in the aesthetic productions of certain ageing artists, writers and composers.[66] Aesthetically talented or not, from where I look out on the world I hear many angry ageing voices displaying little resignation, but instead persistently determined to keep right on challenging a world still determinedly built around the preservation of injustice and inequalities, near and far. I return to this theme often, but here I will just mention what I notice in relation to one of the sites of struggle I have been engaged with lately – opposition to Israel's illegal blockade of Gaza. In May 2010 it was a few women in their seventies and eighties who were most active in commissioning the first six-ship flotilla which, with many veteran activists on board, and against all odds, vainly attempted to break through the continuing barricades cutting Gaza off from the rest of the world.[67] Despite the violent encounter with Israeli soldiers that ensued, which resulted in nine deaths on one of the boats in the first flotilla, five months later another small boat headed up by Jewish people from the UK set sail with the same goal. On board, the average age of the passengers and crew was over sixty. Older people, in particular, have often engaged themselves in a broad range of politics, at the forefront of community activist movements, as the writer and scholar Temma Kaplan recorded in her account of diverse grass-roots struggles around the world.[68]

I know that in old age the pathways back to experiencing the emotions and engagements of youth can be blocked, or treacherous: the playfulness, comforts and recognition hopefully at least sometimes provided in intimacies and friendships may elude us; the political passions that perhaps once animated much of our waking hours may be less easy to express, or even retain. Hard times, hard feelings, extreme physical or mental deterioration can imprison people. However, when we are lucky, there are many ways in which our ageing minds are as busy as ever weaving together our memories, still dreaming, scheming, connecting, resisting and, in the process, sometimes regaining once more earlier ludic selves, even if, occasionally, only through tears of rage.

Something of this sentiment is evident as Anne Sexton imagines the thoughts of an old woman awakened in her nursing home, in a poem written shortly before her own suicide at forty-six: 'What are you doing? Leave me alone! Can't you see I'm dreaming? In a dream you are never eighty.'[69] Throughout life, and not only in our dreams, the impact and messiness of psychic life, floating free from chronological time, enables a host of seemingly inappropriate aspirations and emotions to surface. More people today are commenting upon and trying to find ways of confronting our culture's demoralizing lack of imagination in relation to ageing. One of them, the French scholar Anca Cristofovici has been engaged in commenting upon a host of art works that both reveal and also work to undermine the rigid masks of ageing that are clamped upon us, for instance by counterpoising one facial image upon another from differing ages. This leads her to conclude that there is no true older self, but only 'permanently fluctuating relationships between younger and older selves'.[70] This feels right to me. I know that I fluctuate all the time, and not only in the company of much younger friends, who at times enable me to experience once more much of the energy of youth; at other times, usually quite accidentally, they make me all too aware of the generational gaps between us.

Many of the themes I will be addressing in the pages that follow focus upon these fluctuating ties between younger and older selves, and the pleasures and miseries this can create. First of all I survey the way in which age groups are so routinely lined up against each other, with damaging consequences for everyone, but particularly the old. I then venture into the hazards of desire in old age, and the apparently contrasting situation of ageing men compared with ageing women. By and large men see themselves faced with the challenge of how to keep desire visibly alive, many seeking assistance for maintaining the sexual potency of youth. Quite differently, women often appear to find it more convenient to eschew sexual passion altogether in old age, especially if and when they are living alone, though what exactly lies behind this gender contrast is in need of further elucidation. In looking out for ways of affirming old age I will be paying heed to the many ways in which older people generally, up to and including very old age, sometimes find ways of surviving the hurdles of humiliation and disregard they are likely to stumble upon. Here, women are more visible in the lead, their flags of resistance evident, when confronting the legendary aversion the 'old woman' has hitherto faced largely on her own.

The one thing that both young and old people, men and women alike, seem most to hate about the notion of old age is that it symbolizes forms of 'dependency'. What is rarely culturally acknowledged, least of all in any imprints of masculinity, is that differing modes of dependence are essential to the human condition. From our very first breath, we only come into existence, and then acquire any kind of subjectivity at all, through our dependence on others. We are never truly the self-made, independent creatures our culture likes to celebrate, as in the karaoke and funeral favourite, '*My Way* ... I did it my way' (even though this self-absorbed song apparently remains the top favourite for funerals in the UK and is, disappointingly, seen as the most suitable epitaph for a life well lived).[71]

Thus it is precisely our founding, and then life-long, dependence on others that many have argued makes its acknowledgement most unbearable, and therefore so routinely disavowed. For it threatens not just the vanities but also the

very substance of selfhood, often seen as requiring the enduring disavowal and hatred of dependency.[72] I also suspect that
the hidden stigma around 'dependency' was one of the main
reasons the people interviewed by Paul Thompson so often
insisted that they 'do not feel old'.[73] As we shall see, it is also
why 'old age' is still largely seen – ironically, even amongst
those people most eager to eliminate ageism – as something to
be 'transcended' rather than in any way affirmed, if at all possible. A large survey of elderly Americans conducted in 2009
found not just a gap between actual age and the age people said
they felt, but found that this disjuncture increased with age:
most adults over fifty claimed to feel at least ten years younger
than their chronological age, while a significant minority of
those over sixty-five reported that they felt up to twenty years
younger.[74] It is surely our aversion to the cultural diminishment
we believe ageing entails that lies behind that sense of distance
from it.

Thus another theme in this book will involve looking again
at issues of care and dependency, seeing the notion of 'dependence' as an intricate, interactive phenomenon, one in which
carers in different ways may be both invested in and dependent
upon the presence and the needs of those they care for, whatever their age or condition. However, the cultural framework of
individualism has little time for notions such as this. Meanwhile,
it is those who are already thinking differently about issues
of care and dependency who are also most likely to describe
ageing, and even very old age, as a time when we may well still
be learning new things, deepening existing relationships and,
if spared harsh material deprivation (which many, shamefully,
will not be), continuing to savour life – though probably a little
more slowly and often facing several new pitfalls.

Pursuing such thoughts, in this book I will not be singing the joys of 'agelessness', but rather listening out for alternative stories of ageing, confronting some of my own fears, as well as tackling the routine 'jovial' dismissal of 'dementing oldies'.[75] Acknowledging the habitually disavowed mutual dependence necessary for sustaining the human condition, while querying our cultural obsession with notions of 'independence', just might help us to see that those most disparaged in the circuit of human interdependence, or largely abandoned within it, call into question the humanity of all of us.

'How old am I?' is not a question we usually dare to ask aloud, except in jest. Soon after we learn to talk we come to know exactly how old we are. Today, however, I can easily find myself genuinely wondering exactly how old I am, lurching around between the decades, writing the wrong date on cheques. Ageing is still a topic that many hope to dismiss. Both my own fears as well as the defensiveness I hear all around me ('you don't look old') confirm its unpopularity. Nevertheless, addressing old age is not as forbidden as it once was. In my experience, by the time we start reading that certain topics are unmentionable, we can be fairly certain that old taboos are already collapsing, often indeed that the floodgates are opening.

Simone de Beauvoir, whose voice travels along with this text, said that when in the 1960s she searched for books on the condition of the old she could find hardly any at all, a situation that encouraged her to write her own book on old age. This state of affairs is shifting. Starting up my computer today, I see an interview with the impressive, politically engaged actress Juliet Stevenson, now fifty-six. She is asked whether there are fewer parts for older actresses compared with older actors. We know the answer. But she is quite precise: 'Yes, way fewer.

And it becomes increasingly difficult. As you go through life it gets more and more interesting and complicated, but the parts offered get more and more simple, and less complicated. That's a battle we still have to fight.'[76]

It is a battle I want to join. Old age is no longer the condition that dare not speak its name, but we have a long way to go before we can joke that it is the identity that refuses to be silent.

2

Generational Warfare

'What's the matter with him?' whispered Lenina. Her eyes were wide with horror and amazement. 'He's old, that's all,' Bernard answered as carelessly as he could. He too was startled; but he made an effort to seem unmoved.

Aldous Huxley, *Brave New World*

Age and ageing may appear elusive and complicated when looked at from any personal perspective, yet across society they are monotonously orchestrated in terms of a war of the generations, placing us within uniform and competing age cohorts. In the USA, the public staging of generational conflict made it into the popular genre of reality TV with *Battle of the Ages*, aired on NBC in 2010. In the UK that same year, we saw repeated scapegoating of the older generation, now mockingly labelled the 'Baby Boomers', as responsible for all the woes of young people. The indictment was promulgated at government levels, with the high-profile Tory MP David Willetts publishing his emotive polemic entitled *The Pinch: How the Baby-Boomers Took Their Children's Future – and Why They Should Give It Back*.[1]

Historical Underpinnings

There is nothing new about the war between the generations, or the baiting of older people, though it has taken different forms through history. It is sometimes thought that in earlier times the old were treated with far more respect, affection and kindness than they are today. The self-styled cultural critic and ageist resister Margaret Morganroth Gullette, for instance, so attentive to the way in which 'we are battered by the crosswinds of prejudice as we age' in much of today's world, believes that we have seen a steady erosion of the 'cautious veneration that was once directed so unconsciously toward vulnerable old people'.[2] Societies are indeed diverse in their attitudes towards and treatment of the elderly, but there are multiple reasons for this.

One key factor in the difference in attitudes to ageing can be found in the number of people who now manage to reach old age. Where there is a mass of elderly people there is less respect than in societies where there are few, especially when in the past it was more likely to be only the relatively powerful and affluent who survived into old age.[3] Nevertheless, ambivalence, at best, has been the pervasive cultural sentiment surrounding old age even in traditional societies such as those that existed in Ancient Greece. The Hellenic world, with its cultural riches, philosophical scholarship and official respect for old age and the rights of seniority, provides a perfect case study of many of the enduring contradictions in attitudes towards old age, especially in the epicentre of its cultural power and influence, the Athenian city state around 500 to 300 BCE.

On the one hand, Athenian law required children to provide for their ageing parents and imposed harsh penalties on any instances of mistreatment. Owning property, alongside access to other material goods, ensured considerable power for the small number of city elders who had managed to reach the age of sixty or seventy in Ancient Greece. Furthermore, in the philosophies of Socrates and Plato, old age was associated with wisdom. Plato himself, for instance, suggested that fifty was a good age to begin philosophy.[4] That is a pleasing thought.

On the other hand, Athenian culture displayed a consistent distaste and mockery, if not outright disgust, towards what were routinely presented as the miseries and hideousness of 'vile' and 'ugly' old age. All heroism, beauty and sweetness resided in youth, and in youth alone. This is especially prominent in the work of its best-known poets and playwrights, as the surviving plays of Euripides or Aristophanes exemplify. With harsh, caustic wit, both writers showed older men and women, in different ways, as stock figures of ridicule. They depicted old men as locked in conflict with their sons, ending up beaten and derided; old women as helpless and pitiable, if not ridiculous, above all for any erotic desires they might still hold, such desire arousing immediate disgust. In Aristophanes' play, *Ekklesiazousai*, or *Women in Power*, for instance, old women are described as 'dirty old bags', able to offer a man only 'vinegar dregs and a beard and bad breath': 'sex with her is like sleeping with death'.[5] Such cruel ribaldry meshed with the usually pitiless antics of the gods and goddesses of Greek mythology. Immortality aside, these deities were distinguished from human beings above all in the idea that they would never grow old, never experience the misery and doom of human ageing.[6]

If we travel through time, leaping across the centuries from the fifth century BCE to 1600 CE, the conflict between young and old continues, with England's greatest bard famously proclaiming that 'crabbed age and youth cannot live together'. Yet

41

even Shakespeare's haunting description of old age as 'second childishness and mere oblivion, / Sans teeth, sans eyes, sans everything', seems mild compared to other cruel caricatures of the old.[7] Furthermore, however much old men have been lampooned for their ugliness, witless infirmities, or ageing lechery, especially when marrying much younger women, it was elderly women who aroused the most terrifying degrees of horror. Throughout world literature and across historical time down to the present, ageing women have been depicted as dangerous and destructive creatures when seen as having any power, or else as feeble and repellent objects of pity or contempt, when seen as needy and dependent.[8] Even the highly esteemed sixteenth-century Dutch scholar of enlightenment and tolerance, Erasmus, in his famous essay *In Praise of Folly*, fiercely mocked older women who 'still play the coquette' and 'do not hesitate to exhibit their repulsive withered breasts'. It is thought that his words might lie behind the hideously memorable Flemish portrait known as 'The Ugly Duchess'.[9]

The disdainful and denigrating caricature of the elderly can in certain times and places result not just in routine cruelty, but also in overwhelming acts of brutality. It is important to notice that this has been more likely to occur in periods of economic, social and religious change and upheaval. As many will know, this was most harshly evident in the witch-hunts that lasted for three centuries in early modern Europe, especially in central Europe.

From around 1450 to 1750, it was particularly older women, usually widows living alone, who were most easily targeted as witches. Numerous studies of these witch-hunts have argued that the main targets of the accusations were women most detached from patriarchal institutions. The historian Brian

Levack sums this up: 'The limited data we have regarding the age of witches shows a solid majority of witches were older than fifty, which in the early modern period was considered to be a much more advanced age than today.'[10] His work is corroborated by Deborah Willis, again suggesting that it was usually an older woman, living alone, who was most likely to be 'resented as an economic burden' and seen as 'the locus of a dangerous envy and verbal violence'.[11] This meant that around three-quarters of the tens of thousands of victims who were tried, tortured and executed as witches in central Europe were older women.[12]

If witches have had, historically and metaphorically, an ageing female face, it is a visage that continues to haunt us today. In my youth, with Hollywood's dream factories servicing collective fantasies in the West, the most memorable roles available for the ageing actress were women who were either threatening or pitiable, or often both at once. Perhaps most haunting of all was the chilling performance of Bette Davis in *Whatever Happened to Baby Jane* (1962). Here, she plays the part of a briefly successful child star, her fame long gone, now engaged in the increasingly sadistic abuse of her subsequently more successful, but now crippled sister, played by Joan Crawford. Davis' high-pitched cackling and increasingly demented behaviour embodied the precise doubling of old woman and horror. More often, Hollywood's baiting and punishment of the older woman focused especially on the once successful career woman, portrayed in mid-life as someone now as distressing to herself as she was alarming to others and threatening, in particular, to younger women. This was also the theme of the earlier film *Sunset Boulevard* (1950), as well as the sensationalizing 1968 movie about an older lesbian, *The Killing of Sister George*. In all these films, women who have had some professional success are seen stripped completely of any autonomy or dignity as they age.

To what extent, if at all, we have moved beyond these malicious caricatures is another of the questions to which I will return. However, given the well-documented dearth of any leading roles, let alone good ones, for women over forty in cinema, we can be fairly certain that any progress will be slow, at least in that place best known for marketing our fantasies on the cinema screen. Not for nothing do female stars decry the lack of roles for older women. Simone Signoret and Rita Hayworth were just two of the many beautiful screen goddesses excoriated relatively early in their careers for signs of ageing, when male stars retained their romantic leads despite their boozing and increasingly battered looks.[13]

Channelling Discontent

The Battle of the Ages, we can see, has a history, looping us back through time and bouncing us forward into the present. Two decades ago, in his now classic text, *The Journey of Life: A Cultural History of Aging in America* (1992), the historian Thomas Cole warned that the extent of the federal budget deficit in the USA was creating an increasing 'possibility of intergenerational warfare between young and old'.[14] What he did not mention was the extent of the media's complicity in inciting such warfare. His compatriot, Gullette, took up the story. She was soon compiling an extensive register of the ways in which many of the most popular media outlets were busy throughout the 1990s manufacturing a form of homogenized generational combat. While the decade began in the midst of economic recession with the censure of the supposedly passive younger 'generation X' as 'work-shy slackers and whiners', the search for scapegoats soon switched to defending this younger generation, now lumped together as collectively anxious and discontented, against the culpabilities of 'greedy Baby Boomers'. Media headlines targeted all those now in mid-life, whose eager aspirations when themselves young were said to have been responsible for impoverishing those who came in their wake. ' "Crybaby" Boomers "hate their kids" ', opined a particularly abusive opinion piece by Walter Kim in the *New York Times* (July 1997); other media outlets quickly followed this lead, soon summarized in the *Utne Reader*.[15]

Meanwhile, any deterioration in the conditions of life, whether at work or at home, were also blamed on the Boomers, who according to the academic and award-winning investigative journalist, Mark Hunter, had 'done more than any other generation to erase the line between work and private life'.[16] Hunter's comment appeared in the mass circulation lifestyle magazine, *Modern Maturity*, with its proclaimed mission to help people over fifty to live 'fulfilling lives', later provoking a heated exchange between Hunter and Gullette.[17] 'Boomer-bashing' was declared the new 'national pastime' among twenty year olds by Suneel Ratan in *Fortune Magazine* in the mid-1990s, and also used as a source of humour and provocation by fellow journalists, such as Michael Grunwald of *Time* magazine and another popular US journalist, Bruce Farris, in the *Fresco Bee*.[18] It hardly needs saying that such facile generational scapegoating lacked any accompanying economic analysis. In reality, apart from the new millionaires mainly created by what was soon to prove the disastrous fiscal speculation following the removal of all significant banking regulation in the 1980s, the majority of Americans in the USA, of whatever age, were becoming relatively poorer and less secure. There has been rising inequality among all age groups and a relative decline in both the quality of jobs and the value of wages since the 1970s, as evident in countless economic analyses, from academic texts to routine household surveys.[19]

We have long been familiar with a chorus of men blaming women, and in particular feminism, for men's deteriorating working and home lives, accompanied by routine resort to anti-immigrant sentiment, not to mention the abiding visceral racism of white Americans, all serving as conduits for discharging rage. Nowadays, however, cultural incitement of resentment of the young towards the old has become yet another repetitive feature of much of the media's channelling of discontent away from any more useful attempt to grapple with the far more complicated analysis of the socially destructive effects of the deregulation of corporate finance and its impact on the policies of nation states.

In the UK, the surge of media attacks on the sixty-plus generation is more recent. In 2006 the contrarian journalist Brendan O'Neill was given space by the BBC to broadcast his views: 'Baby boomers like to trumpet their generation's achievements. But their fondness for conspicuous consumption and foreign travel has led to many a modern-day ill, from rising debt to environmental woes.'[20] (O'Neill was associated with the maverick *LM Magazine* – short for *Living Marxism* – that in the 1990s leaped, with extraordinary success, clear across the centre ground from being a small intensely sectarian far-left Trotskyist group, the Revolutionary Communist Party, into the lap of the corporate right.) More generally, it was not until 2010, following the global financial crisis, that the upmarket British media joined the chorus of denunciations of the Baby Boomers in any systematic way. 'Crisis? Blame the baby-boomers, not the bankers', was the headline in the 22 February edition of *The Times*, introducing an article by the paper's principal economics columnist Anatole Kaletsky. Kaletsky ended his analysis of the crisis with a warning of the dangers of 'the rapidly escalating cost of government-financed pensions and healthcare as the baby-boom generation, born from 1945 onwards, starts to retire'. The potentially costly needs of an expanding ageing population now combined with a recurring hostility to those who participated in the freedom-loving 1960s to generate a new vituperation towards the older generation: 'The greedy demographic governing body of timid baby-boomers, far more than the fervour of bankers, is the loyal mercantile calamity right away confronting Britain.'[21]

On my birthday in 2010, I logged on to the internet only to find the BBC homepage adorned with a denunciation of 'my generation'. Headline space had been given over this time to Neil Boorman, the author of *It's All Their Fault*, indicting those of us who have reached our sixties for … well, for what, exactly? We have been blamed for every social and moral blight, from housing and fiscal crises to environmental pollution, while also being held responsible for all the insecurities, moral laxities and any other imputed fears, anxieties or vices of the generation we reared.[22] I couldn't clear my head of the refrain of one particular song, containing the trite rhyme 'Every generation, blames the one before, and all of their frustrations, come beating on your door.' Mike Rutherford wrote the words for Paul Carrack's best-selling single, 'The Living Years', at the close of the 1980s, when he was mourning his own father's recent death, before the silence over their disagreements had been broken.

By 2010, however, it had become increasingly clear that it was not just the younger generation individually echoing Larkin's famous filial lament about the ways in which 'man hands on misery to man'.[23] Accompanying any Oedipal drama and personal grievance, there is nowadays a fully orchestrated mainstream media festival designed to direct the resentment of younger generations towards the older. All the quality papers in the UK picked up the same theme. The business pages of the *Guardian* ran with the alliterative headline 'The inadvertent burden baby boomers have bequeathed the young is sending Britain broke', while the *Telegraph* proclaimed that 'Baby boomers made sacrifice a dirty word – but the young are fighting back'.[24]

It should come as no surprise, therefore, that the manipulation of generational conflict reveals the obvious role of shifting economic forces in the portrayal of different age groups. They have been positioned as competing directly against each other for cherished resources. The chief target of assault at any particular moment moves with the impact of job markets, unemployment, social tensions and, especially, calls upon whatever state funding remains available. With life expectancy increasing in most parts of the world, it is obvious that the issue of pensions is indeed one in need of serious attention. However, as the British left historian Robin Blackburn argues, there are many ways of tackling the needs of the elderly and creating a fairer pension system without resulting in any crisis. He points out that, on current trends, by the mid twenty-first century over a billion of the world's ageing population will be living in poverty. However, Blackburn adds that there are ways of funding a global pension for the elderly. He names three in particular that he sees as highly suited to the task: 'a small tax on international currency transactions, a levy on the fuel used on international flights and a mild tax on corporate wealth'. The first source is similar to the much-disputed Tobin Tax, which places a small levy on the sale or purchase of currencies, and which Blackburn estimates could yield at least $150 billion annually.[25]

The idea that the 'politics' of an entire population of the new elderly could be declared 'selfish' might seem obviously rather dim-witted, nevertheless the Minister of State for Universities and Science, David Willetts, regarded as one of the key thinkers of the Tory Party, put his authority behind such attacks in his book *The Pinch*. Ignoring altogether the role of the banks, whose reckless gambling and gigantic accumulation of personal wealth resulted in the UK government taking on a massive burden of debt to bail them out, Willetts blamed the current crisis on 'the self-interest and electoral dominance of the huge generation of baby-boomers', summed up in his provocative subtitle: 'How the baby-boomers took their children's future – and why they should give it back'.[26] Repeating this divisive mantra, iconoclastic journalist Neil Boorman claimed to have found a new myth to trash – it is not the young but the old who are selfish: 'The richest, most powerful generation that ever lived is embarking on a comfortable retirement. But why does it feel like they've pulled up the ladder with them?'

Boorman was promoting his own polemical manifesto inciting generational battle, *It's All Their Fault*, as a call to arms for the young to line up against the older generation:

This is a terrible time to be young. Graduates are joining the dole queue as soon as they leave university, while their parents retire on cosy nest eggs ... Young families are struggling to provide the basics as their grandparents embark on another cruise. The prospect of paying off that debt and saving for a deposit for a one-bedroom flat is remote, and it is all the fault of our parents. Anyone under the age of thirty-five is living in the shadow of the Baby Boomer Generation who grew up in an era of rapidly growing prosperity, drew wages from jobs for life, got their education for free, and bought multiple cars and TVs that they didn't need. The enormous financial debt we've been handed comes from both their megalomania of overspending and their reckless economic and political decision-making.[27]

Mea Culpa

For many young people this is indeed a very hard and depressing time. However, what is perhaps most startling about the careless and pejorative dismissal of the Baby Boomers is that much of it comes not just from the right, eager to divert us from the depredations of deregulation and neo-liberalism, but from public figures who have been associated more with the left, the Labour Party, and trade unions as well. On top of this, the critique is espoused as much by the old themselves, as by the young. Following Boorman's call to arms, inciting the young against the old, the life-long Labour supporter and journalist Francis Beckett, launched his own very similar critique: *What Did the Baby Boomers Ever Do for Us?*, with its now familiar subtitle, *How the Children of the Sixties Lived the Dream and Failed the Future.*[28]

It is the legacy of the '60s generation itself they love to trash, with its counter-culture and alternative media committed to

sexual permissiveness, anti-war activities, notions of partici-
patory democracy and redistributive and egalitarian politics.[29]
However, for many of these mea culpa boomers, the '60s call
for change is bizarrely inverted. Dissident voices are held
responsible for the subsequent victory of those whose whole
political outlook was precisely geared to condemning, and soon
enough successfully reversing, that '60s heritage. Somehow, the
moral conservatism and reification of unregulated markets that
Margaret Thatcher managed to install at the heart of British
government at the close of the 1970s can be rolled into a *single*
heritage, with the losers in this political confrontation simply
swallowed up and spat out as if we had all raced to embrace the
victors. In Beckett's obtuse summary:

> What began as the most radical-sounding generation for half
> a century turned into a random collection of youthful style
> gurus, sharp-toothed entrepreneurs and management consult-
> ants who believed revolution meant new ways of selling things;
> and Thatcherites, who thought freedom meant free markets,
> not free people ... While the philosophy of the sixties seemed
> progressive at the time, the Baby Boomers we remember are
> not the political reformers, but the millionaires.[30]

The Baby Boomers 'we' remember arrive absent of all the '60s
radicals I recall, from Stuart Hall, Tariq Ali, Adrian Mitchell,
Harold Pinter, Tom McGrath and David Widgery, not all of
whom are still with us, to the few women whose voices were
heard in that decade, and which would grow ever louder in
the following one: Margaret Drabble, Angela Carter, Juliet
Mitchell, Sheila Rowbotham, to name only a handful of those
notable in the UK.

Deluged by this flood of denunciations of our generation, some of the scapegoats have joined the chorus. 'Mea culpa' has become a favourite position for ageing media pundits to occupy. Will Hutton, Principal of Hertford College, Oxford, and a prestigious economics journalist, has been pursuing the same theme and himself fanning the flames of resentment: 'A sixty-year-old in 2010 is a very privileged and lucky human being – an object of resentment as much as admiration.' 'I'm at the heart of it – guilty as charged', Hutton continues, 'I have some sympathy with the resentment, marshalled in a cluster of recent anti-boomer books. Individually, we may not have been the authors of today's flux, uncertainty and lack of social and cultural anchors, but we were at the scene of the crime.' I guess we can only hope that this 'judge' is not placed on any actual judiciary. Hutton is wrong when he attempts to amalgamate the different strands of union politics and the counter-culture of the iconic '60s: 'the shop steward movement of the 1960s and its wildcat strikes were inextricably linked to hippies, smoking dope, the anti-Vietnam war movement and the rapidly growing women's movement'. As any study of their publications would reveal, these strands were usually considerably at odds with each other. He is even less convincing in his claim that 'paradoxically the same liberal culture fed the desire to dismantle the regulation of banks and the constraints of the postwar fixed exchange rate system'. Summing up this slippery causal nexus, where those defeated in the battles of recent history are held equally responsible for all they fought against, Hutton concludes:

> Looking back you can see how 1968 led to the futile confusion of the 1970s, the certainties of Thatcherism and the great mindless credit-induced boom of the 1990s and 2000s – credit

rolling out of the great deregulated banks and building societies ... Privatisation and the curbing of the union movement
had grown seamlessly out of our revolts of the 1960s – even
using our language of freedom.[31]

Seamlessly? Only for those who determinedly avert their eyes
from the crooked stitching.

No doubt it is the pervasiveness of this climate of rhetorical chastisement, so expedient in cost-cutting times, that leads
even a few of those who have been dissenters to accept Hutton's
smug declaration of collective guilt on 'our' behalf. When a
sample of well-known ageing politicians and cultural figures
were asked to respond to Hutton's 'guilty' verdict on them all
as a group, they accepted at least part of his argument. Being
themselves all highly successful professionally, these public
figures were perhaps more easily prone to feeling reprimanded:
'I know how lucky my generation has been and how weirdly
we have kept riding the wave of our times and are still out there
... My generation is guilty of heedlessness, I can see that now',
Marina Warner comments; 'We have left this country bank-
rupt', film-maker Nick Bloomfield concurs; 'We have failed
dismally', Labour MP Ken Livingstone agrees, though going
on to add that 'what ordinary people did during that time was
fine. The failure has been at the political level.' More usefully,
the writer Lisa Appignanesi offers just a pinch of historical
complexity: 'Reality is ever recalcitrant to our hopes. We failed
to bring social justice to all or distribute the benefits of periods
of affluence. But many of us still try ... Milton Friedman and
Maggie Thatcher were not baby boomers ... and I don't think
we can be held responsible for all the excesses of an economic
liberalism they brought in their train.'[32] Nor do I.

Without doubt, all sorts of mistakes were made by militant trade unionists, liberation movements, as well as by the organized far left and Labour Party activists. There were, however, very clear dividing lines. Thatcher and her kind were always the harshest critics of each and all the radical movement of the 1960s, while those shop-stewards, anti-war activists, dope-smokers and budding women's liberationists, if they agreed on anything at all, it would be on the need to curtail the power of banks. Of course, they were not in agreement about exactly how to do this, whether by nationalizing the banks or by creating alternative cooperative ventures. Feminists in particular were hardly in favour of dismantling state regulation. On the contrary, we were calling for government legislation on equal pay, anti-discrimination and a strengthening of the interventionist policies of the state to create greater gender equality and more democratically run community resources, as part of a broader promotion of social justice, environmental harmony and an end to all forms of violence, nationally and internationally.

Entering old age, almost all those leftists and feminists I knew forty years ago hold much the same political views now as then. There is no shortage of older radicals who continue to support struggles for justice, equality and a safer, greener, more peaceful world. Where possible, we often contribute to or even help organize resistance – even if we are nowadays banging our frailer heads against far thicker walls, alongside an emerging array of youthful rebels and militants. From what I read, as well as hear at meetings and on demonstrations I attend, it is clear that it is as often as not those over sixty, the supposedly 'selfish' boomer generation, who still worry most about the rising inequalities and other social hazards of our time. Here

is the prominent writer and critic Marina Warner again, recalling the passionate days of women's liberation and left politics
in the early '70s: 'I'm heartbroken that we were defeated, politically, culturally. I'm also sad for the next generation. The kind
of hopefulness, the energy that buoyed one up in those days, is
something nobody with any kind of sophistication can really
entertain now. You can't believe there is something to be done
that can be done by you' – as she explained to that creative
chronicler of the 'psychogeography' of contemporary London
life, Ian Sinclair.[33] Today, she speaks out loudly and often against
the rising inequality and injustices of the present, far more than
she did forty-odd years ago. As Sinclair notes in a series of
interviews with these activists, all now, like him, in their sixties:
'Women, I felt, carried the memory-burden of their cultural
heritage more effectively than men: less ego, less noise, intimate
details of ordinary life lightly held.' There may be something
in what he says, though perhaps it is a little too generalized,
especially when that cultural heritage is one of social and political engagement. Nevertheless, he adds: 'So many men of the
1960s had creased and crumpled, waiting for the tide to turn.
Incubating disaffection. Nourishing unpublished memoirs,
boxes of dead photographs. Unrequired confessions.'[34]

I know some of these men, mourning their youthful days of
righteous rage and self-dramatization. But I also know many
other men who have found ways to continue some of their old
progressive activism for a fairer world, in one form or another.
They remain less prominent than the better known ageing men
of the left who retain both their old political energy and can
still find platforms for proclaiming their former socialist con-
victions, such as Stuart Hall, David Edgar, Tariq Ali, Robin
Blackburn, John Pilger, Richard Gott, John Palmer, Richard

Kuper, and a multitude of other older denizens of remaining left institutions and publications. Nevertheless, I suspect that feminism, among other things, has provided a more durable lifeboat for many women of the left.

Sinclair is thus probably right to detect more disaffected older men from amongst the left. These are those who are not only more likely to agree with Hutton, but also to become far more belligerent castigators of their own generation, joining the latest judgmental chorus. Certainly that is the disparaging tone of the fiercest of the self-styled contrarians of recent years, including the journalist Nick Cohen, or writers such as Martin Amis and the late Christopher Hitchens in the decade before his recent death. All have been regularly full of bile and fury against what they regard as the self-deceptions, faults and follies of the left to which they once belonged. Amongst older women, the only equivalent I can think of is Melanie Phillips, who always hovered at the centre of the political spectrum before lurching violently to the right, whether in relation to socialist or feminist arenas.

There is little or no chance of ever communicating with the new contrarians. It would be instructive, however, if Will Hutton, and those more mildly inclined to agree with him, were to glance, perhaps again, at the memorable words of one our most incisive and poetic forebears, Walter Benjamin. Benjamin condemns exactly those who dismiss the diversity of the seeds of hope that have animated the struggles of the past:

> In every era the attempt must be made anew to wrest tradition away from a conformism that is about to overpower it ... Only that historian will have the gift of fanning the spark of hope in the past who is firmly convinced that even the dead will not be

safe from the enemy if he wins. And this enemy has not ceased to be victorious.[35]

Thatcher and her monetarist friends, even today, especially today, have not ceased to be victorious, as the current Tory-led coalition in Britain returns to her polities of welfare cuts, military ventures, and the expansion of an insecure and deregulated workforce.

Moreover, far from all boomers have shared the luck of their professionally successful peers. Although the number of pensioners living in low-income households has fallen in recent years, over 20 per cent of those who live in poverty are pensioners, rising to around 30 per cent if they are single women, with at least a third of that group being people in their sixties. Many boomers have no good fortune at all to feel guilty about, remaining instead often vulnerable, sometimes isolated, and with meagre pension entitlements. This may be for reasons of class, ethnicity, disability, ill health, or other circumstances; indeed, sometimes among my close acquaintances, hard times have come precisely because they refused to buy into any of the lures of professionalism and the corporate world. We should not need the assistance of the meticulous research of British historians, such as Pat Thane, to direct us to the residual poverty of my generation. Writing a few years ago, Thane indicates that for many women:

> the difficulties ... of providing for their old age have been known for over a century, have changed little and have never gone away ... Our pension system has been characterized by a state pension too low to live on and dependence on occupational and private pensions which cannot provide a comfortable old

age to the low-paid and irregularly employed, most of whom are female.[36]

Other feminist writers, such as the feisty journalist Beatrix Campbell, have been more prominent in confronting the media's misdiagnosis of the causes of the ongoing economic crisis. As she rightly argued, simplistic attributions of generational blame stand in the way of a political understanding of the policies that have triggered the present recession, with its high unemployment, insecure and highly stressful working conditions, and lack of affordable housing.[37] Clearly, today, it is the young who are hit the hardest by the continuing recession. However, to blame the older generation for the effects of policies many of us opposed is merely to foreclose any useful analysis of the present crisis. It also undermines the faltering efforts of those who are still trying to continue what we once began, looking around for and sometimes finding younger voices to support. This also involves wondering how best to remember, as well as critique, the diverse and conflictual histories of political radicalism.

Understanding the present crisis is a task that both younger and older generations would do well to embark upon together. It is the growing inequality *within*, not *between*, the different age cohorts that underpins the current economic and social crisis, especially in the USA. Many leading economists, such as Joseph Stiglitz, Paul Krugman and Thomas Palley, have been making this point for years. Thirty years of comparatively declining wages in the USA, plus the shortage of affordable rented accommodation and above all the new banking policy of lending to the poor (whose growing indebtedness did not allow them to repay their loans) and then selling on the 'toxic' debts to other banks, was what actually triggered the subprime mortgage crisis that generated the threat of a global banking collapse. Larry Elliott, a British economic journalist who stays close to his roots in the progressive left politics of yesterday, regularly points out that in the USA, as increasingly in the UK, it is the concentration of wealth at the top, together with the undermining of trade unions and the eroding of welfare protection, which have all contributed to greater social inequality and instability.

The solution, tragically eschewed by the current UK and US governments, is to support many of the goals we ageing folk fought for back in the '60s and '70s: increased wages for the majority of workers, especially the low paid, stronger trade unions, a platform for movements representing the interests of all those marginalized, whether by gender, race, ethnicity, or other sources of exclusion or vulnerability. In other words, Elliott concludes: 'We need to junk the right-wing dogma that has dominated economic thinking for the past 30 years. And, in the case of the UK government, still does.'[38] This view resonates with the perennial stance of that ageing British medical epidemiologist, Richard Wilkinson. Together with Kate Pickett, he recently once again presented elaborate statistics showing that, across the whole social spectrum, overall inequality produced more social and health problems in highly unequal societies when compared with the more equal (typically Scandinavian) ones. Mental illness, for example, was 500 per cent higher in all social groups in the most unequal societies.[39]

What does my age group of late mid-lifers, or early elderly, have to contribute to puzzling over the dilemmas of the present? Again I return to the ebullient Marina Warner, suggesting that 'it's crucial to recreate the conditions that brought about our generation's energy: the opportunity of free education, the valuing of ideas over profit, because social wellbeing ... will follow imagination and inventiveness'.[40] However, fear eats the soul as threats of redundancy, disregard, abandonment and isolation routinely dampen the spirits of most people as they age, even when they remain economically privileged.

Leaping the Barriers

Fear eats the soul because, regardless of the recent liberal critique evident in the naming of ageism, the present moment remains saturated with different forms of prejudice against the elderly. It can be sensed everywhere in the reiterated statistical panic over the 'greying of the world' as more people are living longer. On the one hand, there is the weight of history, language and culture in its visceral abhorrence of old age. On the other, there is the significant incitement to generational blame evident in the scapegoating of 'Baby Boomers' reaching pensionable age. Both are present in the fears expressed about those over seventy-five, now increasingly living into their eighties and nineties or beyond, and seen as needing expensive care. Nevertheless, despite confronting so much negativity and alarm, there have always been crevices from which countervailing voices have arisen, trying to reach across the generations. They have done this for diverse reasons, though more often than not their efforts remain somewhat muffled by larger, if sometimes subterranean, forces of fear, shame or diminishment.

However, once we set out in search of the varied voices and texts eager to subvert the cultural chorus of age warfare they are not so hard to find. While they may be rarely evident in the oppositional binaries the journalistic mainstream likes to uphold and amplify, the promotion of more harmonious contact between the young and old is apparent nowadays in some of the more creative academic research and across different disciplines. In Britain, the literary scholar Helen Small exemplifies this new trend in her book, *The Long Life* (2007). Writing in her early forties, Small is interested in what scholars and writers have had to say about old age, wanting to explore the chequered relations between a long life and a good life as well as the impediments to conjoining the two. Repeatedly, she regrets the dearth of interesting philosophical reflection on old age in modern times. Such considerations are essential, she insists, because of their 'repercussions for what we deem to be a good life', alongside what old age tells us about 'how we measure happiness' and reflect upon issues of virtue and justice.[41]

More generally, over the last twenty years there has been a rapid expansion of what is known as humanistic gerontology, which aims to move away from the strictly empirical discourse of mainstream gerontology that was primarily concerned with the ageing body and its needs. Those who take a humanistic approach, such as Thomas Cole and Ruth Ray, state that they are more engaged with issues of interpretation, rhetoric and narrative, thereby encompassing what are seen as psychosocial, ethical, existential and spiritual concerns. Indeed, breaking down the barriers between generations has become one of the mainstays of this approach, in its consistent effort to create and sustain a more optimistic view of ageing. From the humanistic perspective the key epistemological question on ageing is: 'what does it mean to grow old?'[42]

Framed in this way, the concern with what it means to grow old, what it feels like to age, dominates the forms of enquiry that have accompanied what is known as the 'cultural turn' in intellectual life, which became ever more prominent in the final decades of the twentieth century in the humanities and some of the social sciences, as attention shifted to the creation and instabilities of subjectivity and meaning. Such questions direct us, in particular, to the proliferation of memoir writing and other forms of autobiography in both scholarly and popular domains during recent decades. Despite all that we know of the inevitable selectivity and distortion of memory in the shaping of life narratives, it sometimes becomes easier, and altogether less threatening, to make connections across the generations when personal lives are narrated in ways that allow us to explore the perils, pitfalls and pleasures occurring in the course of a long life. In the context of memoirs and of certain fictions that mirror them, old age no longer appears as simply a type of foreign country separated off from the rest of a life. Rather, in such texts the experiences of the old unfold and collapse back, like concertinas, into narratives that are rarely reducible to age itself, but reveal multiple threads that can remain visible from the struggles, choices, contingencies of the younger life once lived, their psychic traces enduring to the end. Moreover, these strands are usually evident whatever the unexpected rewards or cruelties of fate, chance, or shifting national or global conjunctures. Indeed, as I will explore in far more detail in later chapters, they are sometimes all the more visible in a person's distinct ways of encountering suffering and loss in old age.

Just a few literary critics have been exploring these ideas of late. One of the first was Barbara Frey Waxman in her study of the autobiographies of ageing people, *To Live in the Center of the Moment* (1997), which she wrote when facing her own middle age at forty-nine. She embarked on this project, she says, with the personal and ethical expectation that combining literary criticism with the reading of autobiographies of ageing might be able to 'transform our fear of ageing and our wariness of elders'.[43] High hopes perhaps, but her own thinking, she reports, was indeed changed by her reading of the words of many of her older compatriots: May Sarton, Doris Grumbach, Maya Angelou, Audre Lorde, poet Lucille Clifton, and others. In the UK, ageing has remained a largely missing topic in literary theory. Nevertheless, providing much of the material I will rely upon, memoirs and related fiction are certainly emerging. As we saw in the last chapter, Jane Miller's elegant reflections on what it feels like to be old suggested she preferred her old age to her memories of being young.[44] Of course, she admits that there are many bad things about ageing, while also pointing to what can often be the difficulties of being young. She knows she has been more than usually lucky, having been happily married for forty years, remaining in the same house throughout this time, a place that was once one of the hubs of literary London, and finding the career she most enjoyed at mid-life. She writes of her own assorted ailments, pains, memory lapses and more, alongside the terrible sorrow surrounding the deaths or calamitous debility of friends. Nevertheless, she and many of her friends, we learn, remain active and mostly cheerful. The difficulties of trying to bridge the gulf between young and old remain, however, even with her own young relatives of whom she is so fond: 'I see that there is really no reason for the young to bother themselves with old age ... Being able to ignore the future and possible endings is what you're young for, after all.'[45]

Expressing her appreciation of this book, Miller's contemporary, Penelope Lively, having herself written so wonderfully on the paradoxical, unpredictable experiences of ageing, both applauds Miller's attempt to undercut the caricatures of the old (condensed into the iconography of two figures bent over walking sticks on road signs warning of elderly pedestrians) and also confirms the obstacles to overcoming them. Illustrating those caricatures, Lively tells us: 'I once judged a children's writing competition in which entries had been invited on the subject of grandparents; without exception, the people represented were ancient, white-haired, knitting by the fireside.' All the stranger, she adds, when 'the average granny in this country is likely to be around sixty, and still at work'.[46] All the stranger, too, when, as Lively goes on to suggest, over the last fifty years the enormous gulf between the generations has seemed to be in decline. As grandparents today, my '60s generation really are likely to be closer to our grandchildren in values and outlook than we were to our own grandparents. Indeed, as Lively herself reflected in her late seventies:

> it does seem to me that there has been a seismic change over the last fifty years in the relationship between the generations. I adored my grandmother, but was aware that a whole aspect of my life was unmentionable – anything that made reference to sex. My own granddaughters know, I think, that nothing they could say would shock me. Where attitudes are concerned, the generation gap has narrowed, for many of us.[47]

Narrowed, perhaps, but still it seems vast effort must be put into the work of trying to counter those fears and anxieties, from within and without, that keep us so wary of each other across age divisions, all the more so when we are up against forces working to enhance them.

It is this persistence of the sharply differentiating and dangerous dynamics of ageism that has triggered the very recent appearance of a field calling itself 'Age Studies', now sometimes

referred to as 'life-course research', to engage with the continuities and disruptions people experience across a lifetime. Thus
Age Studies courses are designed to combat fixed ideas about
discrete age groups, explicitly seeking out best practices for
promoting intergenerational understanding and cooperation.

This was the goal of all the papers presented at a conference
advertising itself as the 'First Global Conference on Times of
Our Lives: Growing Up, Growing Old', which took place in
Oxford in the summer of 2009.[48] The papers presented there
bore optimistic titles, such as Peter Caws and Julia Glahn's 'The
Irrelevance of Chronological Age', in the opening session, and
the following day James Gambone's 'Together for Tomorrow:
Building Community through Intergenerational Dialogue
and Action'. Yet, although in line with the hopes of most of
the other contributors, the 'irrelevance of chronological age'
seems rather whimsical, even if thought desirable, when its
authors also assert that the possibilities for intergenerational
friendship are currently hard to sustain against the backdrop of
persisting cultural preconceptions insisting on their difficulties.
Nevertheless, Caws and Glahn argued that there were many
ways of challenging such prejudices and trying to shift the usual
pattern of perceptions and practices. These begin, in their view,
with highlighting the very high social, political and economic
costs of supporting such generational separation and isolation.

Also aiming to combat ageist stereotypes, other conference
papers pointed out that sometimes the best comes last: Verdi
wrote Falstaff, perhaps his best comic opera, when he was
eighty; Benjamin Franklin invented the bifocal lens when he was
seventy-eight; Frank Lloyd Wright completed the Guggenheim
Museum, one of his masterpieces, when he was ninety-one;
Michelangelo was painting the frescoes in the Pauline chapel of

the Vatican at eighty-nine; Georgia O'Keeffe was still painting until her death at ninety-eight.[49] In London in 2007 many admirers were drawn to an exhibition of the life's work of Louise Bourgeois, the extraordinary French-American artist who kept on painting and exhibiting her work to enormous acclaim right up to the day she died, aged ninety-eight, in 2010. Certainly, as we will see often enough in subsequent chapters, for the most fortunate, life may be lived creatively till the last.

The hope is that the greater our knowledge of the life-long persistence of creativity, at times even of exceptional talent, among some of the already eminent, the easier it becomes to encourage more positive awareness of the potential and perhaps hidden creativity that might be fostered in the lesser-known elderly folk we encounter. Nonetheless, there is also some wishful thinking in the strategic denial of trying to assert the irrelevance of ageing and old age, ignoring what is distinctive about the layers of years lived. At this early stage, though, I imagine these champions of old age feel such simplification is necessary to embolden forces of resistance to routine ageism – rather like the slogans 'Black Is Beautiful'; 'Gay Is Good'; 'Women Are Strong', to which they perhaps hope to add, 'Ageing Is Admirable'. Such rallying rhetoric may indeed be useful, but it is necessary to insist that all forms of prejudice and isolation are cruel and wrong, even if someone is thought unappealing and disagreeable, whatever their ethnicity, sexuality, gender or age. To argue that age is irrelevant thus runs the risk of turning our attention once more away from the varied distinctiveness of old age, with its gains and losses, its demanding challenges and fluctuating temporalities.

Feminist Genealogies

Unsurprisingly, as second-wave feminists grow old, some of us have also wanted to foster greater generational dialogue. We began by stressing our difference from our mothers, those housewives of the 1950s, who appeared to have sacrificed so much to recreate the brittle 'happy families' of the post-war period into which we were born. They were women often barely able to conceal their bitterness over their own diminished lives or, perhaps like my own mother, their resentment over the domestic tyranny of their husbands.[50] However, along with Adrienne Rich and others, some feminists soon came to celebrate the practices of motherhood and maternal legacies as part of the rich texture of women's experience and the feminist imagination.[51]

Feminist texts began highlighting the extent of mother blaming, whether in the classic Freudian case study, or standard Hollywood productions of bad mothers and 'hen-pecked' husbands.[52] Thinking back through our mothers and grandmothers thus became, for some, one way of asserting generational ties. This could mean writing our way back to valuing older women, while rethinking what some feminists today highlight as the complexities of a 'maternal ethics' of care and commitment: the inevitable strains in the shifting needs for holding close, and letting go, within the mother-daughter bond.[53] Thus Kathleen Woodward has stressed the familial ways in which we are not so much divided as connected across generations, recalling the lure her own grandparents held for her as a child:

In terms of age we were separated by more than fifty years and a generation, but I did not feel either then or now that we were separated by generations. Rather I felt connected by them. I felt … an emotional attunement and mutual recognition that stretched across a continuity established by three generations … Missing were the stormy emotions of envy, fear, hostility, guilt and jealousy intrinsic to the nuclear family of Freudian psychoanalysis.[54]

As Woodward points out, she is not alone in idealizing older figures such as her grandparents. Sometimes, indeed, a young person might even adopt older 'fictive kin', perhaps individuals who have been their mentors, or served in other ways to inspire them with the resilience and commitments maintained throughout long lives. Woodward draws upon the writing and film work of the anthropologist Barbara Myerhoff, who in her early forties lovingly portrayed the community life of elderly Californian East European Jews, in the documentary *In Her Time*, suggesting: 'In contacting them, I have found not only my childhood (I was raised by an Eastern European grandmother), but also my future, as an old lady … We are dehumanized and impoverished without our old people, for only by contact with them can we come to know ourselves, and only thus can we stop looking at them as an alien remote people unconnected with ourselves.'[55] Sadly, as Myerhoff knew when making this film, she would not live to enjoy the fruits of her own lessons, dying of lung cancer at fifty.

Elsewhere, in Woodward's significant collection *Figuring Age*, the American literature scholar, Mary Russo, writes of other examples of cross-generational female bonding, seeing it as challenging the ways in which, for ageing women, 'loss is too often accompanied by shame and abjection'.[56] Russo quotes from Gillian Rose's memoir *Love's Work*, written in her late forties when this incisive British philosopher was already dying of ovarian cancer, recalling an earlier visit to New York when she was well. There she had observed the deep understanding between her friend Jim, a young man dying of AIDS, and Edna, an extraordinarily vibrant ninety-three-year-old woman, seeing their relationship as representing a new form of sociality, reflecting: 'She is an annunciation, a message, very old and very new.' What Rose embraces, and Russo also celebrates in her essay, 'Aging and the Scandal of Anachronism', is the determination of some older women, at whatever cost of rejection, loss or humiliation, to keep on seeking out new friends and new lovers, to the very end of life.[57]

Vaulting over, without disowning, traditional age barriers is certainly possible and I suggest that some feminists in particular have begun to value such moves. The feminist philosopher, Rosi Braidotti, for instance, has written of what she sees as both the psychic strength and political importance of understanding and acknowledging the significance of specifically feminist genealogies, as a 'discursive and political exercise in cross-generational female bonding'.[58] However, any such genealogical mapping would surely be hugely contentious, when feminists at any one time have never shared a unified political outlook. Indeed, feminists have disagreed over how to view women and their relationship to their bodies, the issue of sexual risk, the forms of relationship women should have, and the work they should do, or should value. We have even disputed how best to pursue the basic goal of tackling women's subordination as a sex, whether within the symbolic realm of language, or in seeking or eschewing juridical and social reform. As I have written before in *Making Trouble*, and many others have noted, every re-telling of feminism's past reconstructs a political story from the present, eclipsing much of its earlier contextual nuance. Thus, as Dana Heller summarizes, the 'defining moments of feminism's generational identities, and the key debates associated with generational shifts in feminist thought are themselves constantly shifting constructions that are reworked by feminists, non feminists and antifeminists'.[59]

Worse, however, at least within the competitive sphere of academia, we surely must acknowledge that adversarial generational tension often set the tone for much feminist writing, especially during the fierce theoretical debates of the 1990s. Somewhat depressingly, this is the theme of many of the essays in Ann Kaplan and Devoney Looser's anthology *Generations: Academic Feminists in Dialogue*, published in 1997. Most of them highlight the high degree of conflict between feminist 'mothers' and 'daughters', with blame seeming to come from both younger and older feminists alike.[60] It was clearly younger feminist scholars, as much as her peers, whom Carolyn Heilbrun had in mind when she wrote in her memoir of her closing years, *The Last Gift of Time*, that she was glad to escape from what she felt as the 'poisonous atmosphere' of her work in feminist studies.[61] Such tensions between women make me suspect that the familial metaphor may not be helpful, especially when it marginalizes the significance of economic and other cultural shifts that impact upon the confrontations between younger and older feminists. Generational friction between women is not only evident in intellectual debate, but as ever amplified in the popular press and its now ever-diversifying cyber infrastructures for creating and maintaining distinct identities.

Not long ago I noticed the insightful investigative feminist journalist Susan Faludi commenting on problems caused by the enduring tensions between feminists in the USA: 'A

generational breakdown underlies so many of the patholo-
gies that have long disturbed American feminism – its fleeting
mobilizations followed by long hibernations; its bitter divisions
over sex; and its reflexive renunciation of its prior incarnations
… The contemporary women's movement seems fated to fight
a war on two fronts: alongside the battle of the sexes rages the
battle of the ages.' Moreover, she reports that not only does
much 'new' feminist activism and scholarship spurn the work of
older feminists, but that surveys in 2008 reported young women
overall neither wanted, nor trusted, female bosses, while many
young women opposed Hillary Clinton, apparently, precisely
because she reminded them of their mother. 'I've been to a
feminist "mother–daughter dinner party" ', Faludi comments,
'where the feel-good bonding degenerated into a cross fire of
complaint and recrimination, with younger women declaring
themselves sick to death of hearing about the glory days of
seventies feminism and older women declaring themselves sick
to death of being swept into the dustbin of history.'[62]

Of course, one of the problems about aspirations for bridging
generational divides comes from the way in which generations
are falsely homogenized in the first place. Cross-generational
ties can appear or disappear, sometimes fleetingly, in other
situations, leaving their mark across a lifetime. However, it is
only when we return to the distinctiveness of particular affiliations, aspirations or struggles in specific times and places that
we can understand how unexpected bonds can sometimes be
forged, perhaps according to the sudden interests and needs of
the moment, or else flowing from more enduring familial or
other bonding relationships. I suggested earlier that in some
ways people become more rather than less different from each
other with the accumulation of time, especially in the manner in

which we handle the apparently shared fears and difficulties of facing old age and death. This is just one reason why it can be harder to form new ties, even amongst our own peers, let alone across generations, as we age. It is something Auden, that poet so sensitive to the desires of the human heart, encapsulated with characteristic evocative exaggeration: 'At twenty we find our friends for ourselves, but it takes Heaven / To find us one when we are fifty-seven'.[63]

It is often possible to detect, or at least for others sometimes to perceive, how the frustrations, humiliations, guilt, losses and abandonments of the past live on to haunt and disrupt our connections to others in the present. This is of course at the heart of psychoanalytic thought and practice, which is why embarking upon analytic treatment can prove painful, especially in the early years of analysis. Discussing conscious states of memory in her reflections on ageing, Jane Miller comments on the persistence of negative experiences: 'I am especially puzzled that memory is much better at unhappiness than happiness.'[64]

It is a depressing thought, though clearly we do also retain memories of happy times, especially when they are invoked by those with whom we shared them. However, a slightly different question nags at me, which I hope to explore further in subsequent chapters: can the recognition, status, pleasures and satisfactions of our remembered past, or perhaps I should say our reconstructions of what we once had or achieved, sustain us in later life, as times change and the rewards of the present often become more elusive? Or do the satisfactions of the past serve more to magnify and mock whatever might be felt as the losses and limitations in the ageing present? I am not yet at all sure of the answer, and sometimes rather compelled by Robert Frost's lines in 'Provide, Provide': 'No memory of having starred / Atones for later disregard, / Or keeps the end from being hard'.[65]

Quite how hard, manageable, or at times, in the words of another prescient poet, Seamus Heaney, 'still vulnerable to delight', the process of ageing can be is something I hope to elucidate when pondering more closely how others have reflected upon the most intimate dilemmas of ageing. However, I feel I can say already that despite the inevitable tensions, being able to retain certain ties and affiliations across generations, without too much envy, bitterness or sense of exclusion and loss, usually has something to do with how successfully we manage old age.

3

The Perils of Desire

Understanding across the generations may indeed help us see old age as more of a gift than a shipwreck, but contradictions remain. 'Life becomes progressively stranger as we get older – and we become increasingly frantic to keep it familiar, to keep it in order', wrote the erudite psychoanalyst Adam Phillips.[1] However varied our experiences of ageing, this attempt to recognize ourselves as in some sense still the same person we always have been is certainly one of the challenges of old age. Nowhere is this task more fraught than in matters of sex and intimacy, where distinctly gendered apprehensions arise. We have seen already that for many, and certainly for most feminists, it is women who, first and last, have more reason to fear and lament the frustrations and deprivations they encounter with ageing. Women have written movingly, and often, of the many ways in which they are marginalized and diminished when youthful looks depart. Yet several voices, and not only male, have suggested that old age torments men more than women.

Ageing may be part of the human condition, but every statistic bears out the truism that the double standards of ageing mean women are judged to enter middle and old age far earlier than men. Accordingly, in the media generally, older men are represented significantly more often than older women. Indeed, in 2010 in the UK, the fifty-two-year-old TV presenter, Miriam O'Reilly, was the first employee to successfully sue the BBC for ageism, after she was dropped from their series *Countryfile*, together with other middle-aged female presenters. As she protested, men decades older than her were still regularly appearing on this and similar programmes. She won her case, yet subsequently still felt obliged to change career. Reflecting on this, one of Britain's indisputably aged female media crusaders, Katharine Whitehorn, mentioned 'the lopsided mirror to life', in which only men are allowed to grow old on screen.[2] Similarly, surveying decades of mainstream film in the USA, Elizabeth Markson and Carol Taylor analysed a sample of over 3,000 motion pictures made between the 1930s and 1990s, finding little change in the way in which leading older actors were portrayed throughout those years. Older men's roles were likely to play down signs of physical ageing, portraying elderly male actors as vigorous and engaged with the world (whether as heroes or villains), while the opposite was the case for older female figures, if and when they did appear.[3] Such information makes it all the more striking that what scholarly literature there is specifically addressing masculinity and ageing has tended to emphasize men's relatively greater miseries heading towards mid-life and coping with old age.

Just Like a Woman

'What should a society be, so that in his last years a man might still be a man?'[4] The first person who officially posed this question on behalf of men was not in fact a man, but that woman who keeps appearing in these pages, Simone de Beauvoir. Surprisingly, in her book *La Vieillesse* (*The Coming of Age*), published when she was sixty-three, Beauvoir said very little about women in old age, focusing primarily on the experiences of men. She concentrated on men because she was convinced that it was men, not women, who suffered most from growing old, and she held this view both despite, and also because of, the feminism she by then espoused.

In her view, men suffered more because the ageing process in most men, particularly after retirement, reduced them to the situation she had earlier scrutinized in *The Second Sex*, the situation of a woman: that of being rendered an object, denied agency in the world. What is significant about ageing, she felt, was not just that Western societies so readily refuse to acknowledge it other than as a problem to be avoided, but that it changes our relation to time. For as we age, the weight of the past must be measured and valued in comparison with the increasing flimsiness of any certainties about our future. However, she argued, modern societies, which train us to be always future-oriented and profit producing, fail to recognize as fully human those who have a far stronger sense of their extensive past than of how they should relate to their much shorter future. In her view, the ageing man, when he loses his power, 'becomes, and to a far greater extent than a woman, a mere object. She is necessary to society, whereas he is of no worth at all' (89).

Illustrating her argument with quotations from interviews with mostly retired working-class men, in various cities of Europe and the USA in the late 1960s, she notes the boredom and humiliation that many felt when they were no longer wage-earners: 'Life's not worth living once you've retired'; 'I give her [the wife] less than nothing – I'm ashamed.' Such accounts led Beauvoir to conclude: 'From one day to the next domestic tyrants may become so timid that they no longer cut a slice of bread without asking permission. Others sink into hypochondria' (268). In contrast, she believed that older women usually continued to be more involved with their children and grandchildren, just as they had been before, and were used 'to living for and by means of others': 'Age does not bring women down from such a height; there are more things they can still do; and not being so embittered, so demanding, they "uncommit" themselves less' (475).

Again in the sexual arena, developing a theme we will soon see dominating much of the ageing literature on men by men over the last few decades, Beauvoir explored men's narcissistic trauma over their waning and unpredictable sexual performance. She provided evidence to suggest that neither men nor women lose their sexual interests as they age, finding affirmations of ageing desire not so hard to uncover, though they may be differently expressed in line with gendered practices. In Beauvoir's view, older women take as much pleasure in sexuality as younger ones, while physiologically women experience fewer problems because they can always find sexual pleasure one way or another, if properly stimulated. Men's huge anxieties over their faltering erectile capacities as they age therefore have far greater force than women's fears of sexual failure.

A woman, Beauvoir noted, will 'identify herself with the total image of her body from childhood on, [whereas] the little boy sees his penis as an *alter ego*; it is in his penis that his whole life as a man finds its image, and it is here that he finds himself in peril' (321). Imperilled, indeed, as we will soon be hearing men lament and the experts of psychological wellbeing testify. In Beauvoir's analysis, the dangers women face arise not from the waning of desire or ability, but from the psychological effects of rejection. Beauvoir was all too well aware that an older woman is likely to be dismissed as an object of desire by men because of her body's ageing, often experiencing intense shame in the process, when at the first sign of coldness from a man 'she feels her ugliness in all its horror, she is disgusted at her image and cannot bear to expose her poor person to others' (349).

Beauvoir, however, is far from the only writer to sense a particular crisis for men in relation to ageing. Indeed, the Canadian psychoanalyst and organizational psychologist, Elliott Jaques, coined the term 'mid-life crisis' almost fifty years ago to describe the anxieties of the ageing man.[5] He, and other clinicians and writers since, have made the notion of mid-life crisis almost synonymous with the situation of ageing men in Western societies, using it to describe the shorter or longer periods of dramatic self-doubt, anxiety and worthlessness that some, maybe many, men feel with the passing of their youth and the imminence of old age. Indeed, with the emergence of Men's Studies in the 1980s, researchers had begun highlighting all the difficulties men face in trying to establish and maintain their identities as 'men', when notions of 'masculinity' are supposed to ensure they emerge as the socially dominant, tougher sex.[6]

In this literature, the challenges men face are seen as beginning early. One way or another, a boy has to renounce his first attachment to and dependency on his mother if he is to assume an acceptable form of masculinity, suggesting strength, independence, dominance, and above all the ability to be in control of his own life – a journey requiring displays of what may prove somewhat thin layers of bravado and competence.[7] However, the whole performance can of course become much harder, if not break down altogether, as a man ages, at least if or when his ageing is accompanied by obvious losses of financial and other forms of power and authority.

This is exactly what Susan Faludi – one of many to survey the process of men's sense of growing decline in the late-twentieth-century USA – reported in her book *Stiffed*.[8] Her compatriot, Gullette, has also pointed out that in recent decades men's traditional patriarchal privileges have been further eroded in the USA. Once it was the case that men, though not women, found that their wages kept on increasing until late middle age. However, the emergence of turbo-charged capitalism in recent decades has meant the years after early middle age are increasingly seen in terms of 'obsolescence rather than experience', undermining the workplace seniority and security that once privileged white, middle-class men – skilled working-class men had already lost this age status privilege in the 1980s. After mid-life, Gullette's figures also indicate, men are the most dramatic losers in ongoing age battles.[9] This specific context adds to the reasons more scholars and clinicians are suggesting that some level of male crisis has become nearly inevitable for the ageing man.

The Harder They Fall

Meanwhile, rather differently, although reiterating Beauvoir and many others on the topic, the latest clinical literature includes an ever-greater emphasis on the apparent 'narcissistic mortification' accompanying the ageing man's failure to control the very thing that remains enduringly emblematic of his masculinity across time and place – the erect penis. Masculinity and the functioning penis are symbolically inseparable, the penis as substituting for the man, a truth condensed into the metaphor and iconography of 'impotence'. It is the commercial amplification of this symbolic doubling that has recently also fuelled the extraordinary level of medicalization and commodification of the ageing male body, most dramatically since 1998, with the mass marketing of Viagra and other erectile dysfunction drugs. The virile nirvana promised by pharmaceutical companies is that, whatever his age, a man can retain the sexual capacities of his youth and indeed must do so if age is not to destroy his masculinity.[10]

However, if Viagra and related treatments can provide some medical remedy for one of men's main fears of ageing, their higher suicide rate compared to women's suggests that it cannot offer any complete panacea for other problems of the ageing man. Just for a start, of course, men usually need some appreciative intimate partner to enable any fully satisfactory sexual performance. And though it seems clear that the early signs of men's physical ageing – greying hair or balding heads, the appearance of wrinkles – are not greeted with the same cultural horror as are equivalent signs of women's ageing, there is evidence that men who face divorce or widowhood can be especially vulnerable to extreme depression or even suicide.

Of late, it has become fashionable in Western countries to undertake grand statistical surveys of the demography of 'happiness', or the lack of it. The researchers carrying out the most ambitious of these global analyses have been confirming the existence of a mid-life crisis, although their data suggests, rather unsurprisingly to me, that women as well as men start to suffer from higher levels of depression from mid-life onwards. Indeed, overall, women's higher levels of depression start younger than men's, at least according to the evidence amassed by two economists, Andrew Oswald and David Blanchflower, surveying thirty-five years of data on no less than two million people from eighty different nations. Everywhere, apparently, reported rates of depression were highest during mid-life, although women on average are most miserable at age forty, whereas men's blues kick in when they hit fifty.[11] However, from other studies, it would seem that while older women are more likely than older men to develop depression, and from a younger age, some research suggests that depression for older men may have more devastating effects on mortality. As in all age groups, including the young, male rates of suicide tend to be higher than female rates of suicide, and they have been rising.[12] Men's depression is also seen as more troubling because of the evidence that clinically depressed older men neither seek nor receive treatment as often as older women, presumably because more stigma attaches to mental health issues in men. It is this stigma that is thought to place older men more at risk for committing suicide, with around 85 per cent of all suicides among older adults in the USA, for instance, being by men.[13]

We now have considerable data on the demographics of men's increasing dissatisfactions with ageing. We can also make certain comparisons between the onset and the degree of men's unhappiness compared with women's. However, as these sophisticated bean-counters Oswald and Blanchflower themselves admit, significant as their data may be in suggesting shifting levels of personal misery across a lifetime, it tells us little if anything about the precise nature or diversity of men's, or women's, experiences of ageing. Bald statistics hardly reveal any details about the ruptures and alarm that so often shadow the chronologically evolving, inconsistent and contradictory images of who and what we think we are, have been and are likely to become, as we age. For any fuller description of the tribulations of ageing we surely need the broadest spectrum of resources from across popular, scholarly and literary cultures. The need is all the more urgent given that the scholarly material available for describing men's experiences of ageing remains limited, far sparser for men than for women, at least outside the clinical domain of full psychological breakdown.[14] Fortunately, however, if we consult the overlapping resources of fiction, memoir and autobiography, the richest and most varied images of men and ageing leap vividly to life. Turning to fiction, we are spoilt for choice, which makes it a little hard to know where best to begin.

Phallic Fault Lines

Reflecting on his own feelings at sixty-six, and performing one of his grand sweeps across older men's writing, the once celebrated literary critic Leslie Fiedler suggested that men's feelings of impotence, whether metaphorical or literal, can easily trigger devastating phallic narcissistic injuries.[15] My own explorations confirm his, at least when looking at those male writers who have most assiduously focused on old age. One obvious place to start is with the writing of Philip Roth, winner of the Man Booker International Prize for fiction in 2011 and, though a controversial figure – especially with some female readers – often hailed as America's greatest living novelist. Roth has been expressing his fears about and preoccupations with the effects of time from quite a young age, and his reappearing protagonists mostly age along with their creator.

Indeed, Roth sees himself as speaking on behalf of all his fellow men when he depicts the fears and yearnings that trouble and endanger them as they journey from youth into middle and old age. Thus in his twenty-seventh book, *Everyman*, he characteristically sets out once more to tell the story of the ageing male psyche. It is one in which the often painful, inappropriate and rash desires of youth last the whole life through, but become increasingly unrealizable. In Roth's view, the precise aim or object of such desire changes very little, if at all, as men age. This remains the case even when, as he depicts in abject or hubristic detail in every recent book, the men who continue to be importuned by lust for young women possess no more than a useless 'spigot of wrinkled flesh' between their legs.[16] That spigot, emblematic of masculinity, marker of sexual difference, and hence the thing valued above all else, Roth sees as always on men's minds. Its presence is felt, even when entirely out of action, 'like the end of a pipe you see sticking out of a field somewhere, a meaningless piece of pipe that spurts and gushes intermittently, spitting forth water to no end, until a day arrives when somebody remembers to give the valve the extra turn that shuts the damn sluice down'.[17]

It is easy, just a little too easy, perhaps, to apply Freud to Roth's unflinching examination of masculinity and the degradations of male ageing. The young boy's early 'castration anxiety' is once again intensified in Roth's depictions of the life of the ageing man. Here, it is the anchoring of masculinity in sexual performance, real and fantasized, that underlies the unravelling of men's ageing identities. If turning to Freud, however, we need to realize that Roth has already got there before us. His novels read, knowingly, like Freudian case studies, and analysts feature prominently in many of his books, beginning with his early runaway success, *Portnoy's Complaint*. In all of them, manhood must be affirmed in 'sexual conquest', which somewhere before the end must lead every man into perpetual mourning for the loss of a former imagined phallic prowess: 'Nothing any longer kindled his curiosity or answered his needs ... nothing except the young women who jogged by him on the boardwalk in the morning. My God he thought, the man I once was! ... The force that was mine! ... Once upon a time I was a full human being.'[18]

In Roth's writing, a man's ageing desire is never able for long to eroticize the comforting familiarity of a lifetime companion. However bereft and lonely, it would seem that Roth's men have little choice but to die as they have lived, as lecherous mavericks. Or rather, since we are discussing Roth's depictions of phallic bravado, which is inevitably, and as he keeps telling us, fundamentally illusory, Roth is determined to portray men who will die as they would like us to believe they have lived, as sexual predators, if only in fantasy. Nor is Roth, at least in old age, unaware of the price he pays for what he summed up in one interview as 'the circus of being a man ... [where] the ring leader is the phallus'.[19] Ever the dutiful scholar, he can also sense something of the artificial or performative nature of the gender enactments he so obsessively describes.

But any real transgression of these conventions, at whatever age, seems beyond Roth's imaginative purview. Nor can he find anything to admire in the ageing body, male or female. It is this visceral dismay that makes his fictionalized projections of the situation of the elderly so disconcerting. Yet he remains for me an excellent writer to think with, to think through, and to think against, given his pellucid prose and his constant testing of what he sees as the shifting boundaries between art and life, between what can be said, and what remains hidden in life's journeys.

Moreover, the phallic longings that loom so stubbornly in Roth's depictions of the lives of men, whatever their age, echo sentiments that have certainly been just as fiercely communicated by other ageing men with the gifts to depict their own dreams, fears and frustrations, not least in the words of the Irish poet W. B. Yeats, who mourned, at sixty-one, that he lived with the soul of a man 'sick with desire / And fastened to a dying animal'.[20] Roth borrowed Yeats' words for the title of a novel in 2001, about the lust of an ageing professor for his young student, around four decades younger than him, though here it is she who is dying, his phallic prowess apparently still intact. Roth's late writing also resonates with the 'total disillusion' and 'inner ice age' of Freud's lunar landscape, when he tells us in *Everyman*: 'Old age isn't a battle; old age is a massacre.'[21] I do not actually accept that Roth (or Freud or Yeats, before him) is *Everyman*, although I think he does capture something about the distinctive fears of many men. Not least because very similar imagery can be found in Roth's most admired and popular fellow male writers.

Also from the USA, the novelist John Updike was seen by many as Roth's equal or superior, precisely in his own life-long scrutiny of the inner working of men's hearts and minds. He was, moreover, quite as concerned as Roth with depicting men's masturbatory and adulterous fantasies and the 'power and mobility of the penis' in men's prime, soon to be followed by the inevitable frailties and fears men face when ageing.[22] The novel, *Toward the End of Time*, for instance, was one of Updike's most ambitious meditations on temporality, mortality and ageing, written in his mid-sixties in order, as he later said, to cope with his own ageing: 'Sex dies hard; even when the apparatus of sex fails.'[23] In that novel, the protagonist's declining physical powers are accompanied by a frantic eroticism, fantasizing lubricious encounters with ever-younger women, even as the effects of prostate cancer leave him, like Roth's older protagonists, mortified by 'the pathetic shrunken wreck' his beloved penis has become.[24]

In the UK, Martin Amis, described by one male reviewer as 'his generation's most astute documentarist of ageing', delivers the same message.[25] Like Roth and Updike, Amis is early on achingly troubled by the passage of time. Indeed, few people have expressed a more visceral and consistent horror of ageing than Amis, or offended more people in the process. Like Roth too, Amis not only sees masculinity as his special subject, but also writes to encompass what he understands as the universal male predicament. As Joseph Brooker notes, his books survey what happens when 'the swaggering lad' all too quickly morphs into 'the crumpled bloke'.[26] The theme of imperilled masculinity is centre-stage in the book Amis wrote in his mid-forties, *The Information* (1996), which depicts the trauma of men, just like him at the time, reaching middle age: 'the whole thing is a crisis'.[27] Here, his main protagonist is a blocked, unsuccessful novelist, weighed down by envy, humiliation and a sense of failure, leaving him chronically depressed, self-destructive and, of course, impotent.

Like Roth also, Amis courts publicity through provocation. Yet once again, in his terror of ageing, and chagrin about mortality, Amis does seem to capture something about fears other men have expressed. In *Experience* (2002), the memoir in which he returns once more to his own crisis on reaching forty, he writes: 'Youth has finally evaporated, and with it all sense of your own impregnability.'[28] Of course, however powerful the fantasy, men have never possessed any authentic inviolability any more than women have. Nevertheless, in their youth it is perhaps easier for some of them to *imagine* themselves invulnerable, or at the very least, easier for them to perform in the world *as though* this were the case. It is this performance that is likely to falter as men age, hence the devastation. Amis sees no way to recover from the shock. In the opening pages of another of his highly autobiographically resonant recent books, *The Pregnant Widow* (2009), published as its author turned sixty, old age is likened to 'starring in a horror film'. He returns to this metaphor in its closing pages, with the narrator, the fifty-six-year-old Keith Nearing, suggesting 'the horror film, was set to become a snuff movie, but long before that he would be its trailer. He would be an ad for death.'[29]

It is instructive to compare these authors with a recent work by the ageing American gay writer, Edmund White, offering his own witty account of the disruptions and continuities of male ageing. At sixty-six, writing another of his prolific texts, which are almost always at least semi-autobiographical, White evokes his doppelganger protagonist, Jack, a gay writer of identical age, inclinations and attributes as his creator. He describes him slowing down, dozing off, forgetting names, and mourning that 'his [own] name was now more celebrated than his books, his blurbs more solicited than his stories'. Yet this Jack, though HIV positive for over twenty years, and fearing that 'maybe his wits were slowing down in the same way as his vision was dimming and his hearing becoming less acute', also reflects that one thing had never changed: 'His sex ambitions were still the same – to have sex with every man in the world. He would have been a perfect whore, since he found every man *do*-able.'[30] Unlike the straight men I have mentioned, however, it seems he *can* find ways of actually 'doing' them, or perhaps, to the sheer terror of men fashioned in the normative mould of Freud, Yeats, Roth, Updike or Amis, being 'done by them'. Oh no: 'Just like a woman'!

One thing that no male writer ever seems to suggest, however, is that men lose their longing for sexual encounters as they age, even as their erectile capacities falter. Quite the opposite! This information is in agreement with all the empirical studies of sex in old age, in which older men are twice as likely as women to say that they are still extremely interested in sex. Although, as the British health reporter, Jeremy Laurance, suggests: 'It is hard to be sure whether the gender imbalance shows the resilience of male interest in sex or the resilience of their propensity to boast about it.'[31] Either way, disappointment shadows putative phallic vigour.

There is one Swedish study that does attempt to highlight an alternative to the dominant vision of phallic sexuality imperilled by ageing. However, this comes not from any well-known male author, with his fictional or autobiographical representations of ageing masculinity, but from an altogether different source. It is the data collected by a young feminist scholar Linn Sandberg, discussing masculinity, sexuality and embodiment in older men. Sandberg interviewed twenty-two heterosexual men of around seventy and older, and supplemented her interviews with diaries she asked the men to write about their bodily experiences and physical encounters. In both the interviews and diaries the men stressed the significance of intimacy and touch in their experiences with wives or partners. They did not report any waning of sexual desire, but they did often describe a certain shift away from the phallic preoccupations of youth to describe instead far more diverse possibilities for shared physical pleasure and satisfactions.

In Sandberg's analysis, these old men's emphasis on their pleasure in the mutuality of touch and intimacy in their relationships – perhaps in bathing or stroking one another – present a clear alternative to 'phallic sexualities'. Indeed she sees older men's affirmation of such pleasures as suggesting a possible way of rethinking masculinity and its pleasures more generally, as something 'less clearly defined and more fluid': 'The case of old men may in fact be illustrative of how to think of male sexual morphologies more broadly. Touch and intimacy could then be understood as a potential for the becoming of masculinity altogether; the non-phallic body is not a characteristic of some men but a potential in all men.'[32]

However, if the rush for Viagra is anything to go by, I fear much more will need to change in the still obdurate symbolic and social hierarchies of gender and ageing before such accounts of the 'softening' of older men's activities can begin to undermine the phallus as the privileged marker of masculinity. Meanwhile, if it is still sexual (con)quest and the comforts that a woman's (or occasionally another man's) body can provide that reinforces a man's sense of self, and then threatens to undermine it as he ages, how different is the situation of the older woman?

All Passion Spent?

At first glance, the difference in women's recent writing on ageing compared with that of men lies in its relatively cheerful tone. It owes much to the rhetoric of feminism and its desire to celebrate the lives and agency of women, as evident in one of the first American anthologies of old age with its triumphant title, *Fierce with Reality* (1995).[33] More generally, women's popular writing on ageing over the last decade or so tends to stand in stark contrast with men's precisely in its reflections on the life of desire. This is especially noticeable in the writing of familiar voices from the literary or media mainstream, such as Germaine Greer, Gloria Steinem, Irma Kurtz, Jane Miller or Virginia Ironside. Beginning with Greer, all these writers distance themselves from sexual desire, indeed they usually speak of their 'relief', rather than panic, at leaving sexual passion behind them as they age.

Greer set the tone with her popular book, *The Change* (1991), in which she insisted that women should celebrate old age as a time when we are 'free at last', free from the shackles of sexuality. The book was first of all keen to expose a market-driven misogyny in the rhetoric of those she labelled the new 'Masters of Menopause', aggressively peddling the necessity of hormone replacement therapy (HRT) for older women. However, Greer was also disdainful of those late-middle-aged women she now saw among the 'gallery of grotesques' still trying 'pathetically' to please and satisfy men by denying their own ageing. This was not the way to age with grace and dignity, she chastised, despite having once tried to inspire women into greater erotic rebelliousness through her own exemplary sexual assertiveness over twenty years earlier.

Indeed, turning the usual tenets of ageism on their head, along with her own prior views, she asserted that older women benefited from abandoning altogether the whole clamorous arena of sex and relationships: 'To be unwanted is to be free.' The lucky ones who manage this are liberated, just as they had been before adolescence forced them to become tools of their sexual and reproductive destiny: 'You were strong then, and well, and happy, until adolescence turned you into something more problematical, and you shall be well and strong and happy again.' In short, as she concludes in her final chapter, entitled 'Serenity and Power': 'The climacteric marks the end of apologizing. The chrysalis of conditioning has once and for all to break and the female woman finally to emerge.' Like the 'final girl', the actress left standing in all horror movies, this ageing female figure in Greer's writing could surface once more, 'shiny and new ... like a Virgin', but free from the desire to be touched by any man, ever again.[34] I am not so sure.

Greer does not admit to any mythmaking when she determinedly presents her life as one for others to emulate as she ages. Indeed, she told readers that she finds herself saying: 'The best time of life is always now ... You can't live regretting what's past, and you can't live anticipating the future. If you spend any amount of time doing either of these things you never live at all.'[35] Two years later, a similar rejection of the abiding fears of ageing was also evident in the late Betty Friedan's *Fountain of Age* (1993), which was launched with US government endorsement and much media fanfare. Friedan called for a 'new paradigm' of old age, emphasizing its potential vibrancy and wisdom, rejecting its associations with neediness and dependency.

At the same time, at last in perfect harmony, her former feminist rival, the equally formidable Gloria Steinem, was writing about the 'unexpected liberation' that comes with growing older, as in her brief upbeat memoir, *Doing Sixty and Seventy* (2006).[36] In celebrating the coming of old age, the cheery chorus provided by these popular avatars of feminism contained what seems to me a very loud silence on any experiences of loneliness, loss, envy, fear or anger. Nor are issues of frailty, dependence and cognitive deterioration allowed to surface. These women could be a different breed from me, but I must confess I find a crafted disavowal in those omissions. I am reminded here of the New York literary scholar, Carolyn Heilbrun's thoughts before she died on what she eventually came to see as the waste of effort she spent writing a biography of Gloria Steinem, about whom, she came to think, 'to become the public, generous, productive person [she was and remains] … required a personality ill at ease with introspection, or indeed any deep sense of a self in conflict with her mission'.[37] Indeed, I suspect that what these three very public figures of feminism – Greer, Friedan and Steinem – have all at various points shared is a certain blithe complacency in their self-presentation.

The buoyancy of these spokeswomen insisting upon the joys of old age, especially in their celebration of the rebirth of self-sufficiency, seems to me to promote the illusion that we can age agelessly. False optimism, as Barbara Ehrenreich explored so wittily in her book, *Smile or Die*, can rob a person not just of feelings of rage and disquiet, but also of the capacity for critical reflection.[38] Such resolute sanguinity is just one of the reasons I am wary of a pattern I see amongst older women, especially those in the public eye, eager to impart their secrets for ageing well, who proclaim themselves happily celibate. In Britain at this moment, it is the journalist, author, agony aunt and, belatedly, actress, Virginia Ironside, energetically promoting her belief that 'growing old is great'. On her website she affirms that the years after turning sixty have, 'no question, been the happiest years of my life'. That is why she published and has taken to the stage to perform *The Virginia Monologues: Twenty*

Reasons Why Growing Old Is Great. One aspect of this, she too emphasizes, is 'the freedom of no sex'. Having had far too much sex in the past, she explains, she is now 'older, wiser and luxuriating in [her] single bed'. Moreover, 'one of the really positive effects of being less interested in sex', she adds, 'is that one can have so much better relationships with men than when one was young'.[39] She quotes the views of other ageing sex idols, such as Diana Rigg, agreeing that having had 'quite sufficient sex' in the past, she is 'happy not to go there again'.[40]

Her fellow agony aunt, Irma Kurtz, in her seventies, and who like Ironside has spent most of her adult life advising others about sex and relationships, says much the same thing in her recent book, *About Time: Growing Old Disgracefully.* She may be wishing to age *dis*gracefully, but Kurtz tells us that she decided to become celibate at forty-eight, and now the only 'romantic' attachment she wants or feels is to her infant grandson.[41] Another pioneer of women's liberation in Britain, the late Eva Figes, when in her sixties, was equally dismissive of any form of erotic life. She too urged women to find release in their grey hair, wrinkles, cultural invisibility and long-gone sexual allure: 'She may be alone, but she is no longer lonely, since her body no longer craves what she cannot have.' Unlike men, she argued, 'her body has been liberated from foolish longings, and perhaps she could find it in her heart to pity the men of her generation who are led by their penises into all kinds of foolishness'.[42] Now, I don't doubt that some older women may well feel more freedom from the unrelenting cultural chorus coupling 'real' happiness and sexual fulfilment. Likewise, some women in old age, if in relationships, may feel less constrained by former 'obligations' to satisfy a male partner, unless he is taking Viagra: thus it is possible to read about 'Viagra wives' of husbands previously unable to perform, who are 'not excited to be asked once again for sex'.[43]

Yet I doubt this is the full picture. Giving up on sex is an easy claim to make, if we think its meaning is straightforward, presumably on the assumption that 'sex' reduces to some particular physical action or engagement that is no longer performed. It is true that this is how sex tends to be conceived in sexology, especially from the mid-twentieth century, when researchers such as Alfred Kinsey began quantifying the different routes to orgasm. In this literature, tellingly, masturbation became paradigmatic of 'the human sexual response', when other people, and in some sense sexual desire itself, were seen as getting in the way of genital orgasmic climax.[44] However, I suspect this is not exactly what these older women have in mind in reflecting back on the 'quite sufficient sex' they had in the past, which I imagine would be likely to have involved the full panoply of joy, hope, longing, frustration, disappointment, pain, and more, coalescing around physical intimacies that may or may not involve genital contact or orgasmic climax.

Pronouncements of cheerful sexual abstinence look much less compelling for anyone used to delving more deeply into the curious and bizarre world encompassing sexuality and desire. Here, sex is never best seen as any one thing, or singular event. Viewed more thoughtfully, whether by way of psychoanalytic conjecture, clinical observations, discursive musings, or unguarded personal reflection, sexual feelings permeate an infinite cluster of keen, anxious, stifled, blocked, voyeuristic desires popping up in all the secret spaces within and between people. From these perspectives, sexuality in the form of desire is an all-pervasive aspect of our physicality. Its aims are endlessly varied, from wishes to be noticed or needed by another, to remain close to and able to please or receive pleasure from them, through to seeking out patterns of domination or humiliation that reiterate, in ways we rarely recognize, the pleasures and pains of past intimacies with others.

The situations that trigger desire are diverse and unpredictable, with or without any hope for or interest in direct physical contact. Seen in this way, rather than simply reduced to a version of genital interaction, it would never be straightforward to declare sex 'safely' over, least of all, as in Ironside's reflections, because of any prior orgasm count (or the lack of it), except perhaps when pain or morbidity rule the body entirely, obliterating every other sensation. Moreover, as we've seen, old men are far less likely to make this claim than women, but instead, just like young men, tend to exaggerate their engagement with and interest in sex.[45] Something more complicated than any notion of the rise and fall of physical drives is surely in play when we speak of 'sex'.

Nevertheless, it is easy to grasp why it may be comforting, perhaps even seem necessary, for older women to declare themselves 'post-sex', especially if unpartnered and, for reasons we'll see, strictly heterosexual. Few adjectives combine faster than ugly-old-woman. It is not only Beauvoir who internalized the prevalent shame around ageing female flesh. Despite recent declarations rejecting ageism, ongoing research confirms older women's continuing shame, disgust and guilt at surveying ageing female bodies.[46] In one recent study of women's display of such affect, the New Zealand gender theorist Tiina Vares reports that in lengthy discussion groups with older women and men, it was, surprisingly, the women in particular who expressed verbal and bodily signs of disgust when commenting upon the visual portrayal of an older woman's short liaison with a young builder in the film adaptation of Hanif Kureishi's play, *The Mother*. This was despite most of these women objecting more generally to the invisibility of older women as sexual agents in cultural representation, and in principle supporting their right to be in sexual relationships with anyone they choose, including young men.[47]

With these culturally freighted, unconscious dynamics in play, it may therefore be 'wiser' (consciously or unconsciously) if as older women we tell stories about ourselves that deny any personal interest in sex, insisting, like all the women we heard from above, that sex is something safely behind us. Those who care for old women (or men) with dementia, either at home or in care units, might suggest something rather different. They are usually all too aware that as former inhibitions disappear, along with the cognitive capacity for rectitude and restraint, significant levels of sexual interest are routinely displayed by older women, often accompanied by distress or anger when sexual overtures are rejected – as likely as not made to complete strangers.[48] As the British writer Sara Maitland notes: 'To acknowledge and address the sexual desire of women who can no longer bear children is to expose the whole structure; it is better to act as though they did not desire, and if they do, it is peculiar, tasteless and neurotic.'[49]

In this situation, false optimism, perhaps better seen as illusion or mythmaking, may indeed help people to survive more cheerfully. Yet feminists have always loudly objected to the view that the infinitely puzzling domain of intimacy and desire can be reduced to genital heterosexuality. However, it seems clear that we have not (yet) managed, and only rarely tried, to change the youthful iconography of what it is for a woman to be a desirable sex object. Searching for role models for the older woman, Maitland invokes that of the fairy godmother. But this takes us straight back to youth, yet again, since it is the desirable and impoverished young woman whom such fairy godmothers assist. Furthermore, when applied to females, the 'fairies' in Western mythology conjure up the delicate and ethereal, rarely the physical and sexual.

Who or what, then, might come to the aid of the old woman wanting to feel visible, desiring and desired, before she dematerializes – apart from those demented oldies who are, quite clearly, not post-sex, but rather, post-decorum: 'Drop 'em', was what an acquaintance of mine, a young gay man, reported as a typical greeting when he arrived to work on his old people's ward in Brighton. Similarly, in her beautiful family memoir, *Losing the Dead*, the British author Lisa Appignanesi describes her mother's 'demented fragility' in her mid-eighties, at the same time pointing out that one aspect of her mother's 'character' never changed. Whenever they visited the doctor together, all her mother's aches and pains would disappear, as she sat seductively on the edge of her chair, her old self again: 'Her eyelids fluttering, she tells him what a wonderful man he is … She flirts. She charms. For a brief span nothing but that matters.'[50]

Let me return for a moment to Beauvoir, that arch-rationalist, so committed throughout her lifetime to promoting and exemplifying the importance of the autonomous, self-critical, examined life. Yet her book on ageing is dense with ambiguities and contradictions, which is perhaps not so surprising given the theoretical tensions within her transdisciplinary sweep. Moreover, Beauvoir herself always understood ambiguity, contradiction and unpredictability to be inevitable features of the tensions between autonomy, contingency and the situational constraints in which individuals are located, whatever their age.[51] As I have highlighted from the beginning, for Beauvoir, as for most of us, the intellectual stumbling block around ageing is that in some compelling sense we feel we remain always the 'same', while also knowing that we have changed and will continue to do so. As she wrote in her book on old age: 'All we can do is waver from one to the other, never managing to hold them firmly together.' Aware of the atemporality of the dynamic unconscious, with its inability to distinguish between true and false, Beauvoir was also dismissive of what she regarded as the 'mystical twaddle' from those, beginning with Plato, who liked to suggest that old age releases us from the shackles of sexual desire into a more spiritual life, however incapable the flesh may prove of consummating desire. Beauvoir cited Freud to point out that adult sexuality is not simply, or even primarily, a genital affair. In her book she also provided many examples of the continuity of desire in old age, in both men and women, suggesting that sexual passion is never entirely spent, whatever our age, and whatever our fragilities: 'The old person often desires to desire because he [*sic*] retains his longing for experiences that can never be replaced and because he is still attached to the erotic world he built up in his youth or maturity – desire will enable him to renew its fading colours.' The old woman too often desires to desire, and remains attached to her erotic world, as Beauvoir knew all too well, despite also knowing, and often articulating, the extra degrees of shame she is likely to feel when she realizes that the man she wants no longer desires her. It is then, Beauvoir says, that she can no longer 'bear to expose her poor person to others'.[52]

Bodily Shame and Narcissistic Mortification

The scandal for some of Beauvoir's readers was that she believed that women too would come to share what often seemed men's horror of their bodies, as she herself did. She projected the revulsion she felt about her own middle-aged face ('I often stop, flabbergasted, at the sight of this incredible thing that serves me as a face ... I loathe my appearance now') onto the world at large, adding for good measure: 'It wounds one's heart to see a lovely young woman and then next to her her refection in the mirror of the years to come – her mother.'[53] It wounds one's heart, her critics may feel, to read Beauvoir saying this, even though there is nothing unfamiliar about her thoughts except the frankness with which she expresses her own recoil from the ageing female face. However, there is a certain tension between her refrain that 'we only learn that we are old from the outside' and the repulsion Beauvoir felt about her own body in middle age.

It may seem even stranger when from the many photos others have reproduced of her Beauvoir appears an impressively attractive older woman, despite female beauty and allure being made synonymous with youth. It is worth noting, however, that in the 1960s, when Beauvoir was expressing her bodily mortification, the self-conscious anti-ageism articulated in the later mantra of 'ageing well' had yet to emerge. That newer narrative, which we heard above from Greer and other women, would never openly admit to any such dread of the ageing visage, but emphasizes instead the possibilities for life-long health and creativity. Nevertheless, I suspect that even had she heard such voices, Beauvoir would not, could not, have echoed their optimism, but would probably have dismissed them as a form of disavowal, bad faith, or evasion. In her early middle age, the only way Beauvoir knew of dealing with those periods in her life when she felt rejected by men was to try to accept, sorrowfully, rather than with any sense of release, that she would never again be allowed to love or be loved once more. As she aged, whenever she felt herself desired again, her ageing sorrows instantly retreated. This happened for her unexpectedly, at forty-four, when she started a seven-year relationship with one of Sartre's follower's, Claude Lanzmann:

[His] presence beside me freed me from my age. First it did away with my anxiety attacks ... And then his participation revived my interest in everything ... a thousand things were restored to me: joys, astonishments, anxieties, laughter and the freshness of the world. After two years in which the universal marasma had coincided for me with the break-up of a love affair and the first warnings of physical decline leapt back enthralled into happiness.[54]

As mentioned in my opening chapter, just under ten years later, completing the third volume of her memoirs *Force of Circumstance*, Beauvoir was once more without a male lover and consumed by the tragedy of being an ageing woman: 'I have lost my old powers to separate the shadows from the light ... My powers of revolt are dimmed now ... but my joys are paled as well.' The reason for her sorrows, we quickly learn, is her anticipation of the inevitable failure of erotic passion: 'Never again a man'.[55]

Some of her critics accused Beauvoir of distancing herself from the lives of ordinary women. Such censure was levelled at her final work of fiction, the three novellas constituting *The*

Woman Destroyed (1968), which deal with older women's vulnerability and loneliness, deserted by husbands, and facing the process of old age alone.[56] Others, including many women who wrote to Beauvoir herself, suggested she 'was merely presenting the reality of what happens to women in our society'. In actuality, Beauvoir did manage to distance herself from the bleakness she saw awaiting her abandoned female protagonists, and not by eschewing passion, the fate she most feared, but by beginning a mutually enduring 'intense and total' relationship in her sixties with a much younger woman, Sylvie Le Bon, as she told her biographer, Deirdre Bair: 'now I have Sylvie, and it is an absolute relationship, because from the beginning we were both prepared to live in this way, to live entirely for each other'.[57]

Though both women publicly acknowledged their love for each other, neither spoke of themselves as 'lesbian', as such, despite Beauvoir telling Alice Schwartzer in 1972 that she believed women were 'more desirable than men', and despite her public support for lesbian and gay relationships, not to mention her own admitted practice of sexual relations with women.[58] Moreover, Deirdre Bair, among others, makes it very clear that Beauvoir was never free from the hurt of Sartre's continuous affairs with the nubile young women who flocked around him, nor from the effects of his early indifference to her physical being as soon as she began to age, or from her own attachment to and identification with him. Thus, she did know something about the plight of many an older woman who still desires men but who, especially when single, notices how often the men they are attracted to either fail to register them, or turn away from the physical presence of their mature embodiment.

Beauvoir was surely right that such a woman is likely to find it impossible to remain confident about her desirability, even though she was sure that passion itself was rarely extinguished. She points out, for instance, that the persistence of desire is often confirmed within long-term lesbian relationships, in which women may 'continue their erotic activities well into their eighties', proving, she adds, 'that women go on feeling desire long after they have stopped being attractive to men.'[59] Beauvoir was also persuasive on the jealousy older women feel towards younger women (or men) who attract the attention of older men. It is again something she wrote about in her fiction, beginning with *She Came to Stay* through to *The Woman Destroyed*. Thus it seems to me that the nub of one of the most contentious issues around ageing for women is the space that exists for love, intimacy and passion. It is certainly a topic that is often on my mind, although both personal experience and opinion surveys make it clear that older women express varying degrees of interest in the subject, relating especially to whether or not they are comfortably partnered or living alone.[60]

Even more popular than Beauvoir, and more widely read internationally, it was the novelist Doris Lessing who in her many books quickly became another key narrator of the hazards, tensions and ambiguities of women's experiences through life. Her writing both influenced and reflected the way in which many women came to assess their situation, especially those young white women who were first drawn to women's liberation from the late 1960s. Roughly a decade younger than Beauvoir, and still being published in her nineties, Lessing's prolific output includes her determined attempts to delineate women's personal, political and, in recent decades, spiritual voyages at different stages of their lives, from girlhood through to very old age.

Her best-known novel, *The Golden Notebook* (1962), quickly became a landmark text, often described as one 'that both changed and explained a generation', as the British cultural critic Natasha Walter wrote forty years later. Lessing agrees: 'I still get women writing to me saying, my grandmother and my mother read *The Golden Notebook* and I'm the third generation reader.'[61] Moreover, from her autobiographical writing, it is easy to observe the interweaving between Lessing's fictional and autobiographical texts as she ages; indeed, she is keen to provide her own versions of these connections. Her early narratives of political activism, betrayals and disappointments were always explored alongside the hazards women face in their personal life, from conflict with mothers to later frustration with men and with children. However, most significantly for my interests here, for over three decades the issue of women's ageing has been centre-stage in Lessing's texts and public pronouncements, whether in her autobiographical voice, or in her fiction.[62]

Lessing is far more candid than most women in addressing the narcissistic injuries of ageing: whether dramatically highlighting her own or her fictional characters' sense of confusion, loss, loneliness and regret. Lessing says she first experienced these forms of distress in her late thirties, despite and seemingly also because of the status she has achieved globally as one of the most prominent women writers of her time. This was some forty years before she won the most prestigious prize of all for a writer, the Nobel Prize for Literature in 2007.

The nature of the loss and regret Lessing experienced approaching middle age is consistent in her memoirs and fiction, with narcissistic wounds very much to the fore. Persuasively, Lessing suggests that, at least for her, it is not so much the end of any specific attachments but rather the loss of her own former self that provides the key to the sorrows of ageing. Somewhat unusually, she says that when young she was always confident about her own physical attractiveness and its magnetic effect on the men she encountered: 'I used to stand among people, knowing that my body was strong and fine, under my dress, and secretly exalt, or look at a naked arm, or my hair in the mirror, and thrill with pleasure.'[63] Again in her memoirs Lessing depicts her own youthful arrogance, even cruelty, towards others who desired her, up until her late thirties. It is a cruelty she attributes to young women generally in her writing. However, her own most passionate attachments, we learn, were to men who always made it clear that they were promiscuous seducers, who would never love her alone. It is the abandonment by two such lovers, one after the other, first by the Jewish psychiatrist she calls 'Jack', then, after a three-year relationship, by the American writer Clancy Sigal, which Lessing says caused her to have a breakdown. For several months, aged thirty-nine, she became alcoholic, suffering what is probably, she says, the 'clinical condition' of many another discarded middle-aged woman: 'who slides into drinking, feeling abandoned, unloved, unwanted'.[64]

Revisiting her young self, Lessing later reflects upon the particular forms of gratification she found in those earlier attachments, as with her former lover 'Jack': 'what I loved was his loving me so much'.[65] Consistently, it is the loss of self-love that she emphasizes in describing her own ageing miseries. She is mourning the disappearance of her young self, and the pain she experiences from witnessing what she sees as the self-absorbed aggression of so many of the young women she encounters – which she almost admits is a form of projection. However, if there seems a surprising degree of narcissism in

Lessing's description of her younger self, the nature of narcissism is itself always ambiguous. The longing for love, in its most romantic sense, is never unrelated to some form of narcissism. In his essay 'On Narcissism', Freud argued that the ego or self is formed through the narcissistic experience of being the loved object of another, creating a form of 'primary narcissism' that later 'gives rise to a vigorous attempt to recover that state'. This, he continued, is why falling in love always includes aspects of narcissism: 'To be their own ideal once more, in regard to sexual no less than other trends, as they were in childhood – this is what people strive to attain as their happiness ... Being in love consists in the flowing over of ego-libido onto the object.'[66]

In Freud's view, it is when our sense of self-worth, the fundamental narcissistic satisfaction that is sustained by the ongoing love of another, encounters frequent obstacles that a person begins to invent forms of 'secondary narcissism', falling back on attempts to love only what we once were, or what we imagine that we might have been, but no longer are. Lessing narrates her life-story as though she is presenting a case study of this form of secondary narcissism, with her insistence on loving what she once was – she loves herself, but only in so far as she is the object of desire for another. A further comment Freud made in his essay, suggestive of the perils of love at whatever age, is that 'another person's narcissism has a great attraction for those who have renounced part of their own narcissism and are in search of object-love'.[67] Again, this could help explain why certain people are more likely to fall in love with the young, the beautiful and the self-absorbed, that is, those least likely to be able to sustain any reciprocity in mutual attachments.

One thing that is certainly evident in Lessing's

autobiographical writing, as in descriptions of the male lovers in her fiction, is that she offers little that is especially positive in her account of the men who become objects of desire. Moreover, just as she sometimes mentions her own guilt over the men she once teased or rejected, in all her writing Lessing identifies with, and yet also reproaches, what she sees as the cruelty of young women who remind her of her youthful self. It is they who are responsible for the pain that devastates older women. In her first formal memoir, she reflects upon an encounter she has as an older woman with a 'pretty girl of twenty' in a changing room, whom she describes as provocatively displaying the back of her beautiful body for Lessing's inspection: 'Deliberately, she allowed the towel around her to fall, displaying a beautiful back. She half-turned ... so that I could see her breasts ... She smiled at me, cool, triumphant, and went out. Pain was slicing through me for what I had lost. And, too, because I knew that I had been every bit as arrogant and cruel as that girl.'[68]

Older women, she often comments with weary resignation – in her memoirs as in her fiction – lose men of their own age to younger women, because such men are the inevitable prey of these younger women. Meanwhile, mature men are pro-grammed by their own nature to respond to these predatory girls, whether they really want to or not. Further absolving men, while keeping a baleful eye on young women, Lessing adds a further Freudian flounce to her dour Darwinian dogma, commenting that men have had to 'fight so hard to free them-selves from their mothers, but then circumstances and their natures make their wives into mothers, and they free themselves again'.[69] It is a pitiful unfairness she sees as biologically rather than culturally encoded.

Back to basics, for Lessing, means always returning to the

narcissistic injuries of ageing. This is perhaps most explicit in the crafting of her novel, *Love, Again*, which, like her memoirs, she wrote in her late seventies. It is here that Lessing fully explores what she sees as the full force of the disaster shadowing the eruption of sexual longings in any woman on the brink of joining what Lessing elsewhere refers to as 'old hags' in their chairs.[70] A complex and troubling text, its protagonist, Sarah Durham, is an energetic and successful theatre producer in her sixties who was widowed decades earlier. At the novel's opening we see her cheerfully industrious, announcing that having been an attractive young woman, who once 'always had people in love with her', she had experienced the anguish of love all too often and was now thankfully done with all that: '"Thank God it can never happen to me again. I tell you, getting old has its compensations"' (39). We know what to expect. Soon enough, Sarah has lost all her carefully nurtured serenity, with old passions rekindled when, during the theatrical production of an exceptionally poignant, tragically romantic musical, she finds herself falling in love again, though never wanting to. In quick succession she is emotionally undone by her desire for first one young man, then another, after each of them had seemed to respond to her own ageing charm and wisdom.

The novel thus creates a platform for Lessing to share her views on the near catastrophe attending any upsurge of sexual desire in an ageing woman: she is forced to remember and relive her past loves, taking her right back to the first losses and emotional deprivations of childhood. Again, however, Lessing is most evocative when describing the tragedy of thwarted narcissism she sees accompanying falling in love in old age: 'One falls in love with one's own young self – yes, that was likely: narcissists, all of us, mirror people ... it can have nothing to do with any biological function or need' (104). In the novel, the unexpected and violent need Sarah has for these men's attentions soon has her experiencing corrosive shame, dread, humiliation and guilt, despite and because of the ways in which it also rejuvenates and energizes her. She feels she is 'ridiculous', but above all, she is destroyed by her searing jealousy of the young women she sees as her competitors: 'She was poisoned ... Certainly she was ill ... She felt in fact that she was dying' (133). As Lessing takes pains to clarify, Sarah had fallen in love with the pride, arrogance and cruelty of her younger desiring self, which she sees reflected in the young man she has fallen for, who has brought her former self back to life. Wallowing in, yet knowing the painful futility of such projected identification, Lessing keeps illustrating the ways in which this sudden eruption of burning passion is a reliving of her own youth and *amour propre*, the desire to avoid old age, to close the gap between the body she had been living in apparently 'comfortably enough', as she has aged, but which had always, at the same time, 'seemed accompanied by another, her young body, shaped in a kind of ectoplasm' (94). Seemingly, it is against her conscious wishes that Sarah falls in love, triggered by these two men's unexpected interest in her, making her yearn again for the existence of that desirable woman she once knew she had been and making her feel 'like a miserable old ghost at a feast' (137).

Avoiding sexual passion therefore seems essential to Lessing if the ageing woman is not to experience 'atrocious suffering': 'I simply can't wait to go back to my cool elderly self, all passion spent' (180). However, as Lessing also realizes, so long as it is at least conceivable that an ageing woman might once again feel or imagine herself to be noticed and appreciated by another, however fleetingly, she surely risks the reigniting of passion. Indeed, Lessing suggests in this novel: 'old women by the thousand – probably by the million – are in love and keep quiet about it. They have to. ... A secret hell populated by the ghosts of old loves, former personalities' (171). The problem, Lessing notes, echoing Beauvoir, is our sense that we have some unchanging inner core, making us never able to feel simply the age we are.

In *Love, Again*, for instance, Sarah keeps returning to the mirror, forcing herself to absorb the age she really is,

> because the person who is doing the looking feels herself to be exactly the same (when away from the glass) as she was at twenty, thirty, forty ... the same as the girl and young woman who looked into the glass and counted her attractions. She has to insist that this is so, this is the truth, not what I remember, this is what I am seeing, this is what I am. This. This. (236)

In Lacan's account of the infant's mirror phase, it is one's reflected image that forms the basis for establishing any sense of a unitary self. However, inverting this formula, in later life it can seem that it is the mirror that lies to us, obscuring the true self, which seems to exist somewhere within. I am reminded here of a recent witticism about old age from the British writer Will Self: 'in modern western societies, "acting our age" is something that requires an enormous suspension of disbelief'.[71]

There is, however, another feature of Lessing's writing that makes desire so impossible for an ageing woman such as herself, and it is that the body she wants to embrace is, specifically, a young person's body. Sarah, for instance, mourns: 'I shall never again hold a young man's body in my arms. Never. And it seemed to her the most terrible sentence Time could deal her' (260). Why the emphasis on youth? Because it is only youth that can gratify the narcissistic identification. Interviewed by the Irish scholar Billy Gray, at eighty-four, a decade after writing *Love, Again*, Lessing is still wondering why people fall in love at all. However, by this time she has joined those older women claiming she is 'happy to be invisible', feels 'much more free' and able to talk to men without any presumption that you desire them: 'I mean it's a great deprivation to cease to be a sexual being but not as bad as you think it is because ... by then it's only a deprivation if you happen to be in love which thank God has only happened to me once ... a total disaster I can tell you!'[72] I detect some tension between becoming happily 'invisible' and the presumption that men will still notice and freely talk to her – not altogether invisible then, though perhaps invisible *as a woman*.

Nevertheless, I too can see that if and when women do genuinely start to feel 'invisible', we are safely, indeed definitively, spared the dangers of imagining ourselves the object of another's desire, however briefly. When Gray presses Lessing on issues of ageing and sexuality she finally says: 'But what I really mean is ... quite simply, if you have been young and beautiful, the idea aged fifty, of going to bed with someone, is too much of a blow to your pride.'[73] Lessing can feel no joy in any man actually seeing her ageing body, and here she is referring to a firm, attractive, middle-aged female body. What she loves, and has always loved, was her sense of being young and beautiful. Early on in her memoirs, Lessing also mentions the pathos of ageing women displaying old photos of their youthful selves for visitors to survey, suggesting that what they are secretly saying is: 'Don't imagine for one moment that I am this old hag you see here, in this chair, not a bit of it, *that* is what I am really like.'[74]

Lessing thus shares the passion of men such as Philip Roth, though she must *be*, rather than *have*, that young and beautiful object, or as the Lacanians would say, she must be the thing that promises men phallic completion. Hence the sense of aggression, even cruelty, she always attributes to young women.

Lessing's personal escape from these narcissistic wounds came from her embrace of the spiritual guidance of Idries Shah, whose Sufi teaching helped her, she said, to move away from individual cravings, towards a transcendental, mystical domain.[75] However, other women, who claim never to have had the assertive self-confidence about their own youthful beauty that Lessing recalls, nevertheless suggest that it may well be a type of failed narcissism that has diminished, if not removed, their interest in sex in old age. In her thoughtful memoir written in her mid-seventies, Jane Miller reflects: 'I wonder whether desire for things and people, covetousness, longings, are all aspects of narcissism ... all feelings in some way related to pleasure in one's self.' Nowadays, Miller continues, feeling no pleasure in her own body, it is impossible to find enjoyment in the thought of others' desiring it, however unlikely they might be to do so. Although she knows there are women her age who would disagree, she adds: 'It can't be a coincidence that one should be stripped of desire and being desirable and desired more or less in one fell swoop.' She does admit that although it makes for a more peaceful life, sustaining one's pride from the turmoil of rejection, jealousy and more, it also 'feels like an absence ... perhaps even a loss: though perhaps not a loss of any greater significance than the loss of a front tooth'.[76] The loss of that front tooth, clearly, is first and foremost, a blow to one's sense of self. However, I wonder if Miller's equanimity over the abandonment of sexual desire is not related to her being still, as she writes, happily married for over forty years to a man of significant eminence – the writer and critic Karl Miller.

This returns me once more to thoughts on the complexity of sex, and all that it symbolizes. The contrasting experiences it embraces are so impossibly diverse that they easily move us beyond words. These range from the soothing pleasures, or alternatively fierce relief, of desired physical contact, to the sense of self-affirmation that can be generated by the concentrated attention of another or, in particular, and most critically for a sense of connection to the world as we age, the promise – illusory or otherwise – of the comforts of enduring intimacy with some chosen partner. In heterosexual couples, at least, such partnerships usually confer social status and acceptability as well, all the more so if a woman is partnered with a man admired by others. Just what it is that an older woman who lives alone (as I do much of the time) might be wanting when experiencing differing shades of desire can therefore be rather hard to unpack. At least, I find it so.

'Better to act as though we older women do not desire', suggests Sara Maitland, and many older women clearly agree. Not so, however, those experts who nowadays conduct empirical surveys on the sexual lives and wellbeing of the elderly. Indeed, quite the contrary. The information that in earlier times sex in old age was not only seen as sinful and immoral, but capable of leading to madness, blindness and the shortening of life, only adds to the eagerness with which such advice is inverted by professional voices nowadays.[77] However, nowhere is the relativity of human mores easier to see than in shifting perceptions of just when a person should be seen as 'old'. This accompanies differing understandings of the behaviour thought appropriate to old age, with women in some countries already excluded as objects of desire in their forties and therefore categorized as uniformly old. Sociologists, such as Edward Laumann and his co-workers in Chicago, have for some years now been spreading the message that ageing well usually means, and they argue should mean, engaging in regular sexual activity, with orgasms seen as both the definitive marker of sexuality and also a powerful demonstration of overall health.

Orgasms are good for you, and good to have often. Establishing their case, in 2004, these researchers interviewed over 3,000 'older adults', between the ages of fifty-seven and eighty-five, for a National Social Life, Health, and Aging Project in the USA.[78] In a related report, we learn that over two-thirds of men in that age range had active sex lives whereas, over seventy-five years of age, almost two-fifths of men, compared with only one-sixth of women, were sexually active.[79] Lack of a sexual partner was the main problem women faced; in Laumann's words: 'It turns out that healthy people are sexually active if they have a partner, and that this is an important part of the quality of life.'[80] Despite these researchers having some awareness of the diverse realm of the erotic, sexuality here is conveniently identified as something researchers can isolate and (purportedly) measure, reducing it to forms of genital intercourse. Moreover, it is not hard to see that their goal of accurate measurement accompanies the long process of medicalization of sexuality, especially the labelling of sexual 'dysfunction', begun at the close of the nineteenth century. Its related commercial ramifications have expanded exponentially in recent decades with the commercial success of Viagra as a treatment for erectile dysfunction. However, while it is possible and exceedingly profitable to promote technologies to 'banish' what are seen as physical impediments to sex in old age, primarily those restricting penile performance, it is not so easy to change a situation in which older women, if single, find that they are no longer viewed as potential sexual partners by men.

When an earlier global study of the sexual practices of over 27,000 people over forty was conducted by Laumann and his team between 2001 and 2002, the majority of both men (four-fifths) and women (two-thirds) said that they were still sexually active. Nevertheless, among those over seventy, well under a quarter of the women compared to more than half the men reported having sexual contact in the previous twelve months. Since the overwhelming majority of both older women and men expressed the view that they would still like sexual contact, this would seem to leave many women short-changed and frustrated.[81]

One must be aware of the limitations of social statistics, which convey little of the complexity or nuance of desire. As the acerbic biologist Richard Lewontin suggested some time ago, self-reports of sexual activity are already contaminated by personally loaded, culturally acquired expectations of how people think they should appear to the world, making them 'an indissoluble jumble of practices, personal myths, and posturing'.[82] For certain, quantitative measures of genital performance lie oddly alongside the always ambiguous intricacies of what people might feel able to say about differing psychosomatic yearnings, which is why I prefer to explore the life of desire via introspection, memoir or fiction. Nevertheless, reliable or unreliable, posturing or not, empirical surveys do indicate how people report their situation in relation to ageing and sexual practices, information that clearly leave so many women out in the cold, or else needing to disown their potential for passion.

Apart from bare social statistics declaring the existence of sexual activity in old age, however, there is tellingly all too little reflective literature on women's sexuality in late life. It has become fashionable nowadays to suggest that our sexual desires and practices are not static. Yet we have no more control over, and still little understanding of, the nature, resurgence or retreat of erotic desire. Furthermore, it can be hard to grasp just how dependent what we understand and feel about ourselves is upon our social context and what it encourages, disdains or ignores. As we shall see, this seems to be especially true in relation to women. Never in my lifetime was this more evident than in the early years of women's liberation. Suddenly many women, young women for the most part, began to look more powerful and alluring to other young female rebels, whatever our sexuality. As Lillian Faderman recorded, never had lesbian encounters, for instance, been quite so popular.[83]

Still Looking for Love

At seventy-seven, the lesbian poet and novelist Maureen Duffy ended one of her playful poems about ageing with the line, 'Help us all then Lady, Sappho's own goddess, / to sing your song until the last bittersweet note'.[84] Just one of the lasting impacts of feminism in nurturing its own diverse audiences has been to make it a little easier for women of all ages to celebrate their desire for each other. Moreover, in my own experience, it is often easier for an older woman to feel herself the object of desire in situations that exclude men. As we have seen, the old woman is usually all too aware of the ways in which her image has classically brought fear into the hearts of men, whether running from their mothers or recoiling from the mythic witches and gorgons that have frightened them since childhood, as Medusa rages in Carol Ann Duffy's compelling rendition of her bitter tears: 'But I know you'll go, betray me, stray / From home. / So better by far for me if you were stone'.[85]

Looking around my own ageing feminist milieu, I can see that I am far from the only older woman who has enjoyed and, in my case, celebrated the delights of a heterosexual partnership that ended in her late fifties, who has subsequently found unexpected erotic pleasure in a relationship with a woman. This is not so surprising, according to the research of the American social psychologist, Lisa Diamond, in her book *Sexual Fluidity: Understanding Women's Love and Desire*. For over a decade she tracked the sexual accounts provided by eighty-nine women across the USA, concluding from the reports they gave of themselves, and their very varied and shifting experiences, that while they did have a sense of predispositions and intrinsic orientations, these proved 'less of a constraint on their desires and behaviours than is the case for men'. Both Diamond's own research, and several others she cites, suggested that unlike men's, women's sexual desires prove more responsive to context, or as she puts it, 'the types of environmental, situational and interpersonal factors that might trigger her fluidity'.[86]

Consistently, many more gay men than lesbians or bisexuals report already feeling 'different' in childhood, claiming they were always 'gay'. However, self-identifying lesbians show far greater variability than men in when they first become aware of an attraction for another women, and also in how fixed such desires remain.[87] 'Who'd want to be a man?', Adam Phillips asks, reviewing Diamond's book. Despite his scepticism about the limitations of empirical research, he is convinced that she and others are right in suggesting that what is most 'mysterious' about women's desire and relationships is that they are less narrowly focused and more flexible. Indeed, although Diamond herself is not at all disparaging about men, Phillips concludes that 'after reading her book it is hard to see the attractions of being a man', when all the research suggests that, compared to women, men must remain 'more relentlessly themselves', 'more determinedly themselves'.[88] 'Masculinity' and its constraints remain a powerful cultural force.

In thinking about desire and ageing, these findings might help us understand why some women in old age feel able to claim that they have happily abandoned sexual activity, while others, who may be – even unconsciously – waiting for something new to happen, sometimes find that they experience rather different forms of desire. Somewhat remarkably, given some of the views mentioned on older women as contentedly post-sexual, the lesbian writer and organizer Amber Hollibaugh reports that during her advocacy work with SAGE (the largest organization representing older lesbians, gays, bisexual and transgender people in the USA) she was astonished by the number of very old women turning up at the 'coming out' groups. Indeed, she writes that she 'watched in fascination as SAGE was forced to close admissions to a "coming out" group for women over the age of eighty because there were so many who wanted to attend'. This was true for all the different groups serviced by the organization, including women of eighty-five and ninety years old, crossing lines of class, ethnicity and urban or rural locations.[89]

Moreover, those older women still looking for love have sometimes managed to write lyrically about the joys of ageing passion. 'I see ageing as a wonderful time to question everything including gender', another American lesbian writer, Joan Nestle, announced when she was sixty. Defiance was always on her agenda, and when I think of the old slogan, 'the personal is political', it is Joan Nestle's name that usually pops up first. It is quickly followed by a multitude of other feminists, gays, queers and more, from around the globe, all of whom know that there is a politics to personal life, and a place for personal life in politics, without ever wanting to collapse the two. Given their cultural visibility, it was always likely to be the Americans who were first out, and stood most prominently, under that banner of personal politics. Nestle herself began questioning gender from a very young age, early on tied in with her sexual radicalism. However, today in her seventies, having lived in a body struggling against the ravages of three consecutive cancers and their treatment for well over a decade, nothing is more challenging for her than the enduring determination to keep entwining her interest in left feminism and sexual radicalism with thoughts on ageing, ill health and dying.

Nestle tackled this most directly in her moving collection *A Fragile Union*, which she describes as a type of memoir, written after she had been fighting colon cancer for a year, in her late fifties. As she later commented, this made it a very intense book, in which she struggled to build a bridge between her old life as a publicly visible sex radical, a type of sexual 'warrior woman', and the realities of living with a terrible illness and its effects on her life and sexuality. She was by then not only a fifty-eight-year-old woman living with cancer, but one still sharing an apartment with an ex-lover, who had just left her for 'a younger, prettier woman'. Moreover, she was now jobless, the illness having forced her to retire early from work she had loved – thirty years of teaching writing skills to poor, mainly black and minority students at a state-funded college in New

York: 'It's a cliché. I was feeling pretty sick from my chemo-therapy and I felt like I didn't know how to go on with my life.'[90]

At the book's opening she lists the questions that will keep recurring throughout her memoir, which seem so pertinent for any ageing feminist, wondering how it is possible: 'to love when I keep failing ... to be brave when I am so fearful ... to protest injustice when I am so tired ... to embrace difference when I do not even trust myself'. Yet, remarkably, with a body often racked by pain, she writes of enjoying loving sexual encoun-ters, while asserting, with all her old conviction: 'I find this to be a time of great passion in my life, a time of deep commit-ments to the forging of fragile solidarities that, if of the body, may last only a night, and if of a more sweeping kind, carry me more humbly than ever into the historic processes.'[91] Although her determination is often threatened with defeat, the one thing she simply will not resign from altogether is a certain hunger for future embraces, however often she recalls having turned away from her erstwhile lover's desire over the previous year. Towards the end of these stories, Nestle had not fully recov-ered from her cancer, but she had begun a new relationship. This was with the dynamic Australian activist and human rights professor, Dianne Otto, ten years younger than her: 'She's just brought me so much all wrapped up in this incredible love and caring', as she later expressed in an interview.[92] A decade on, in the spring of 2011, Nestle said much the same thing to me when I met her in London. Although often weak, she is still, when she is able, speaking out publicly for social justice around a myriad of issues, as she did reflecting upon her Jewish roots while visit-ing Israel in 2007 and spending time with women committed to ending the occupation of Palestinian territories and working for peace in that troubled land.

Above all, however, in what she sees as her final years, Nestle retains her roots in radical sexual politics, though today carefully trying to thread her way through the tentacles of the capitalist commodification of sex and its incitements of desire, which, as she says, is hardly the same as a culture genuinely open to sexual differences. What is special, and inspiring, about Joan Nestle is the way in which she continues, with whatever level of bravado, to present a sexual self to the world, to fashion an erotic identity that recognizes its bodily weaknesses, its dependency on others, while still hoping, indeed still managing, to be herself the object of others' desire. It was in her late fifties that she announced: 'Grey hair and textured hands are now erotic emblems I seek out.' Then as now, she pursues, and she finds, at least a little of what she wants, affirming 'a glory in love-making', despite also experiencing 'fear and change and loss'.[93]

Nestle's writing brings to mind other audacious, if often foundering, efforts from the heyday of feminism to eroticize women's lives – indeed, the voluntaristic determination to declare all women desirable and significant, whatever their age. Another North American lesbian writer from that era, who helped found a feminist press, was the late June Arnold. Almost forty years ago I first encountered and recall enjoying her book, *Sister Gin*, with its portrayal of sexual desire for a much older woman. In this book, published in her fiftieth year, Arnold depicts her menopausal, middle-aged protagonist, Su, also approaching fifty, falling in love with Mamie Carter, a poised and self-confident woman in her eighties. In this surprising yet compelling narrative, we read of Su's yearning to stroke the parchment skin of the one she loves, 'I would sand the whorls off my fingertip to avoid scratching that silk'. Her desire is gratified, and continues after the two women do eventually spend a night together: 'Su sunk her face into the ageless curve of her love's shoulder and smothered a giggle "I never imagined the delights of age would include the fact of endlessly drawn out orgasms. Did you always know?"'[94]

Although Su wants co-habitation, Mamie Carter decides that she will never live with her much younger lover, but this in no way diminishes Su's desire, which only deepens as she reaches out to age itself, to 'lust after a final different dry silken life and so much grace and elegance from all the knowledge of the day … There is no more beautiful word in the language than withered.' There's defiance writ large! I recall reading this novel at the height of my feminist conversion, and although identifying as a straight woman at the time, and entirely distanced from Arnold's lesbian separatism, I found it exciting to ponder this direct assault on what had been the unbroken landscape of ageism I inhabited, with its exclusion of the old as conceivable objects of desire. It was a backdrop that had been barely named as such back then. 'My darling's face has been walked on by life', Su reflects, as her aged lover teases her that she must not worry about her relative youth: 'The truly free is she who can be old at any age … It has been said that geniuses are forever old.'[95]

For many people, however, and not only feminists, it will be the American poet Adrienne Rich who for over forty years was one of the most influential voices in fashioning a space for celebrating the bodies of women, whatever their age. Rich's poetry and prose was usually written to express her commitment to identifying and opposing the complex fabric of entrenched inequality and injustices, near and far, noting the destructiveness of much of US global policy, especially over the last two decades.[96] Sometimes, however, this ageing poet, who lived in a

body permanently enduring the pain and impairment of rheumatoid arthritis, simply expresses the sustenance she gained
from the mutual love and desire enduring in the relationship she
shared for decades with the Jamaican-born novelist and editor,
Michelle Cliff. In her poem 'Memorize This', which she wrote
at seventy-three, Rich celebrated their lives together:

> Love for twenty-six years, you can't stop
> A withered petunia's crisp the bud sticky both are dark
> The flower engulfed in its own purple
> So common, nothing like it.

The poem continues, describing their daily emotional support
and enduring desire for each other over the years, concluding
in joyful wonder:

> Sleeping with you after
> weeks apart how normal
> yet after midnight
> to turn and slide my arm
> along your thigh
> drawn up in sleep
> what delicate amaze.[97]

(Returning to edit this chapter, I receive the sad news of Rich's
death, in March 2012, but she was very much alive, and inspiring me, during the years I was writing this book).

I have suggested that, as vividly exemplified in the writing
of Beauvoir and Lessing, it is in heterosexual contexts that
women, at least when single, are likely to find it hardest to turn
around the pernicious effects of the picture of old women as

sexless and undesirable. Certainly, it is not easy to find instances of men expressing their desire for older women, even though I don't doubt that such passion exists. Here is Seamus Heaney, at seventy-two, with a somewhat chaste image of the mutuality of love in old age, in his collection, *The Human Chain*: 'Too late, alas, now, for apt quotation / About a love that's proved by steady gazing / Not at each other but in the same direction.'[98]

It is almost as difficult to find evidence of older women publicly celebrating their passion for the man, or men, in their lives. One of the few novels I have found that depicts sexual passion between a couple in their seventies is *Age: A Love Story*, written by the late American writer, Hortense Calisher, published when she was seventy-five. The novel opens with a declaration, written by the wife – approaching seventy-seven, and four years older than her husband – explaining that against expectations they still make love: 'Our performance is like memory, sometimes faint, sometimes strong. Often dampened by the daily rhythms, or refreshed by the slightest novelty.' The wife describes their naked bodies, commenting 'to me the aquiline of his nose is still a kind of physical poetry', while telling us that her husband says he finds the lines on the loosening skin of her arms 'like a Greek wave etched by an artist adept at those border patterns'.[99]

The novel is also an account of the anticipation of loss, and a defence against future loneliness, since the alternating entries of this loving couple, both keeping an anxious eye out for 'each other's hurts', are being written to be read by the surviving spouse. Fearful of loss, yet still able to embrace what remains in the present, the book closes with them deciding to read each other's entries together, while they are still alive, as the husband reflects:

Our nest here still smells of the sexual. I touch her there.
So the bland wall darkens. As we ride toward it.
Our bed a skiff.
As any child can see.[100]

If and when women writers do describe sexual desire in old
age it is never through the dramatic moans or revulsion of a
Roth, Amis, or even Updike, with their tales of impotence,
prostate procedures, and incontinence. Despite their frequent
sense of the world's indifference to them, and whatever their
private anguish, in general women appear to have mastered the
art of losing a little more easily than have men. Maybe something about our existence as women in the world as we have
known it has always suggested a certain sense of loss and failure:
'Better luck next time!', as my father, a doctor, would 'joke' to
any woman he had assisted in giving birth to a daughter. The
Lacanians might say that, with language, every woman knows
she is born into lack, whereas men have to pretend otherwise.

Another woman writer, who could elegantly combine sexual
passion with her own gentle wit and wisdom about the ambiva-
lences of ageing, is the late Grace Paley. Decades before my
own generation thought we had invented women's liberation,
Grace Paley, like another American Jewish writer, Tillie Olsen,
was busy chronicling women's typically undervalued labour of
love. Paley's first prose fiction, *The Little Disturbances of Man:
Stories of Men and Women at Love* (1973), was written during the
1940s and 1950s, depicting hard-up, harassed housewives and
mothers daily confronting the temper tantrums of agitated children and the deficiencies and desertions of husbands. Between
sporadic outbursts of helpless rage over their round-the-clock
responsibilities, Paley's feisty housewives have surges of desire

for the men in their lives. Revisiting Paley's writing today, at the advanced age she was when I first encountered her forty years ago, I notice thoughts on ageing that I barely registered back then (illustrating that it is readers and their contexts as much as authors and their work that determine what we attend to in reading).[101]

In the opening narrative of this collection, 'Goodbye and Good Luck', written in 1955, an old woman cheerfully recalls the joys of her youth: 'I was popular in certain circles', says Aunt Rose, 'I wasn't no thinner then, only more stationary in the flesh.'[102] Shifts of the flesh are memorably mapped by Rose: 'I noticed it first on my mother's face, the rotten handwriting of time, scribbled up and down her cheeks, across her forehead back and forth – a child could read – it said, old, old, old.'[103] And yet, refusing the flesh-loathing so pervasive in our time, this is not a tale of woe. Despite her wobbles and her weight, Rose retains the capacity to love and be loved again: the story ends with her returning to an old lover she had adored but forsaken half a century earlier, because he was married, now that he has become a widower.

Over thirty years later, in a poem written at seventy-nine shortly before she died, Paley mentions her enjoyment of her own now 'heavy breasts' and 'nicely mapped face', but most of all she reveals her capacity to express her continuing keen love and desire for her husband of many decades, the poet and playwright, Robert Nichols:

> that's my old man across the yard
> he's talking to the meter reader
> he's telling him the world's sad story
> how electricity is oil or uranium

and so forth I tell my grandson
run over to your grandpa ask him
to sit beside me for a minute I
am suddenly exhausted by my desire
to kiss his sweet explaining lips.[104]

With neither her political nor her personal passions ever desert-
ing her, the enduringly activist, feminist, pacifist, anti-Zionist,
Grace Paley could truly write, 'It's all life until death.'

The current British doyenne of old age, Diana Athill, would
certainly agree. In her mid-nineties, she still regularly appears
in our media, having written her memoir *Somewhere Towards the
End* in her ninetieth year. Although she has lived alone for the
last thirty years, only recently moving into a retirement home,
she recalls with pleasure her last seven-year, weekly liaison in
her sixties, with a man she calls Sam: 'to be urgently wanted at
a time when I no longer expected it cheered me up and brought
me to life again – no small gift'. Decades later she still enjoys
the memory of her late-life affair: 'I feel him lying beside me
after making love, both of us on our backs, hands linked, arms
and legs touching in a friendly way. His physical presence is
so clear, even now, that it is almost like a haunt (an amiable
one).'[105]

Athill mentions the power dynamics present in all erotic
attraction, though this is an aspect of desire which is usually
repressed or disavowed, especially by feminists, even as it shifts
dramatically for women as we age. In Athill's case, she raises the
complicated way in which status can feature in interracial relations, while knowing it is a difficult matter for white people to
raise without courting accusations of racism. From middle age
her two sexual relationships were with black men, the first and

most long-lasting and passionate with the artist Barry Reckord. She in no way condones the cultural hierarchies in play, but suggests that they explain why certain older white women, such as herself at that time, may still have an allure for black men. At any rate, she believes that for Sam, as for many black men from his background at that time, it was probable that her being a 'well-bred' white woman gave her a certain prestige that she no longer had for white men. She is grateful for its consequences, even as she deplores the underlying racism that gave her this advantage: 'Sam was not a man of vulgar instincts so he didn't want to show his woman off, but it gave him private satisfaction to feel that she was worth showing.' Like Beauvoir, Athill also writes of the importance of staying in touch with younger people, so as not to slide into 'a general pessimism about life': 'Always we are reflected in the eyes of others ... So if and when we are old a beloved child happens to look at you as if he or she thinks (even mistakenly!) that you are wise and kind: what a blessing!'[106]

I read these women's words, and I ponder my own life. I can see that I identify with those women who keep doors open to passion of all kinds as they age. At the close of my sixties, I am still pushing on doors myself, still in need of attention, affection and praise, fearing that one day I will lose them all. Yet while I know I am hardly unique, I can see others making different accommodations with ageing. I do not share the tranquillity of those who feel that they are freed from the perils of physical desire, or who say they no longer fear the loss of the world's regard, but as I will explore further in later chapters, perhaps they are following pathways I have yet to find.

4

The Ties That Bind

There is another side to intimacy that does not involve the kindling and consummation of sexual activity. Instead it includes all the diverse forms of attachment, commitment and the many personal responsibilities we feel towards others, with their promise of comfort and support, and their risk of encumbrance and loss. There is little doubt that the symbolic ideal of such attachment, as well as its often-messy actuality, comes first and foremost from the original maternal encounter. The woman giving birth to a baby for the very first time is jolted into a reality where she will find that she is no longer the autonomous being she was before, but rather someone who must be 'there for another': 'Yes, motherhood', as Lisa Baraitser writes, 'is the pitilessness of the present tense … The [baby's] cry pulls me out of whatever I was embedded in, and before I have a chance to re-equilibrate, it pulls me out again.'[1] In Freudian thought, which so often mirrors aspects of folk wisdom, we love in order to be loved, telling us that there is always a narcissistic component to our love for another. Yet love, in any depth, also necessarily means surrendering something of oneself to another person.

What we may come to love and nurture, and in turn receive

satisfaction from, also extends beyond the interpersonal to other living creatures and even specific spaces, activities and situations, as we project ourselves into familiar surroundings and events, animating them with properties that soothe and comfort us in our own care and attention to them. The gay American poet Mark Doty, for instance, in his lyrical memoir *Dog Years*, describes how his attachment to the two dogs, Beau and Arden, he loved for sixteen years, helped him to bear the grief of caring for his lover, Wally, as he died from AIDS.[2] As we will see, Donna Haraway also writes eloquently of love and forms of intimacy that extend from humans to animals, especially those interacting most closely with humans. It is these enduring ties, whether to people, places or pursuits, that can facilitate ways of visualizing the process of ageing as a time of preservation and possibility, quite as much as one of devastation and decline.

Forging Myths

'Old age can be magnificent', the redoubtable May Sarton wrote in one of her prolific reflections on the topic in her journal, *The House by the Sea*, published in 1977 when she was sixty-five.[3] Sarton was so resolutely drawn to recording her experiences of ageing over many decades that she can be seen as America's poet laureate of ageing, commanding our attention if only for her determination to live passionately to the very close of her life and influencing others who would attempt to follow in her footsteps. Sarton died in 1995 at eighty-three, maintaining till the end such a large readership that she often complained that answering her fan mail would kill her off. Yet, ironically, it was long periods of solitude and immersion in the beauties of the natural world that Sarton famously said she longed for. Her ties, she alleged, were to her animals, her gardening, the joy of seeing her plants in bloom, arranging her flowers in vases, planning her writing, recording her reading. However, in what was just one of her many contradictions, Sarton relied upon the acknowledgement and love of her friends and admirers in order to fight off depression, even as she resented them for interfering with her solitude.

Opening *Journal of a Solitude*, the first and perhaps best known of her published journals, written when she was fifty-eight, Sarton reflected on living alone in Maine, suggesting 'Whatever peace I know rests in the natural world, in feeling myself a part of it, even in a small way.'[4] Nevertheless, in just one of her contradictions, she longed for recognition of her work from the literary establishment, which she only received in old age, and then, especially, for her memoirs and journals so vigilantly depicting the creative challenges and triumphs of ageing. Sarton seemed not so much to fear ageing, or death, as to worry about not being adequately recognized as a poet and writer, aware that she would never 'feel secure enough no longer to crave praise'.[5] In my experience, this longing for recognition and acceptance from those in whom we have invested power and authority rarely fades over the years, nor the particular delight of receiving praise from people we most admire, unless such longing is violently stamped out of us. If extinguished, as it may well be from lack of any sort of nourishment, what goes with it is usually the ability to feel any desire at all.

Born into the American upper middle class, Sarton knew that it was her financial and imaginative resources that enabled her to separate her physical dependence from the common disempowerment of ageing. Suffering quite early on from various degenerative diseases, she sometimes indicated, unusually, that old age had enabled her to appreciate the joys of dependency on her closest friends for support and comfort: 'Here's a good thing', she told one interviewer at seventy-nine, 'I've certainly become much more passive.'[6]

Moreover, she registers the plight of those less fortunate than herself, with no one to lean on, evident in the novel she wrote on reaching sixty, *As We Are Now*. This happened to be the first of Sarton's books I read and admired in my own late thirties. It forced me to think in ways I had hitherto evaded about the extreme dispossession and humiliation faced by the old if they end up helpless and alone when in need of care. In this novel, the dehumanizing treatment in a nursing home is described in chilling detail, with its protagonist arousing the reader's sympathy and concern throughout, even as her despair and final loss of all hope facing the bullying by the staff leads her to commit the terrible crime that closes the book, burning down what Sarton has depicted as a type of 'concentration camp for the old'.[7]

However, Sarton herself was most loved by her admirers – or censured by her critics – for the more characteristic stress she placed on depicting her own spiritual ties and cominglings with the natural world, remaining forever open to its aesthetic joys, while also describing how she tried to surmount the challenges each new day might offer. Though some critics saw her writing as overly self-absorbed, when looked at from the perspective of ageing it seems to me that there was always a type of politics to Sarton's personal predilections. This involved her determined self-presentation as lacking any deep fears about ageing, combined with her love for those older people, usually women, who served as her main mentors, friends and lovers from her teenage years. Certainly, the American literary critics now concerned with ageing, including Kathleen Woodward, Anne Wyatt-Brown, Barbara Frey Waxman and Silvia Henneberg, all suggest that her work is critical for anyone interested in old age.[8]

In so many ways Sarton seems to have spent her whole life rehearsing for a creative old age, and throughout her adult life she claimed that 'I have always been fond of old people, and I always wanted to be old.'[9] Or at least, what she always wanted were fresh chances to reinvent and re-imagine herself, something she felt she could learn from those older people to whom she was attracted. It was old age, she would say, which provided her with a deepening awareness of the fleeting transience of things, a thought she found moving rather than depressing, as long as she could capture it in memory and in writing, which for her slowed down the passing of time. It is not that Sarton was free from the fear 'of dying in some inappropriate or gruesome way', but that she was simply determined to hold on to what life offered her. It was this quality she used to beat back life-long threats of depression. She summed this up in her poem 'Gestalt at Sixty':

> I worked out anguish in a garden.
> Without the flowers,
> The shadow of trees on snow, their punctuation,
> I might not have survived.
> ...
> How rich and long the hours become,
> How brief the years,
> ...
> I live like a baby
> Who bursts into laughter

As a sunbeam on the wall,
Or like a very old woman
Entranced by the prick of stars
Through the leaves.

I am not ready to die,
But I am learning to trust death
As I have trusted life.[10]

Having subverted the routine denigration of old age, Sarton later admitted that she tended to romanticize it.[11] Nevertheless, given her life-long attachments to older women, any idealization on her part was not a self-serving outlook, acquired only when joining the ranks of the elderly herself. Throughout her life she was a genuine saboteur of the cultural segregation which most of us practice in our youth. She pioneered an approach decades before it was publicly politicized, first of all by just a few feminists, such as Cynthia Rich, younger sister of poet Adrienne Rich. In 1983, aged fifty, Rich co-edited the trailblazing book, *Look Me in the Eye: Old Women, Aging, and Ageism*, with Barbara Macdonald, her much older lover. There she presented rallying calls echoing Sarton's conviction that:

It is not natural, and it is dangerous, for younger women to be divided by a taboo from old women – to live in our own shaky towers of youth ... It is intended, but it is not natural that we be ashamed of, dissociated from, our future selves, sharing men's loathing for the women we are daily becoming. It is not natural that today ... old women are still an absence for younger women.[12]

It may be in a sense 'natural' for us to reach across the generations, given that as young women we will always have a strong, if usually ambivalent, connection to at least one older woman: our mother. However, it seems that it has been easier for certain lesbians, though far from all, to experience lasting love and friendship with older women, even as many straight women have found it easy to love and remain with older men.

Sarton was, famously, one of the first to celebrate her lesbian passions in fiction, at a time when this was still risky for a writer. In *Mrs Stevens Hears the Mermaids Singing* (1965), Sarton depicted her formidable heroine, Hilary Stevens (a character resembling her creator), reflecting upon the many women she has fallen in love with in the past who, although often unattainable, have always inspired her poetry. Sarton wrote this book when she was fifty-three, although tellingly she makes her eponymous heroine a woman already in her seventies.

It was always clear, however, that Sarton's determined belief that creative reinvention can be intensified with ageing, even when very old and facing serious illness or death, extended well beyond her enjoyment of any erotic ties with women, many of which she had found anguished. Indeed, when she opens her journal, *At Seventy*, asking herself, 'What is it like to be seventy?' she at once supplied a string of cheerful responses. 'I do not feel old at all, not as much a survivor as a person still on her way', while adding: 'I suppose real old age begins when one looks backwards rather than forward, but I look forward with joy to the years ahead and especially to the surprises that any day may bring.' She admits to being haunted by the mistakes she has made in the past, but this only seems to lead her to repeat more strongly: 'This is the best time of my life. I love being old ... I am surer about what my life is about, have less self-doubt to conquer.'

It was the difficult process of writing itself, her daily entries in her journal and the labours they recorded, but above all what she saw as her receptivity to change and the unpredictability of the future, that gave new meaning to her life. Sarton believed she coped with life far better at seventy than when she was fifty: 'I think this is because I have learned to glide rather than to force myself at moments of tension.' Moreover, she continued to form new emotional attachments at seventy, though she knows these erotic ties with women may no longer involve the same sort of physical sexual connection. Towards the end of this journal she described a delightful day she spent with her much older friend, Lotte Jacobi: 'we talked and teased each other about our mutual propensity to become violently attached to someone, she at eighty-seven, me at seventy, the living proof that love is always possible, that special kind of love that always brings poetry with it'.[13]

Sarton's writing set the tone that many other women have followed, hoping to bring poetry into their own lives when dealing with the dilemmas of ageing. 'She was ... deluged with adorers, fans, visitors and letter-writers in love with her life, fulsome with praise', as Sarton's literary executor, the author and feminist scholar Carolyn Heilbrun commented.[14] What is less clear is the degree to which these admirers and followers noted what Sarton herself always acknowledged, namely the degree of *invention* she put into her self-making: 'We are all myth-makers about ourselves', she wrote in her mid-fifties, embarking on her first memoir, *Plant Dreaming Deep* (1968).[15] Indeed, she later confessed, one reason for writing her popular *Journal of a Solitude* (1973) was that she worried that she had given the wrong impression about her 'solitary' life in that earlier book: 'without my own intention, that book gives a false view. The anguish of my life here – its rages – is hardly mentioned. Now I hope to break through into the rough rocky depths, to the matrix itself. There is violence there and anger never resolved.'[16] The degree of fabrication, and all that was left unsaid about the difficulties of her 'solitary' life – a life that was actually often filled with friends and helpers – is also evident in a later interview for a documentary film about her work made when she was seventy-nine: 'We have to make myths out of our lives in order to sustain them and I think this is partly how one handles the monster.'[17] The monster being life itself.

Sarton made myths about her life, and many people tried to emulate them. Her fellow American, Alix Kates Shulman, for one, experiencing a writer's block and general loss of confidence in her fifties, managed to regain her serenity and find spiritual renewal, so she wrote, restoring her old hope and confidence in meditative solitude, in relating to animals, the earth and the sea, when living for a summer in a cabin on a rain-swept beach, also off the coast of Maine. She recorded this new sense of joy in her memoir *Drinking the Rain* (1995), feeling herself in tune with the rhythms of life in the plants and animals she tended. Indeed, she closes her book contemplating the ocean, somewhat ecstatically expressing her by then firm embrace of ecopolitics: 'Perhaps the tides will heal the hole in the world.'[18]

The buoyancy of these public spokespersons, insisting upon women's capacity for ageing 'liberation', is somewhat at odds with any closer reading of Sarton's memoirs or journals, with their indications of suppressed rage and recurring depression. For all that, ageing remained an 'adventure' for Sarton, and in her final journal, written at eighty-two, she could still depict the 'lovely glow of happiness' she experienced meeting friends, or simply sitting on her terrace, although she also confessed that much of the time she was suffering from 'a serious depression', which she had always found it 'hard to talk about' and avoided putting into her diaries.[19] Sarton did less to hide the complexities of ageing than many she has influenced.

The Art of Losing

Second-wave feminists were mostly young and busy struggling for more choice and control over their lives – whether in the home, the workplace, or the world at large – when they first found their voices around the start of the 1970s. This meant that it was childcare and housework, not old age or debility, which came to the fore when questions of intimacy and care were brought into the political arena. Feminists then also devoted much of their young lives to trying to build supportive friendship and community networks, sometimes experimenting with alternative family arrangements. It was the division of labour in the traditional family, feminists argued, that had for so long defined, subordinated and constrained women. Nowadays, however, earlier feminist attempts to politicize personal life are usually dismissed as foolishly utopian. What caused the most disapproval, however, was the criticism of marriage and the family.[20] For it is this institution that has remained the authorized way to live, still seen as providing the only haven in a heartless world, with the politics of the moment geared more to expanding its parameters to include same-sex couples than to any attempt to overthrow it.

Conventional families are indeed often the crucial bulwarks

of defence against worldly stresses, yet in relation to ageing it is worth revisiting some of the problems of the overriding respect and importance given to that institution. As we have seen, through choice or circumstance, one of the most common experiences of older women is that they live outside any nuclear family, or even coupledom. This means having to confront a situation in which, as Michèle Barrett and the late Mary McIntosh wrote in 1982, it can be hard facing the pervasive ideology of pity or contempt for all those outside the remit of the traditional family: 'It is indeed a place of intimacy, but in privileging the intimacy of close kin it has made the outside world cold and friendless, and made it harder to sustain relations of security and trust except with kin. Caring, sharing and loving would be more widespread if the family did not claim them for its own.'[21] Moreover, just as feminists had revealed the domestic misery, violence and abuse once kept well hidden behind the closed doors, nowadays it is increasingly necessary to reveal the frequent distress and isolation of elderly caregivers and those who depend upon them within what can be profoundly fraught family settings. This is all the more necessary today when for some time the social supports for domestic life have been chipped away both by state spending cuts and the greater isolation produced by job mobility undermining old extended family and neighbourhood relations.[22] As things turned out, feminists could not solve the problem of how to make caring and sharing better resourced and more widespread, beyond family ties, but it was not for want of trying, and we were certainly adroit in raising the problems.

Sometimes it is the very same feminist voices that were once most passionate about women's isolated situation in the home as young mothers that can be heard again rethinking the politics of personal life as they ponder the hopes, fears, anxieties or rage they feel entering old age. One feminist who posed such 'burning questions' over forty years ago is the indomitable Alix Kates Shulman, mentioned above.[23] To huge controversy, she published 'A Marriage Agreement' in 1969, when her children were young, insisting that her then-husband share responsibilities for household chores and childcare. Today Shulman writes of all the readjustments she has had to make in her life over the last few years of caring for her much loved current husband, Scott, after he suffered a traumatic brain injury from a fall, at seventy-five, causing a form of dementia similar in its effect to late-stage Alzheimer's.[24] In her latest memoir, *To Love What Is*, Shulman says she is often teetering on the verge of despair. Having no short-term memory, Scott is now unable to concentrate on anything, or to pursue his old art work, and requires her constant and unwavering attention.

As Shulman struggles for time to read, write, chat with a friend or just for moments to herself, Scott struggles for her attention: 'And there it is, the paradox of our predicament. The relentlessness of his needs and the frustration of mine are one', she writes.[25] When things go well, she is able to hire Scott-minders, although it is hard to find ones whom he will accept, and in the time she has to herself Shulman is usually busy writing about the continuing joys and many sorrows, the constant hazards and remaining passion, of their ongoing life together. In the two years she spent writing that book, we learn that Scott retains his old gentleness, charm and affection much of the time, at least when she is paying attention to him. If he sees her crying, she writes, 'he reaches out an arm to comfort me, exactly as he always has ... he kisses me and says, "Don't be sad. You've made me so happy. I didn't know I could be so happy"' (171–2). Every moment we're together, she reflects, 'in battle or harmony: he is my hub' (166). They still cuddle up at night, and by day they go to movies, free chamber concerts, opera or dance matinées, while Shulman consoles herself about the losses his dementia causes:

> That he forgets the concert or dance the minute it's over hardly matters; even in undamaged brains sensual pleasure fades quickly. Like the flavor of an exquisite dish or the quality of a given orgasm, the sound of a particular performance, however transporting, won't usually outlive the week. Whereas once I kept whole libraries in my head, nowadays I can recall only vaguely the contents of a book I read a month ago, but that doesn't diminish my passion for reading in the slightest. (170)

I've heard most recently that things have got worse, leading Shulman to search for further sources of sustenance as she continues to care for Scott at home. She wrote about her support group in the *New York Times*: 'Monday morning can be a downer, but for the dozen women and men in our support group, it's a highlight of our week. That's when we gather to speak candidly of what is unspeakable in polite society or even among closest friends and family ... Often down or drained when we assemble, we part after 90 minutes buoyed and energized, week after week, year after year.'[26]

Alix Shulman's book immediately brings to mind John Bayley's thoughts on caring for his wife, Iris Murdoch, in her final years with Alzheimer's disease. Seamlessly moving between past and present, Bayley's account of the tribulations of the present are placed alongside romantic or peaceful reveries of their life together over the previous forty years. They were so often together, and yet in many ways 'together apart', each always allowing the other the space to do their own work, think their own thoughts, even during mealtimes, where they'd sit together, each with a book reading. In those final years, however, everything reversed, and though in some sense they were increasingly apart, as the husband could not easily follow his wife into the anxieties and fears of her amnesia, they were at all times 'together': 'It was very different from the life we live today. It was like being alone, and yet we were not alone … We were separate but never separated … Now we are together for the first time. We have actually become, as is so often said of a happy married couple, inseparable.' Bayley does not ignore the rage he occasionally feels when his wife's behaviour becomes intolerable, as on a bus trip they have to take. More often, however, he claimed to be satisfied, as he remained ever present accompanying Murdoch's disquieting journey in those final bleak years. Especially at night, in bed, he feels free to hold and remember the wife he has always loved: 'It is wonderfully peaceful to sit in bed with Iris reassuringly asleep and gently snoring. Half asleep again myself I have a feeling of floating down the river, and watching all the rubbish from the house and from our lives – the good as well as the bad – sinking slowly down though the dark water until it is lost in the depths.'[27]

Interestingly, I read that in Australia today there are more men over sixty-five than women caring for partners with dementia, and there are certainly a few other books by men providing accounts of this challenging journey.[28] More generally, as seen in Linn Sandberg's research, many of the older men she interviewed in Sweden stressed that the pleasure they received in touch and intimacy with their partners was a large measure of their fulfilment in later life. Nevertheless, the language and world of caring, and indeed of letting go and loss, is still more often associated with woman's world, even as more men come to share it in old age. Certainly, some women work especially hard to find just the right words, the right stories, the right rhythm even, to encompass and hence to try to surmount their losses. They are not, of course, always successful, even when their words move others to greater understanding of their own predicament.

With mordant humour, Elizabeth Bishop wrote one of her most celebrated poems on loss over seventy years ago, 'One Art', with its sharply parodic refrain, before naming the suicide of her lover as the ultimate catastrophe:

> The art of losing isn't hard to master;
> so many things seem filled with the intent
> to be lost that their loss is no disaster.
>
> Lose something every day. Accept the fluster
> of lost door keys, the hour badly spent.
> The art of losing isn't hard to master.
> …
> I lost my mother's watch. And look! my last, or
> next-to-last, of three beloved houses went.
> The art of losing isn't hard to master.
>
> I lost two cities, lovely ones. And, vaster,
> some realms I owned, two rivers, a continent.
> I miss them, but it wasn't a disaster.

– Even losing you (the joking voice, a gesture
I love) I shan't have lied. It's evident
the art of losing's not too hard to master .

though it may look like (Write it!) a disaster.[29]

It may look like, and sometimes it is, a disaster. At other times, the continuation of forms of love, compassion, attachment, even desire, can accompany the most extreme challenges and losses of ageing. Some women writers have skilfully rehearsed in fiction the unexpected joys as well as the difficulties of caring for fragile and ailing elderly partners, friends or lovers. At fifty-six, the late North American writer, Jane Rule, wrote her remarkably compassionate novel, *Memory Board*, a moving account of a lesbian couple in which one partner, the recently retired medical practitioner, Diana Court, suffering, as Rule did, from bad arthritis, is learning how to manage to care for her partner, Constance, now afflicted with Alzheimer's disease. Despite the increasing confinement in which the independent and argumentative Diana now chooses to live to keep Constance secure and relaxed, she says she can still feel considerable contentment in her life. As she explains to her twin brother David: 'It's as much for my own sake as for hers that I don't want it disturbed. I have had to cut off friends who have wanted to rescue me from it.'[30]

Entering his sister's world after forty years of estrangement, David does not try to 'rescue' her, but is instead fascinated both by his sister and for him the still beautiful Constance. After working hard to rebuild his childhood closeness with his sibling, while struggling to win Constance's trust (becoming, for instance, whichever person she takes him to be, from plumber or gardener to garbage man), David eventually moves in to help his sister cope with Constance's growing needs. Constance, like her carers, Diana and David, still finds much mutual pleasure in music, and other forms of physical beauty and contact, as Diana notes one time when joining her old lover in bed: 'Constance turned and welcomed her into a sleeping embrace, the body's memory flawless' (35). Aware of what she owes to all the old friends and family members now helping her care for Constance, Diana reflects, more than once, that there are 'miracles' that became easier to recognize when everything else failed:

> Jill [an old friend and lover of Constance] stayed to cook, for which Diana was grateful. She sat with her drink, listening to a violin concerto, while Constance gently rubbed her neck. To be cared for and cherished in this kind of domestic harmony was something that perhaps couldn't be learned except in old age where the needs of the flesh, though humiliating, were rarely competitive. It was an accomplishment that came out of failure. (207)

Making an Exit returns us to yet another compelling memoir of caring for a woman with Alzheimer's. This time it is a daughter's narrative, that of the New York academic and theatre critic Elinor Fuchs, who ends up mothering her mother Lil, through her final years with dementia. Lil was a once a vivacious, beautiful woman who, unusually for the 1930s, left an unhappy marriage to pursue an ambitious career, travelling the world and leaving her only child, Elinor, to be raised by her grandparents until adolescence. Half a century later, both mother and daughter are transformed by Lil's rapidly increasing dependence.

With humour, anguish, insight and empathy, Fuchs recounts the new love flowering between them, perhaps for the very first time, as she learns to respond to her mother's playfulness (as well as to her fears and tantrums), decoding the poetry and meanings in her mother's disintegrating thoughts:

> The more reduced you are, the more loving you are, every-thing else washed away – success, money, glamour, clothes, 'things'. 'My love!', you say, 'the one I love' … I'm sitting here weeping and weeping for you and for myself. Oh, little lamb! It hardly matters now which of us is the mother and which the daughter. Taking care of as good as being taken care of. My job, to keep the little flame alive for just a while, to keep the little spirit in the world.[31]

As she readily acknowledges, it was important, of course, that Fuchs had relatives, especially a loving uncle, as well as money and resources for helping her with the task. This memoir joins the previous narratives in seeing the mother's deterioration not merely as a period of loss, but as a type of spiritual rebirth, as the daughter learns the skills of connecting with her mother's daily life: 'I call her "Little Bones" and sit her on my lap. "I love you," she purrs. I talk comforting baby talk. "Little pussycat, my little pussycat." ' 'The last ten years: they were our best', she writes, as she ends her memoir.[32]

Another thoughtful and extremely informative memoir on the shifting feelings of love and commitment towards a parent with Alzheimer's is a daughter's reflections on her complicated relations with the suffering of a father. In *Do You Remember Me?: A Father, a Daughter and a Search for Self*, the American writer Judith Levine explains that she had always been, at best, a 'reluctant daughter', spending much of her young adulthood as a feminist at war with her overbearing father, while also rejecting any form of traditional family life.[33] Now, however, as she watches the cognitive deterioration accompanying Stan's Alzheimer's disease, she finds herself 'warily beginning to love' him again, even to enjoy his company in unexpected ways. His mind wanders but his senses remain intact, sometimes returning him to some of his earliest pleasures. Father and daughter have fun visiting galleries together, or when he starts drawing with crayons: 'When I'm with him, I enjoy a kind of contact dementia. The rational world snookered, I respond directly to colors, shapes, and images, the irrational reason of the contemporary visual', she writes (89). They listen to his favourite music together, and he gets up to dance with her, a slow and serious waltz. The father's inability to hold a rational conversation distances him from his wife, her mother, who is with him all the time until she eventually leaves him, though continuing to arrange for his support. But strangely it allows the visiting daughter to draw closer to him.

As Fuchs found with her mother's cognitive breakdown, Stan wants to communicate, he attempts to make conversation, though his wife can barely listen. So he chats to strangers he hopes might prove friendly, and sometimes they are. Despite his cognitive fragilities, when he feels relaxed with people, Stan animatedly repeats old phrases from the past, and his daughter listens: '"I'm saying to myself, Jesus Christ!" a playful look on his face, then he chuckles and shrugs just like before, or he'll say, "how are we going, I'm asking myself. You have to ask yourself"; when anxious he might yell, in ways that are easily meaningful, "I have no boat, I have no money"' (161). He becomes aggressive with some people, but he is good-natured with those who treat him kindly and gently. He is kind and courteous with the person who becomes his paid carer, Nilda, who barely speaks any English. They sit together watching television, holding hands contentedly, as she brings out Stan's best self: 'Dad now has more room to express his gracious-ness, his yearning to be liked, and his pleasure in the pleasure of others' (310).

What seems obvious to Levine is that the medical standardi-zation of dementia care misses all that is creative and important in offering good treatment. So much money goes into finding a 'cure' and so little time and effort into providing the best care for those who suffer from dementia, she writes. Levine looks at the research of the American neurologist David Rothschild, half a century ago, or the more recent work of the late British-based psychologist Tom Kitwood, who both stressed that the type of care a sufferer receives makes so much difference to the outcome of dementia, making it a social as well as a biologi-cal disease. There are ways of shoring up the personhood of the dementia sufferer, and ways of smashing it faster.[34] What is evident from various studies is that at any stage of cogni-tive deterioration, good quality provision leads to emotional improvement and can even impede cognitive decline.[35]

Nevertheless, tales of caring for others with dementia in late life are not often so redemptive as those told by Fuchs and Levine, neither of whom had to shoulder the burden of care on their own. The majority of those afflicted with what is cur-rently the most feared of all diseases will end up in care homes, when assisting them at home is no longer possible. Life may look like, and indeed it may become, a disaster for other carers of older people with dementia. In her prize-winning memoir, *Keeper*, Andrea Gillies describes the impossible toll on her and her family in a harrowing tale of trying to look after her mother-in-law, Nancy, after making what turned out to be the devastating decision to move to a beautiful retreat in the far north of Scotland. Instead of Nancy being moved by the beauty of the landscape (when her memory and language kept failing), as Gillies had hoped, Nancy became increasingly unmanageable. She was unhappy, angry and afraid, hostile especially towards Gillies herself as she tried to care for her: 'Nancy's ranting about me to helpers and carers has become ubiquitous and vicious', with Nancy accusing her daughter-in-law of stealing from her, hitting her, and worse.[36]

Gillies, like Levine, makes ample use of her medical researches into the disease. However, in the end no amount of knowledge can enable her to keep on loving someone who seems to hate her and, perhaps, she comes to feel, has always secretly hated her. Before she finally gives up, admitting to herself she's tired of dealing with everything to do with Nancy, she feels herself to be a failure, suffering from what she later discovers is called 'caregivers' dementia', becoming herself intolerant, bad-tempered and demanding. It is a painful narrative, and relief comes only when Nancy is safely in a nursing home, though Gillies, now engaged in speaking out to improve conditions in care homes, ends her book: 'As for me, I've arrived, already, at a state of self-protective forgetting. People are good at that, at moving on, dwindling the past into a story we tell ourselves, into parables, and choosing the future over the past.'[37]

Alongside those who experience forms of love, significance, distress or pain – rarely free from ambivalence – caring for the frail elderly, there are many situations that afterwards leave the survivor cherishing memories they wish only to preserve and to share. In another tender memoir, *Endnotes*, Ruth Ray describes falling in love, at forty-two, with Paul, a man of eighty-two, with Parkinson's disease, living in a care home.[38] Already a creative writing teacher, but in training to be the gerontologist she will become, Ray is giving classes to the residents of the care home where Paul lives, encouraging them all to narrate their lives. The first thing she notes about this open, insightful and engaging man, Paul, is his sensuous, witty prose and gentle, humorous ways as, for instance, he looks down, ruefully, ordering his uncooperative feet to move, or arrives late to class, with toilet paper stuck to his neck, apologizing softly: 'Someone volunteered to cut my throat, and it took a while' (22).

To her own surprise, Ray sees nothing disturbing in Paul's extreme frailty, or when he starts to express his admiration and affection for her. However, already a divorced woman, with suitors of her own age, she was not, she says, looking for love. Yet when Paul takes her hand to declare his love, she finds herself returning it, replying at once, 'I love you too', kissing him back when he kisses her (26). Ray's memoir of their love affair, which took her ten years to complete, covers the period until Paul's sudden death, with the couple seeing each other or telephoning almost every day.

In ways that are challenging to the reader, but not to Ray herself, she writes of their delight in each other, even as she candidly reveals his many impairments, including his shakes, memory loss, incontinence, difficulties in walking, and more. Together they confront all the pleasure and problems of their sex life, the difficulties of planning for the future and the limitations of nursing homes. They speak to each other of the closeness of Paul's death, as Ray tells Paul he will be 'watching over her' after his death, from wherever he is: 'Paul sighs contentedly. "That was a true lover's speech"' (129). So this is a love story about living apart, together, as some describe that alternative form of intimacy today, giving Ray a very special platform for addressing the constraints of nursing homes and offering her own practical suggestions for improvements to make nurses and other carers more attentive to residents' needs for autonomy and choice, as well as for privacy and the recognition of diverse sexualities.

Reviewing this memoir, Margaret Gullette notes, 'in fiction this would scarcely be credible; on film, [Paul] would have to be tall with a full head of hair and no perceptible shaking'.[39] When Ray, who became a friend of Gullette's, had first told her about Paul years earlier, she confessed to her new friend: 'his was "the best loving" she'd ever had'. Gullette is not slow to draw the lessons of this moving narrative, noting how Ray is able to present Paul as lovable, despite a much feared impairment: 'As a result of making a man with Parkinson's lovable', Gullette concludes, 'Ruth Ray can show where value lies inside later life – in unsuspected places. Lovingly, she shows us how to write touchingly about – and quote as often as possible – people with disabilities who also happen to be old.' As ever, Gullette emphasizes that ageing and disability, let alone such a debilitating one as Parkinson's, are far from the same, even though we confront social anxieties that tend to equate them. Rightly, if perhaps somewhat optimistically, Gullette suggests that books such as Ray's might help us to withstand such cultural horror of old age, drawing us closer to all older people, whatever their fate: 'Having empathetically read *Endnotes*, now I can imagine not only being Ruth but being Paul, and even thinking, as Paul does, "How lucky I am." '[40]

Our luck, or misfortune, after we first confront the 'stranger' who begins to look back at us from our middle years is hardly predictable. Of course, material privileges or deprivations will be accentuated as we age, cushioning or worsening our fate, as will our embeddedness or lack of it in supportive communities, and not just inside conventional families. Nevertheless, neither the sociology nor the biology of ageing is the chief concern of this book. It is rather the stories we tell ourselves given the strange or bewildering predicament of not really knowing how to *be* our age, as we age. The confusion remains, even when we attempt, usually belatedly, to tackle the noxious flow of prejudice and inner fears most of us face in old age. Illness and disability will age some people prematurely, leaving them to face the process of dying when still young relative to the average life span of their time and place. Even so, the psychic resources we can call upon are rarely predictable, though we can learn much just by listening to the account others give of the process.

The late, influential American literary scholar, Eve Sedgwick, wrote of finding new resources for living with illness, confronting mortality and appreciating the joys of daily survival after getting breast cancer at the age of forty. This was first evident in the book she wrote soon after learning about her cancer, *A Dialogue on Love*, with its medley of poetry and prose, providing an extraordinary account of the healing therapy she began months after her diagnosis. Her therapist, Shannon, was a man who shared little of her intellectual passion but with whom she felt able to share her fear that in facing mortality she might stop knowing how to like and desire the world around her.

The opposite happened. As the therapy proceeded and Sedgwick recorded the ways in which the ties between patient and therapist deepened, she wrote again and again of the 'sheer pleasure' she gained reviewing all the most difficult, grubby episodes of her life and the loneliness and isolation of her childhood as 'a dorkily fat, boneless middle-child', with this attentive witness to accompany her – an observer who gave her access to his own case notes. For instance, recounting her complicated, sadomasochistic fantasies with 'sheepish pride' in therapy, she writes: 'Somehow Shannon develops a way of listening to fantasy that leaves me feeling I've revisited it accompanied by a friend.' In what quickly became itself a type of healing love relationship, Sedgwick struggled to find words for her new attachment to life: 'I don't know how to put it. But there's some circular reciprocity between these holding relations: your ability to hold me inside you, and mine to hold you inside me.'[41] During the therapy, Sedgwick also discovered two other sources of joy: the pleasure she gained from texture, in the craft of weaving, and from the practice of Buddhism, immersing herself in *The Tibetan Book of the Dead*.

By the time she put together her last collection of essays, *Touching Feeling*, Sedgwick clarified her distance from some of her earlier influential engagement with poststructuralism, work she now referred to as critical theory's 'hermeneutics of suspicion'.[42] That earlier work covered her nuanced semiotic readings of the hidden, often-repressive meanings of texts – especially those disavowing dissident sexualities for a privileging of what she referred to as the 'homosocial' bonding of heterosexuality. In her later writing, she expressed her liking for the notion of the 'senile sublime', borrowed from fellow academic Barbara Herrnstein Smith, referring to possibilities for conveying the more inchoate performances of brilliant old people, or what Sedgwick refers to as 'an affective and aesthetic fullness that can attach even to experiences of cognitive frustration'.[43]

This takes me back to my opening thought that what we may come to love and nurture, and in turn receive satisfaction from, extends well beyond the human to other living creatures. It was the presence of his two beloved dogs, Mark Doty realized, that helped him care for and then cope with the death of his lover, Wally. As he explained: 'Love for a wordless creature, once it takes hold, is an enchantment, and the enchanted speak, famously, in private mutterings, cryptic riddles or gibberish.' Years after Wally's death, however, and in a new and happy sexual relationship, Doty later comes to find his renewed anguish hardly bearable when he faces the approaching death of the last of his most beloved dogs, Arden. Later, mourning Arden, he hovers between feelings of constant loss and recuperation: 'He's an absence and a presence, both – the way he will be, to greater or lesser degrees, for years to come … Wouldn't you know that the most misanthropic of poets would write the warmest of elegies for his dog?'[44]

Donna Haraway, that formidable feminist scholar and philosopher of science, also living in the USA, has written similarly about her relationship to her own two canine companions. In her *Companion Species Manifesto*, for instance, Haraway describes how she and her two dogs have been mutually training each other: 'In acts of communication we barely understand. We are, constitutively, companion species. We make each other up, in the flesh. Significantly other to each other, in specific difference, we signify in the flesh a nasty developmental infection called love. This love is a historical aberration and a natural–cultural legacy.'[45]

However, just as one person, even in moments of loss, finds a way of trying to move beyond speech to attend to more enigmatic, affective states, another experiences only an increasingly bitter cynicism: 'Is that all there is?' Short of belief in an afterlife, sooner or later we will all realize, whether with humour, resignation or fear, 'yes, that *is* all there is'. A certain cynicism about life and its legacies is surely appropriate. Yet, as Angela Carter once suggested via the fabulations in her last book *Wise Children*, not even our closeness to death need preclude moments of pleasure, as we recall, if only from the images we see and the sounds we hear in our heads, 'What a joy it is to dance and sing!' Or, as she added, writing as she was dying of lung cancer approaching fifty, 'Comedy is tragedy that happens to *other* people.'[46]

Confronting Mortality

There may, however, be no way of redeeming the particular horror of ageing we saw expressed by some of the men confronting old age in the previous chapter. For instance, when promoting one of his recent books, *The Pregnant Widow*, Martin Amis seemed to be almost satirizing himself in feeding fears of the cultural and economic crisis caused by the ever-rising 'silver tsunami' of old people: 'There'll be a population of demented very old people, like an invasion of terrible immigrants ... I can imagine a sort of civil war between the old and the young in ten or fifteen years' time.' His solution, obviously courting much of the publicity it garnered, was to suggest 'euthanasia booths': 'There should be a booth on every corner where you could get a martini and a medal.'[47] Some writers, most of them men, are determined to maintain their ability to shock, whatever their age, but the banality of Amis' proposal, familiar from science fiction, seemed to render his provocation more tiresome than shocking.

That old iconoclast, Quentin Crisp, did it better, almost forty-five years earlier:

there should not be this undignified element of hazard about the date of a person's demise. There ought to be a Minister of Death, though, in Orwellian terminology, it would be named the Ministry of Heaven. This august body of men, all preferably under thirty years of age, would deal with the chore of exterminating old people ... they would have to agree on a time limit (say, sixty) to live beyond which would be an offence (punishable with life?).[48]

Writing this at sixty, that celebrated old rogue lived on for over another thirty years.

In contrast, although Philip Roth also likes the notoriety of scandalizing his readers, we can just occasionally glimpse another side to his routine depiction of the woes of ageing phallic hubris, at least in the portrayals of old age in one of his books, *Patrimony*. Here, in a memoir of his father, we are given a very different portrait of the ageing author, who was already fifty-eight when this book appeared. In these pages, Roth is himself the caretaker and comforter, the one who is presented as both willing and able to console and reassure his father immediately after the death of his mother. He depicts himself enjoying the physical and emotional closeness he can now offer this overbearing, obstinate, obsessive and opinionated old man, even being prepared, literally, to take up the place of his mother in the bed:

We took turns in the bathroom and then, in our pajamas, we lay down side by side in the bed where he had slept with my mother two nights before, the only bed in the apartment. After turning out the light, I reached out and took his hand and held it as you would the hand of a child who is frightened of the dark. He sobbed for a moment or two – then I heard the broken, heavy breathing of someone very deeply asleep, and I turned over to try to get some rest myself.[49]

Roth later hears that his father has said of him: '"Philip is like a mother to me" '; a mother, he notes, not a father (181). In other ways too, it is in this book that Roth is able, for once, to shed much of his masculine carapace, revealing the softer, supposedly 'feminine' traits it exists to hide. In dreams, once his father has died, he sees his own weaknesses emerging in what he takes to be the stunned and bereft image of his father arriving in the USA, when still a child: 'my own pain so aptly [captured] in the figure of a small, fatherless evacuee on the Newark docks' (237). As we discover in this book, there was much the son had to learn to hide: 'People don't realize what good girls we grew up as, too, the little sons suckered and gurgled by mothers as adroit as my own in the skills of nurturing domesticity' (40).

Nevertheless, any such excursions into the possible satisfactions or challenges of nurturing domesticity, or indeed any form of care and commitment, are rare in Roth's portrayals of men and the dilemmas of ageing. First and foremost, he focuses on what he sees as the loneliness of the productive man when, post-retirement, he realizes he has lost all trace of his old sexual allure: 'There was an absence now of all forms of solace, a barrenness under the heading of consolation, and no way to return to what was.'[50] Other male writers, however, including John Updike, have found more varied modes of escape from similar accounts of the perils of priapic obsession that their writing elsewhere depicted. For in Updike it is possible to find consistently gentler, affectionate images of men's old age, including his own, especially when pondering mortality, which makes his thoughts worth returning to. Updike often writes lyrically of old men losing themselves in contemplation of the moment, enthralled by particular landscapes, as well as by their sexual reminiscences. This is most evident in Updike's writing in his seventies, when his own preoccupations with ageing encourage him to project more benevolence, more complacency perhaps, but certainly, greater possibilities for enjoying the pleasures of kinship, connectedness and hope, onto his characters as they handle the travails of old age.

Most people, like me and my friends and acquaintances, face our own ageing by moaning, mulling it over, or reading about it, though usually, for as long as possible, by simply disavowing it. Updike, so he tells us, learned how to age by writing about it: 'I never thought of myself as old until I wrote this book about an old man', he said in an interview at sixty-five. He was referring to his novel *Toward the End of Time*: 'I used to look at people my [current] age and I would think how can they stand being that close to death without screaming in terror? And now I'm of that age. In some odd way you adjust to the proximity of death. But something else in you fights it.'[51] Screaming in terror is the thought that another word-spinner, the British poet, Philip Larkin, saw as appropriate when pondering old age in his mid-life: 'What do they think has happened, the old fools / Why aren't they screaming?'[52] However, as I've suggested often enough, and as Updike illustrates, we aren't all screaming partly because we are never fully convinced by the age we are, the age that others, including one's own mirror, together conspire to bestow upon us. In his memoir, *Self-Consciousness*, written in his late fifties, Updike expresses many times the thought that we never quite accept mortality: 'As we get older we go to more and more funerals, and sit there in a stony daze, somehow convinced that it will never happen to us, or if it does, we will be essentially elsewhere.'[53]

In one of the most evocative of the short stories from his final collection, *My Father's Tears and Other Stories*, published posthumously, Updike has the nameless narrator reflecting: 'Approaching eighty I sometimes see myself from a little distance, as a man I know, but not intimately.'[54] The protagonist in this story, 'The Full Glass', feels he is not so intimate with the old man he sees in the mirror, since he is in many ways a less familiar creature than many of the former selves he can more readily recall. Although this man is depicted as very ordinary, a person not given to introspection, yet with so much time on his hands, and so many memories hanging around, he cannot refrain from sometimes 'digging deeper'. He recalls past pleasures, experiences occasional bouts of remorse when flashes of unpleasant choices he has made come to mind, then again he summons up times when life seemed completely full and precious, as in childhood, remembered as a time of perpetual eagerness 'for the next moment of life, one brimming moment after another'.[55]

As ever with Updike, the life explored in this tale largely mirrors that of his creator, especially in the recollections of adultery and its destructive effects, primarily on the other woman involved.[56] The narrator in 'The Full Glass', however, as in most of the other stories in this final prose collection, still enjoys the care and comfort of a (second) wife who has forgiven and supported him over more than thirty years. Updike depicts this old man, swallowing the pills that now keep him alive, as someone who still finds immense pleasure in surveying the busy maritime life he observes on the full, flat ocean visible from his bathroom window, as he calmly anticipates the next day with all its boring routines: 'If I can read this strange old guy's mind aright, he's drinking a toast to the visible world, his impending disappearance from it be damned.'[57]

If I can read Updike aright, he is able to capture here something of the experience of having lived a full life, a relatively satisfied life, in which the comfort of receiving the constant love of another helps to overcome fears of death and dying. Some of the verse in his last book of poetry, *Endpoint* (again published posthumously), is written about, and often for, his own (second) wife Martha: 'My wife of thirty years ... I need her voice; Her body is the only locus where / My desolation bumps against its end.'[58] Updike realizes that these supportive wives, who appear regularly in his fiction, may sometimes have a harder time. 'I'd give anything not to have married you', a husband describes his second wife repeating when she is 'angry or soulful' in 'Personal Archeology'; she is only partially consoled by her husband's reassuring words, 'You've been a wonderful wife. Wonderful' (23).

Updike is nevertheless able to depict a certain tranquillity in the face of ageing, and even imminent death, in his older men who manage to enjoy the present, while living only for the next brief moment: 'Give me another hour, then I'll go' (3). In *Self-Consciousness*, feeling himself already old at fifty-seven, Updike provides some disparaging reflections on what he sees as his former egotistical, attention-seeking, ambitious, faithless or distracted selves, yet also manages to find a certain solace in the process: 'when I entertain in my own mind these shaggy, red-faced, over-excited, abrasive fellows, I find myself tenderly taken with their diligence, their hopefulness, their ability in spite of all to map a broad strategy and stick with it'.[59] Neither Updike, nor Roth, however, had any experience of or showed any real interest in how ageing might affect the far grimmer lives of men without status or money.

Even so, the potential desolations of old age are real enough in some of Updike's descriptions of men's ageing in his fictional world. He is less bitterly corrosive than Roth, but convincing in his depictions of men, post-retirement, coping with a sense of isolation and child-like helplessness, especially as they watch their often younger, usually second wives, still active as ever with 'committees and bridge groups and book clubs and manicure appointments' (148).[60] Indeed, Updike sometimes depicts the situation of the ageing man as not so much that of a 'woman', as Beauvoir and others have seen it, but rather as a return to the helplessness of childhood. Either way, whether seen as more like a woman, or sensing his own weakness, Updike once again captures here the distinctly male fear that the ageing man may come to occupy the subordinate position traditionally reserved for the woman or the child.

More often, however, Updike's old men find ways of holding depression at bay in the comfort of the attachments they have finally learned to cherish. In his short story 'Free', for instance, the once adulterous and now widowed husband, briefly experiencing 'the old beast' sluggishly stirring within as he revisits a woman with whom he once had a passionate affair, decides to return chastely home: 'To the repose he found in imagining [his now dead wife] still with him. Since her death she was wrapped around him like a shroud of gold and silver thread'.[61] It was, by and large, the conservative routines of Updike's white, middle-class, patriotic and church-attending American Christians, with their adequate pensions, their memories and usually a wife, all functioning to sustain them, which enabled these old men to live without rancour in a world they now realize exists primarily for young people: 'Their tastes in food and music and clothing are what the world is catering to, even while they are imagining themselves the victims of the old, the enforcers of the laws'.[62] It was also Updike's conformity as a good US citizen that left him untroubled by thoughts that many of the young might also be seen as the insecure victims of the fierce marketing of the badges of status in the contemporary USA, facing futures where home-ownership, pensions and even secure partnerships, let alone soothing ocean views, would remain completely inaccessible.

Finally, however, it is clear that there is one other thing Updike and Roth unquestionably shared in confronting old age: their ties to their creative work, and simply being able to keep on telling their stories of men's lives in the best way they could. Updike died with his pen in his hand, knowing the great consolation he received from the ability to just continue writing, likening it to riding a bike, knowing 'if I were ever to stop pedaling, [it] would dump me flat on my side'.[63] Roth has just recently announced that he will write no more books, and it will be interesting to see whether he can manage life without this support. Beauvoir, we have seen, agreed with Updike. She just kept on writing to the end, declaring: 'There is only one solution if old age is not to be an absurd parody of our former life, and that is to go on pursuing ends that give our existence meaning – devotion to individuals, to groups or to causes, social, political, intellectual and creative work.'[64] Meanwhile, she was clear that part of the problem for the working-class man is that his labour was never highly valued or seen as important when he performed it, hence the meaning of his existence was 'stolen from him from the very beginning'.[65]

Living with Fear

Martin Amis believes that young men lose their sense of impregnability on reaching forty. Some men, however, seem never to have shared his sense of impregnability, even when young, nor to need any reminding of life's brevity. The English writer, Julian Barnes, for instance, could be seen as our leading thanotophobic, having thought about dying every day since he was thirteen or fourteen, with intermittent nocturnal attacks: 'Mortality often gatecrashes my consciousness when the outside world presents an obvious parallel', he tells us, 'as evening falls, as the days shorten, or towards the end of a long day's hiking.'[66] During the night, he experiences 'that alarmed and alarming moment, of being pitch-forked back into consciousness, awake, alone, utterly alone, beating pillow with fist and shouting "Oh no Oh No OH NO" in an endless wail' (126). Yet what is interesting about Barnes is that over his lifetime he has shown little horror of old age itself. He has no problems calmly depicting his fears of death, nor indeed in portraying old age in richer hues than most of his contemporary male writers. He has had a lot of practice: 'The thing about your books, Julian', the late Beryl Bainbridge is said to have announced at a literary festival some years ago, 'is that they're all about *death*. All your books are about dying.'[67]

She exaggerated only a little. Meditations on mortality have featured in most of Barnes' novels, even in the thoughts of the sixteen-year-old narrator in his first novel, *Metroland* (1980), begun in his twenties; while death and suicide appear prominently in most of his subsequent books, including the novel that established his literary eminence while still in his thirties, *Flaubert's Parrot* (1984). However, it is in *Nothing to*

Be Frightened Of (2009) that Barnes tackles his fear of death directly, incorporating reminiscences of the deaths of his parents. In that book, Barnes suggests people are divided into two types: those more afraid of dying, and those more afraid of old age, illness and incapacity. As someone firmly in the latter camp, along with most of my friends, I think he may be right. I also suspect that the former group, the 'thanatophobes', is a smaller one, which Barnes currently heads up – although we learn it has included Philip Larkin, Kingsley Amis and John Betjeman, along with some of the author's own unnamed friends, whom he suspects of competing with each other to be the most death-fearing.

That it is death rather than old age that frightens Barnes also resonates with the absence of any of the customary expressions of horror accompanying the portrayals of old age in his writing. Although he mistrusts the idea that ageing brings serenity, he does think it can bring wisdom: 'The good news is that we do indeed sometimes become wiser as we grow old', even supplying the information that, unless we are among the minority who will suffer from Alzheimer's, 'the higher intellectual functions of the brain are much less affected by the cognitive cellular morbidity causing physical decline' (199).

Barnes never attempts to probe what might be the psychic make-up of the differing psychologies he mentions. He knows all about the tricks of memory and is a sharp observer of surface nuance and fluidity in people's dealing with the contingencies of a life, but he is clearly wary of any form of psychic reductionism, Freudian or otherwise. Rejecting any settled explanatory framework for the perpetual flow of observation, Barnes seems to see as all-too-neat those clinicians with their conceptual tool kits always waiting in the wings, eager to stamp and package us. For Freud, especially in his early work, the unconscious knows nothing of the finality of death, hence fears of dying and death are interpreted as displacements of castration anxiety or, more often nowadays, fear of abandonment by the mother.[68] In *Nothing to Be Frightened Of*, Barnes certainly presents us with an unsympathetic image of a cold, critical, insensitive, narcissistic and controlling mother – his own – whom he would not wish to meet again, even in fantasy. Quite different are the warm reflections on his late father, whose final years he saw as tyrannized by a wife 'always present, nattering, organizing, fussing, controlling' (103). However, unlike Roth, Barnes prefers his readers to refrain from 'knowing' speculation. Indeed, when summing up his life, he reiterates that there is little at all to say about him, suggesting simply that he had 'achieved as much happiness as his nature permitted ... He was happy in his own company, as long as he knew when that solitude would end. He loved his wife and feared death' (178).

Death may be round the corner in Barnes' account of his daily fears, as well as in much of his fiction, but for me one pleasure in reading him comes from his ability to express not just compassion but true affection for many of the old people he brings to life in his texts. This is much in evidence in his collection, *The Lemon Table*, where we learn that in China the lemon is a symbol of death, and the lemon table the place where men gather to talk of death. In one of the stories here, 'Knowing French', Barnes imagines receiving long letters from an unmarried upper-class woman in her eighties, writing to him about the books she reads, including his own, while wittily depicting her daily frustrations in the 'old folkery', all the while ruminating on old age and death. She is forbidden to mention these topics in her institution, hence her need for the sympathetic ear of 'Julian

Barnes', whom she knows will read and respond to her 'senile garrulity'. Whatever dissatisfaction she faces, however, this old lady rejects suicide as 'vulgar and self-important, like people who walk out of the theatre or the symphony concert'.[69] Barnes clearly shares her views. He too will go on, however demanding the challenge and whatever his fear of death. And he has gone on, this man, who claims that there is little that is special about him apart from his love for his wife and his fear of death.

Barnes has continued to write, and indeed won the much-coveted Booker prize for his short novel *The Sense of an Ending* (2011), despite the merciless speed of the unexpected death of his wife, Pat Kavanagh, within a year of the publication of *Nothing to Be Frightened Of*. Since then, two other collections of short stories have appeared, the first, *Pulse*, containing one haunting story, 'Marriage Lines', narrated by a man whose wife has recently died. It explores his feelings revisiting the Scottish island where he and his wife holidayed together every year throughout their marriage, for over twenty years. The story opens with the lines, 'They, their: he knew he must start getting used to the singular pronoun instead. This was going to be the grammar of his life from now on.'[70] He weeps as he leaves the island, realizing his own presumption in imagining the visit could somehow help him manage his grief at his loss: 'But he was not in charge of grief. Grief was in charge of him. And in the months and years ahead, he expected grief to teach him many things as well. This was the first of them' (127).

Reading this story in 2011, it is impossible not to think of it as autobiography, especially given Barnes' belief in the continual slide between fiction and non-fiction. Yet it is almost uncanny to learn that the story was written in 2007, two years before his wife became ill. I do not know if it is presumptuous to hope that this constant rehearsal of fears of death and dying somehow makes it that little bit easier to tolerate when death pays a visit.

It does now seem to me that being able to confront mortality, at least at times and however fearfully, may prove one way of being less disdainful and dismissive of old people. Long before I had begun to think about either mortality or ageing myself, the book that first alerted me to Barnes' unusual empathy with old age was his earlier novel, *Staring at the Sun* (1986). (This was the fourth novel written under his own name, although Barnes had by this time published three crime thrillers under the pseudonym Dan Kavanagh.) I read the book when I had just reached forty, the age Barnes was when it appeared, although unlike him I had as yet hardly ever, knowingly, let thoughts of my own ageing or mortality cross my mind. I was intrigued that Barnes should choose to depict the life and memories of a very old woman, finding his portrayal of the 100-year-old protagonist, Jean Serjeant, utterly compelling. Jean is depicted, and sees herself, as having lived a very ordinary life, apart from her single revolt – choosing to separate from the husband who had never made her feel good about herself when she unexpectedly found that she was pregnant for the very first time, at thirty-eight.

Jean's long, healthy life gave ample scope for Barnes' imaginings of very old age, which here are far from gloomy. Rereading the book today, I see that it encompasses so much of what have since become my own feelings about ageing, although only after much recent thought. The accord is almost total when I reach the opening pages of its final section, when Jean reflects on old age, suggesting that in her fifties 'she was still feeling in her thirties', 'at sixty she had still felt like a young woman; at eighty, she felt like a middle-aged woman who had something a bit wrong with her; at nearly a hundred she no longer bothered to think whether or not she felt younger than she was – there didn't seem any point'.[71]

The novel is set in 2020, and Jean has been able to take the medical advances over her lifetime for granted. She now rarely goes out, no longer keeps up with public events, and has little interest in examining herself in the mirror. She is more fearful, forgetful and stumbling, but is content, she suggests, to live increasingly inside her head, pondering her memories, of which there are now so many, far too many, and noting the smirking paradox of old age: 'how everything seemed to take longer than it used to, but how, despite this, time seemed to go faster' (140). The reason it was all bearable, she reflects, is that

> You never did age instantly; you never did have a sharp memory for comparison ... You grew old first not in your own eyes, but in other people's eyes; then, slowly, you agreed with their opinion of you. It wasn't that you couldn't walk as far as you used to, it was that other people didn't expect you to; and if they didn't, then it needed vain obstinacy to persist. (139)

Meanwhile her son, Gregory, himself entering old age at sixty-two, more closely resembles his creator, Barnes, at least in his fears of mortality and thoughts about suicide. However, when he broods over suicide and different ways of dying, it is in a 'quiet, almost companionable' way (142). What I find particularly interesting about the fictionalized version of Barnes' early mid-life reflections on very old age is their clear contrast with that of almost all the other male writers I have looked at in this book. He shows little dismay over women's ageing bodies, sagging flesh, or other forms of physical decay, making neither sexism, nor misogyny, nor even ageism, particularly evident in his own musings on old age. In this book, for instance, Gregory sees his mother as 'an alert, tidy, sympathetic old lady who, if she hadn't necessarily attained wisdom, had at least discarded all stupidity' (185). He reflects that her apparent eccentricities and random memories are attributable to the absence of any shared points of reference. 'The very old', he realizes, 'needed interpreters just as the young did. When the old lost their companions, their friends, they also lost their interpreters: they lost love, but they also lost the full powers of speech' (156).

Finally, and rather wonderfully, Barnes' own compassion for old people leads him to fantasize not for Amis' suicide booths on street corners, but the opposite. In his imaginings of the future, the disdain shown towards the expanding numbers of elderly evident from the close of the twentieth century has led to old people campaigning for new civil rights which, after a spate of militant public suicides, has resulted in most of their demands being met, making 'old people not just acceptable, but fashionable' (144). The demands included the following fine sentiments: 'Old people are to be loved more'; 'There shall be special series of awards to recognize wisdom and the achievements of old people'; 'Creation of an Old People's day, to be celebrated once a year'; 'Positive discrimination in jobs and housing in favour of old people'; 'Free fun-drugs for the over eighties'. I can only hope that Barnes today, now in his late sixties, agrees with these suggestions dreamed up in his late thirties, for they are surely in need of revisiting.

Old people are to be loved more; yes, and old people often need the opportunity to be able to love other people more, need someone, or something, to take care of, even if only by stroking them, being able to show their affection, or simply concern for, another, knowing that their feelings are appreciated. 'No-one exists alone', the poet Auden wrote in 1939, at the outbreak of the Second World War: 'We must love one another or die'. But Auden wanted not just to be pitch perfect, but to be accurate, as time goes by. He therefore amended his words sixteen years later to read, 'We must love one another and die.'[72] In a similar vein, I have now come to think that dwelling upon mortality can make us more responsive to our bonds with others. Both in literature and in standard empirical studies there is some evidence for this. It was while facing death that the renowned French radical writer, André Gorz, wrote his remarkable love letter to his terminally ill wife, Dorine, whom he chose not to outlive:

> You're eighty-two years old. You've shrunk six centimetres, you only weigh 45 kilos yet you're still beautiful, graceful and desirable. We've lived together now for fifty-eight years and I love you more than ever. I once more feel a gnawing emptiness in the hollow of my chest that is only filled when your body is pressed next to mine.
>
> At night I sometimes see the figure of a man, on an empty road in a deserted landscape, walking behind a hearse. I am that man. It's you the hearse is taking away ... Neither of us wants to outlive the other.[73]

To the extent that we can manage it, awareness of mortality can enhance our sense of our bonds to others and our embrace of the moment. The problem with laboratory studies is their artificiality, hence the difficulties of generalizing from them, and their dependence, often barely registered, on the interpretations investigators choose to make of them. Nevertheless, in some recent psychological research it has been reported that subjects emphasized the significance of relationships and were more likely to be helpful to others after being asked questions about death, or when they were in other ways made more aware of mortality. The psychologists concluded that awareness rather than disavowal of death strengthens social bonds to others, at least inside one's own group.[74] This seems plausible to me, although it is significantly at odds with the general cultural beat encouraging us always to remain goal oriented, with eyes focused on the future. In my view, we may well be extremely anxious about the future, and yet still busy learning from the past in ways that keep us curious about the present, and its endless dilemmas, whether personal or social. However, let me now turn to other forms of resistance to the fears and challenges of ageing and mortality, fears so evident in the usually quite unthinking disparagement of old age, often palpable even in attempts to combat ageism.

5

Flags of Resistance

'Old age is not interesting until one gets there,' May Sarton wrote.[1] Well, most of us will get there, indeed, linger there for quite some time before we die. But can we make it interesting, at least for ourselves, or perhaps even for certain others across the generations? In this chapter I look at further ways of resisting the fear of old age, beginning with a straightforward refusal to acknowledge one's own ageing. However, there are other ways to recognize and value the mixed experiences of old age, in which beauty, pain, resilience and resistance intermingle, while time itself appears more fluid.

That ageing is never straightforward has been a refrain throughout this book. Given our enormous diversity, it is not so hard to challenge most stereotypes of old people, whatever form they take. There are, for instance, always a few formidable figures, including among the very old, who not only stay determinedly in touch with world affairs, but even manage to keep commenting usefully upon them. It is not so difficult, either, to intervene in the battles between the optimists and pessimists addressing ageing and old age. One side, like May Sarton, emphasizes the continued health and vigour possible in old age, stressing it as a period when the experiences of a lifetime offer spaces of openness for meditation and spiritual renewal.[2] The other sees only the losses, regret and sadness attending old age, as Philip Roth and Martin Amis epitomized. Neither side sufficiently encompasses the conflicts and potential, or the ambivalence and paradoxes, of ageing and old age.

Meanwhile, the world races ahead anyway, indifferent to our life or death. That sense of being left behind, losing out, can begin at whatever age we turn around, regretting the loss of the pleasures of yesterday. Indeed, Paul McCartney was only twenty-three when he wrote and the Beatles recorded 'Yesterday', when troubles seemed so far away, which became one of the most popular songs ever made, and with more cover versions than any other.[3] Nostalgia is always with us. Indeed, as the psychoanalyst Christopher Bollas suggests, it is the passing of time itself that is 'intrinsically traumatic': 'the loss of youth, the loss of loved ones, the loss of "futures" ' – some regretfully register these transformations well before old age.[4] However, though sentiments of loss, decline and an inability to keep in touch with the world can certainly occur at almost any stage in adulthood, there is no doubt that such feelings must increase with age, although by then old people sometimes find better ways of dealing with them.

Defying Chronological Age

'You haven't changed at all' are words I love to hear when meeting people I have not seen for a while. Guiltily, I cherish the thought that I don't look my age, and like to believe friends and acquaintances when they flatter. So do all of my friends, I notice, and I've learned to offer these reassuring words myself.

It is a losing game, I know, rather than any flag of resistance to the dread of ageing. This type of personal bolstering is also the mainstay of the current promotion of healthy lifestyles, exercise regimes, beauty treatments, or more invasive surgical interventions, that encourage us to believe that if we strive hard, pay enough, remain sufficiently vigilant, we can grow old free from the standard signs of ageing. Here too, class differences in how we age are deeply etched. Biologists have revealed that, owing to the effects of stress and poverty, such differences are clearly evident even at the cellular level, not just in the most visible signs of ageing.[5] We are urged everywhere to control those telltale signs by the adman's 'body maintenance', similar to the care of a sleek car, which can be kept functioning at the optimal level so long as it is adequately serviced: 'bodies require servicing, regular care and attention to preserve maximum efficiency', as Mike Featherstone summed up the message.[6] Personal worth itself becomes tied up with our ability to match up to approved models of fitness and slimness, whatever our age.

Researching the history of shifting attitudes to ageing in popular culture, the Scottish sociologist Andrew Blaikie similarly encapsulates the current zeitgeist as one in which 'older citizens are encouraged not just to dress "young" and look youthful, but to exercise, have sex, diet, take holidays, and socialize in ways indistinguishable from those of their children's generation'.[7] The commercial implications are blatant, as captured by that caustic observer Hanif Kureishi in his novella *The Body*:

> It was rare for my wife and her friends not to talk about botox and detox, about food and their body shape, size and relative fitness, and the sort of exercise they were or were not taking.

I knew women, and not only actresses, who had squads of personal trainers, dieticians, nutritionists, yoga teachers, masseurs and beauticians labouring over their bodies daily, as if the mind's longing and anxiety could be cured via the body.[8]

In this particular surrealist narrative, where the protagonist Adam is granted his yearning to remain forever young, the fulfilment becomes itself a curse, just as it always has been in its better-known literary precursors, Goethe's *Faust* or Wilde's *Dorian Gray*.

Nevertheless, today it is not any diabolical pact that might offer us eternal youth, but rather paying too much heed to the way scientific research is packaged in the popular press. It is hard to avoid such reckless promises, as they arrive with our morning papers, or with every click of the mouse. 'An "elixir of life" could soon be reality, scientists claim', according to Fiona Macrae, the science reporter for the second largest-selling newspaper in the UK, the *Daily Mail*. Here she tells her readers that cells treated with what she labels the 'forever young' drug – called rapamycin – lived longer than normal cells. This drug had been used successfully on children to reverse the effects of a genetic condition called Hutchinson-Gilford Progeria Syndrome, which causes its sufferers to grow old and frail in childhood, before dying of 'old age' at around twelve. It is a breakthrough that could 'hold hope for the general population', the newspaper celebrates.[9] However, since I have also read that the drug is used primarily for suppressing the immune system in organ transplants, it seems researchers have a long way to go before such claims can be taken seriously. Just a few weeks earlier, Macrae had spied out and reported on a different 'forever young' drug, 'Teperdexrian', which has been used to turn back time in old mice. Here, she quoted Professor Linda Partridge, a geneticist from University College London, who told the Cheltenham Science Festival in 2011 that 'science is moving so quickly that it will soon be possible to prevent many of the ills of old age'.[10] Let us hope she is right, but preventing disease and staying forever young are not the same thing.

It is the dedicated refusal to admit any necessary impediments in people's lives as they grow older that remains at the heart of many narratives of ageing well. It is one thing for me to point out that we can always see continuities across a lifetime, suggesting also that as we age we retain a certain access, consciously or not, to all the selves we have been. It is quite another to imagine that we can remain ageless. Yet this is now the future many like to suggest is imminent. In a recent book exploring life free from any constraints imposed by ageing, Catherine Mayer celebrates what she calls 'amortality'. This is her word for those she interviews and writes about who, according to her, are already managing to live 'agelessly'. Simply by repudiating old age, Mayer's amortals continue to live exactly as they have always lived until they die. They reject any form of dependency or restrictions on their lifestyle by whatever drugs or surgical interventions may prove necessary: 'the defining characteristic of amortals is that they live the same way, at the same pitch, doing and consuming much the same things, from late teens right up until death'.[11]

Mayer interviews and reports upon scores of candidates for agelessness in her book, mostly rich, powerful and successful white men, predominantly from the USA. These include Bill Clinton, Hugh Heffner, Woody Allen, Mick Jagger, Simon Cowell, Bob Geldof, and just a few – very few – women, mostly businesswomen, exemplified by Lynne Franks. We are told that Mayer herself, at fifty-eight, lives agelessly, as did her parents and grandparents – although she made the choice not to have children in her quest to stay always the same as she has been. It helps a lot, she admits, to be affluent, and hence able to afford the latest anti-ageing products on offer, such as Viagra, supposedly enabling men to live in their prime till they die. Her amortals are almost all workaholics, their only lack, if one sees it as such, as I certainly would, being any form of peace and quiet: in the words of one of her interviewees, 'I keep maniacally active because if there's any down time I sit there feeling guilty I'm not doing anything' (11). Here personal growth and achievement, the refusal to decline, must remain a lifetime agenda. 'Research suggests a link between retirement and physical and mental deterioration', she warns us (177).

Grief, mourning, loss, even exhaustion or boredom, let alone weakness, passivity or dependence, make no appearance in this book: amortals deal with mortality by ignoring it. When this is no longer possible, they are likely to seek to control death as well, by checking out assisted suicide: 'In our assumptions of agelessness and blindness towards age, we criss-cross a fine line between resilience and denial, optimism and absurdity' (261).

Mayer is aware of the commercial side of this quest for agelessness, and understands the association between the pervasive emphasis on self-determination and the contemporary rejection of calls upon the public purse to provide a better existence for elderly dependent people in line with the continuing attenuation of welfare provision in the 'developed' world. However, the aggressiveness of market capitalism, and all those exploited and ignored by the pursuit of profit – the majority of the world's population – is completely outside her frame of reference. She is vaguely knowing about, if largely uncritical of, the reigning ideology of neo-liberalism: 'Amortality is a product of a world that has normalized certain narcissistic traits, favours individualism over collectivism, has lost faith in God and public life' (262). Actually, even religion itself is all too easily made to service corporate capital in much of the USA, where it is the worship of God, rather than any support for or from the state, which draws together forms of collectivity beyond family and workplace. Religious faith substitutes itself for belief in public life, as evident in the paradoxically public orchestration of the populist Republican 'Tea Party' movement, with its extreme hostility towards any forms of state provision or redistribution.

It's easy enough to see the dangers of that oscillation between optimism and absurdity, resilience and denial, in the desire for agelessness. Flaunting only confidence, strength and autonomy, when life is inevitably full of losses and sorrows, leaves those who are furthest from the comforts, cosmetic manipulations and elixirs that money can buy all the more subject to humiliation and abuse for failing to conceal the signs of ageing. In its repudiation of actual ageing, striving for agelessness is thus in one sense a rejection of life and collectivity. It is not just that such relentless buoyancy allows no space for neediness and dependence; it is also quintessentially shallow, self-centred and elitist in its refusal to engage with the suffering and helplessness of others. 'Experience consists of experiencing that which one does not wish to experience' is an aphorism that Freud quoted playfully in his book on jokes.[12] It is a form of imaginative impoverishment to refuse to accept the tragic. Freud was surely right to point out that forms of denial operate in most of us, much of the time, in our daily pursuit of personal happiness. Nevertheless, as I will explore later in this chapter and the next, unless we choose unremittingly to close our eyes to the world around us, we need to acknowledge that loss, mourning and grief are inevitable aspects of a full and creative life.

Being in Time

What does it mean to feel in time with time? I can remember occasionally feeling this, usually when I was caught up in something much bigger than myself. What was so exciting about becoming a part of women's liberation as the 1970s kicked off was this sense of immersion in something outside of oneself, a collective identity that felt like it might leave its mark on history. However, the problem with such moments of high collectivity, whether in politics or any other domain, is that they will soon enough be outflanked or disregarded, as new political or aesthetic avant-gardes jostle them for space. A more fashionable location is always waiting, eager to insist upon its own moment of articulation. Moving from the public to the personal domain, instances of true pleasure and passion are usually those in which we manage to escape our gloomy or restless selves, to become completely immersed in something else: whether in absorbing work, imagined or actual fulfilment of sexual desire, in thrall to the beauty of a landscape or other visual delights, captivated by music, or merely caught up in the enjoyment of friends, family, dinner-table conversation – whatever takes us out of the everyday into something else. Even in solitude, those most lyrical about the joys of chosen silence are usually in search of transcendental or sublime states of meditation and arousal, which may be experienced as the necessary precondition for creativity: 'one can never be alone enough when one writes … there can never be enough silence around one when one writes ... even night is not night enough', Kafka declared.[13]

What I am suggesting is that the time we feel most at one with the world is often when we are in a sense *least* our ordinary selves. Paradoxically, being in time with time in these ways means stepping outside of normal temporal patterns, stepping outside ourselves. When the feminist writer, Sara Maitland, for instance, went in search of solitude in her fifties, adopting a reclusive life in Galloway – the landscape of her childhood in south-west Scotland – she recorded the pleasures and joys of the complete silence she found in the depth of its moors or on the peaks of its mountains, surveying the landscapes and skies she had always loved. Combining her treks with prayer, meditation and other rituals, she felt she was breaking down her old self-narratives, creating a new porousness or openness to the world beyond the bounded life she had earlier struggled to maintain. This was not in her view an escape from her former love of noisy sociability, family and friends; these old desires remained with her, alongside her need for silence. It was simply that she was able to add a new dimension in her embrace of the various enjoyments of solitude. She tries to capture all this in *A Book of Silence*, a text she closes with the thought: 'Terror and risk walk hand in hand with beauty. There is terror, there is beauty and there is nothing else ... The rest, I hope, is silence.'[14]

Clearly, there is an alternative sense of time, perhaps better seen as a type of timelessness, which people describe when they feel most at one with the world. This is certainly a feeling not confined to or perhaps even particularly prevalent in the young, eager to display forms of individuality in social contexts that they hope will convey their independence, autonomy and agency. We are more at the mercy of dates and deadlines in projects of personal growth and achievement, whatever our age. Accordingly, some of those more attentive to the experience of ageing, such as Ruth Ray in *Endnotes*, have suggested that the rhetoric of life-long self-building is lacking in imagination, especially so when Ray found it guiding the policies operating in nursing homes in the USA, which set out to keep old people as 'busy' as possible. Adding to the observations of another American feminist, Margaret Cruikshank, Ray described this 'busy ethic' as contrary to the desires many older people expressed. Instead, they spoke of a need for solitude and meditation, although within spaces where they could feel secure, respected and loved.[15] The wish to escape the self and its unremitting intellectual goals was also what Eve Sedgwick mentioned when she wrote of the joys she found in poetry, textile art and Buddhism, as she faced up to the mortal fears and debilities of cancer in her middle age.[16]

There are philosophical routes as well as spiritual ones that suggest more complicated understandings of our relationship to time. In his densely abstract compendium on modern time-consciousness, British philosopher Peter Osborne argued that everyday life is constructed through repetitive cultural practices that valorize only the new. Drawing upon Walter Benjamin, Osborne concludes that in the accelerating pace of modernity the 'new' that is always sought after is actually better seen, like fashion or other forms of commodification, as an endless recycling of 'the ever-always-the-same'.[17] Such a conception of time as the fleeting moment that is always impatiently urging us into the future also exists in stark contrast with the temporal patterns evident in Freud's psychoanalytic metapsychology of unconscious desire and fantasy. For Freud, unconscious processes remain in themselves 'timeless', displaying a life-long indifference to the forms of temporality emblematic of capitalist modernity.[18]

As we saw in the opening chapter, it is this timelessness of the unconscious, the persistence of the psychic past within the present, which ensures that there will always be some sense of temporal vertigo within our experiences of ageing. For if we are never simply our chronological age, we will all nevertheless, one way and another, be kept aware that we are growing old – though for some the effects will be far harsher than for others. Meanwhile, the practices that allow us most easily to acknowledge ageing and old age are those most at odds with exhortations to seize each passing moment and the opportunities it offers for making fresh plans for the future. They are thus at odds with the temporal tunes of our time, usually disdainful of tradition and the wisdom of elders, and thereby fostering disavowal of the experiences of ageing, even when promoting notions of 'ageing well'. In contrast, the ruminations most attentive to ageing include much pondering over all the ways the past has impacted upon the present, or alternatively perhaps reflecting upon how fast things change, often seeming to leave little enduring trace.

Contemplating ageing might include mourning the roads not taken. Or more contentedly, it might involve finding pleasure in the reveries of the moment, as if we might linger there forever, indifferent to the passage of time. For sure, the border between the approach of old age and old age itself is fluid, in general more dependent on our social and economic situation than on genetic inheritance or personal attention to health and fitness. Yet wherever we situate ourselves on the continuum of old age, it is a time when each day brings us more to look back on than to look forward to. By late middle age, we know far more about the past than we will ever know of the future. This may give us a certain freedom from projects of self-making, though hardly total escape from pondering how one should live. We know that time seems to speed up as we age. The most convincing explanation of this sense of temporal acceleration is that in childhood and youth each new day brings the excitement of genuine novelty, making the days seem longer (especially in retrospect), while as we age routine and repetition collapse the weeks and months into each other, year on year. This is also why our memories of youth appear more vivid and enduring.[19] Acknowledging old age means knowing that we are unlikely to remain the autonomous, independent and future-oriented individuals most of us once liked to imagine we were, and in Western cultures are encouraged to think we should remain. It also includes, when we can manage it, finding ways of facing up to loss, and mortality, ideally in a manner we can share with others.

Ruptures and Reckonings

I have heard it said that those who most mourn their youth are more likely to be people who felt confident, loved and attractive when younger. Whatever the pitfalls and losses of ageing they face, those recalling more unhappy feelings about their younger years may therefore have little cause to grieve the passing of youth. One friend who suggested this insists she herself has little regret, despite suffering from the most serious of incapacitating diseases for the last twenty years, since reaching early middle age. The relevant statistics on 'wellbeing' partially confirm the view that people can become happier once safely past middle age. Unsurprisingly, however, these empirical studies offer a welter of inconsistencies depending on the wording and particular methodology of the information being solicited. For instance, overall, women are said to be slightly happier than men, and yet women are generally more prone to depression than men.[20]

Nevertheless, over the last few years the 'happiness' studies I have already mentioned report a U-turn relating to happiness and ageing. They present evidence for a serious global dip in wellbeing in mid-life, when people are in their forties and fifties, and then an upward surge in feelings of acceptance and wellbeing from the late fifties.[21] The researchers explain their accounts of increasing happiness coming after middle-aged misery in terms of people becoming less ambitious and angry about disappointments in life, more tolerant and accepting of any misfortune. Whether a person's verbal report of increasing tolerance of life and its limits can be equated with the sense of leading a fulfilled life, however, takes us down philosophical pathways that cannot be further explored by these studies themselves. Yet it is surely at least pertinent to say that individual lives, even at the best of times, are likely to be a messy mix of satisfactions and frustrations, pleasures and pains, that cannot but be flattened out if we are forced to sum them up on 'happiness' scales telling us that on average people entering old age complain less about their lot in life. It seems old people do come to expect less, but it is surely a moot point if that should be our definition of 'happiness', or indeed of any notion of the 'good life'.

From whatever perspective we look at ageing, however, it is generally agreed that at least for many people mid-life brings with it differing levels of mourning for the loss of what is recalled at this time as the greater physical attractiveness, energy or exuberance of their youth. Yet this mourning for our youth, in particular when it is for lost beauty, is a regret for something most of us did not experience ourselves as owning at the time we supposedly possessed it. This is what the feminist scholar and poet Denise Riley intriguingly calls a form of 'retrospective identification': "'Yes, I suppose in the past I must have been beautiful, as people used to say, although at the time I never saw it.'" [22]

Riley has always been adept at finding just the right words for grappling creatively with the most difficult challenges of identity, change and sorrow. In her reflections on 'language as affect', she ponders the consolations people use when facing up to the disappearance of their youthful bodies and looks, while herself preferring a sort of flinty stoicism surveying the precarious joys and many losses of life, especially her own. She notes, for instance, that while anxieties over what is registered as the steady erosion of looks are exhaustively serviced by the colossal commercial industries of repair and regeneration, our actual dread of the fading of beauty is barely admitted. Personal vanity encourages silence, even as fearful apprehensions are incited by ubiquitous cultural landscapes of youthful beauty: 'consolations of illusion meet and fortify the illusions of consolation'. [23] This leads Riley to ponder other sources of possible solace that people turn to, however illusory.

One panacea can be found in the attempt to fortify the ageing self with images of what we now recognize as our past beauty, though hardly aware of it at the time. This is what we saw Doris Lessing suggest in commenting upon older women placing photographs of their youthful selves for visitors to survey, as if secretly saying: '*that* is what I am really like'. [24] Looking at old photos of ourselves, often together with our friends when young, can induce a strange mixture of belated pleasure and wistfulness, as the British poet Ruth Fainlight depicts in her poem 'Friends' Photos', written when she was sixty-six:

> We were beautiful, without exception.
> I could hardly bear to look at those
> old albums, to see the lost glamour
> we never noticed when we were
> first together – when we were young.[25]

As we saw with Lessing, those who really were aware of their beauty and seductive charms back in their youth, rather than in reconstructions afterwards, are likely to find ageing all the more painful. This is certainly what that keen observer and elegant chronicler of old age, Penelope Lively, has one of her fictional characters express: 'If you have been a beauty, ageing must be intolerable ... The process is bad enough as it is – the ebbing away of possibilities, the awful tyranny of the body – but for those who lose their very trademark, it is savage.'[26]

Other attempted consolations mentioned by Riley include the type of residual satisfaction that might come from knowing that our former beauty lives on in the memory of others, all the more so if those others have managed to commemorate it publicly in visual or poetic form: 'His beauty shall in these black lines be seen / And they shall live, and he in them still green', in the words Shakespeare used to immortalize the youthful charm of a young man he favoured at the time.[27] Best of all, of course, is when such enduring memories trigger emotions of the past in the present, so that even when old and sometimes sad, we might feel confident that we remain desirable in the eyes of a long-time lover. It is again Fainlight who knew how lucky she was that, at seventy-nine, she was still certain that after returning from a trip abroad, 'my husband would look at me / as wonderingly as if / we still were bride and groom'.[28] However, few of us feel, or could remain, so lucky, not even Fainlight, whose husband of fifty years and more, Alan Sillitoe, died soon after she wrote these words.

Then again, as Riley also observes, some of us will be permitted, encouraged even, to take a narcissistic pride in surveying the beauty of our children, or grandchildren, suggesting in the face of time's erosion that they are now what we have been, our genetic stand-ins. Much has been written and said about the delights, especially, of grandparenting, in keeping ageing spirits buoyant. Apart from the testimony I have from numerous friends (having as yet no grandchildren of my own), we can easily turn to any number of literary sources. One of the most memorable for me was Penelope Lively's short story, 'Party'. Here she persuasively recounts the peaceful and creative affinity that can exist between the old and the very young. A grandmother and her grandson feel themselves to be equally the unwanted outsiders at the start of a party hosted by the child's mother as the adults start to drink and chat. Yet as the hours pass, in this story they end up enjoying themselves the most once they retreat happily into building a model plane together, cheerfully whiling the long night away until, in the early morning, having completed their task, they are 'the only ones still capable of celebration ... in silence and in mutual appreciation they drink to one another'.[29]

Even more vividly, the late Tove Jansson evokes the humour, insight and strong mutual support that can exist between a very old woman and her six-year-old granddaughter in her immensely popular *The Summer Book*, which has never been out of print in Scandinavia since it was published forty years ago. This Finnish writer, best known for her enchanting children's fiction, has her characters bonding across the generations as they discuss the meaning of life and death, helping each other to overcome their differing pains and anxieties after the death of the child's mother. Jansson wrote the book in her late fifties as a way of coming to terms with her personal grief after the death of her own mother, drawing upon the nature and importance of her relationship with her young niece, Sophia.[30]

Nevertheless, there can be a more troubling aspect associated with the caring side of grandparenting today, given the increasing expense and shortage of nurseries available to meet the needs of the working parents. Several studies from around the globe have suggested that the demands of caregiving on grandparents are sometimes stressful and exhausting, perhaps exacerbating existing health problems.[31] 'It's exploitation and grandparents are at the receiving end', the Mothers' Union from the UK announced over a decade ago, arguing for more government rights and recognition for grandparents' caring work.[32] Grandparents, even those who have been regularly caring for grandchildren, can also suddenly lose all access to them following acrimonious divorces. Yet despite these dangers, for the most part, people with grandchildren routinely celebrate their pleasure in relating to them, especially during the early years of more regular contact.

Denise Riley herself, however, seems largely to reject these possible consolations. As I have suggested, she turns instead to the thoughts of the ancient Stoics for guidance, including the Roman former slave, Epictetus, and the Roman emperor, Marcus Aurelius. Quintessentially Stoic, Epictetus counselled self-reliance, acceptance and forbearance at all times, famously saying 'Let death and exile, and all things which appear terrible, be daily before your eyes ... and you will never entertain any abject thought, nor too eagerly covet anything.'[33] Similarly, Marcus Aurelius, in his even more celebrated *Meditations*, maintained that people should expect little from the body, which from the beginning is a harbinger of death: 'live each day as though one's last, never flustered, never apathetic, never attitudinizing'.[34]

Riley spells out the implications of such philosophy, for instance that the fleeting strength or beauty of youth, being arbitrarily bestowed, is best seen as something that never truly belongs to its bearer, who should remain indifferent to it. As we have seen many others counsel, we should dwell determinedly in the present moment, aiming for a form of impersonal self-transcendence, disinterested in our own fate and hence free from worries about the future or regrets for the past. Yet however sensible this advice, especially when Aurelius was sending his troops into battle, it seems to me hardly likely to succeed for long in preventing the weight of the world bearing down too heavily upon most of us, much of the time, whatever our age. Nevertheless, there is a certain emotional seduction in such language, as well as a clear affinity with the floating meditations of others I have looked at in search of ways of leading a good life in old age, such as those of Sara Maitland, when merging with the landscapes she loves in the timeless moment of the present.

I also see such Stoic fortitude and melancholic strength beautifully expressed by another somewhat neglected author and elegant stylist, Rosalind Belben. In her late thirties she wrote a wry and compelling confessional novel, its protagonist, Lavinia, sharing Belben's age and circumstances in every detail of time and place. As if laying the author's life on the line, Lavinia reviews her present situation and prospects in its opening pages as a childless woman, without spouse, partner or lover, a condition she realizes will remain unchanged now all the way till the end. Two refrains are repeated throughout the text, '*This is not the life I imagined for myself*'; 'I want to make sense of my life':

> As all bodies do I require and desire to love and be loved; to exert myself, to be stretched; to have demands made upon me, not the kind of demands which, paradoxically, are made upon me. I should prefer not to articulate such commonplaces ... Bother it, I was, I am, lonely ... *I am not the person I could have been.*[35]

Yet her painful envy of conventional families, the raw sexual frustration, the horror that she will never again be loved by anyone, which Belben depicts so precisely, are presented in rich counterpoint to continuing moments of joy and fulfilment, as Lavinia is suffused not with resentment – though resentment often shadows her – but in her pleasure of nature, in the countryside she loves, in travel and sightseeing, in the heightened awareness of her wandering and wondering gaze at expressions and movement in the lives of others, above all, in the texture of landscapes. However solitary, the protagonist's enduring desire for and engagement with the world constantly erupts in poetic engagement with the rhythms of her own life past and present, whether pondering the mother she left her job to care for approaching thirty, or in her love for animals and reflections upon each passing moment: 'Unfamiliar surroundings content me' (7); 'I am helped by the sight of water; rivers and streams; canals; and drops of dew' (73); 'I have discovered an amazing gift in myself, a boon. For the first three or four hours in rural solitude and peace, my senses expand so rapidly that I can smell separate varieties of grass and trees, bracken and gorse or heather, buttercup or vetch. I can sense cow or pig or horse, fox or badger … It makes me giddy' (118).

In the final section of the book, the protagonist writes of her dreams of the dead, conjuring up the two creatures she has most loved, her mother and her dog. In one dream her mother appears, more tender than in life, hunting through her hair for lice: 'I feel a strange, physical soothing all through my body, a purely instinctual response: we never touch; it is a novelty' (132). Thus the book closes, with the protagonist stumbling into a future she had never anticipated, but realizing 'I have fuel enough in me to blaze alone' (145).

The Work of Mourning

Fuel enough to blaze alone is, one way or another, perhaps what most of us are seeking, especially when older and, sooner or later, often on our own. And if not to blaze, for that seems rather a lot to ask, at least sufficient energy to help us welcome each new day, holding on 'stubbornly content', as Elaine Feinstein concluded in the closing stanzas of 'Long Life', the last poem of her recent collection, *Cities*, published as she turned eighty.

These days I speak less of death than this miracle of survival.
I am no longer lonely, not yet frail, and after surgery,
recognize each breath as a favour.
My generation may not be nimble, but, forgive us,
we'd like to hold on, stubbornly content – even while
ageing.[36]

192

However, unless we work hard at gliding superficially over the miseries of life, whether our own or those of others, then the miracle of survival must involve finding ways of mourning our losses and heeding the suffering of others. Significantly, in what has emerged as a new era of mourning and public 'remembrance', much – too much, some have suggested – has been written about mourning over the last few decades. It is all too evident in the sudden popularity of what have been called 'pathographies', a word coined to describe memoirs of encounters with illness, failure and death. At the very least, this explosion of writing about grief, memory and survival means that nowadays we are hardly lacking in material about loss.[37] 'I am no longer lonely', Feinstein declared in *Cities*, which is notable because in her previous collection, *Talking to the Dead*, published four years earlier, Feinstein often sounded painfully alone: 'You were always home to me / I long for home'.[38] *Talking to the Dead* is her moving collection of elegies to her late husband Arnold Feinstein, who had died a few years earlier after fifty years of marriage.

How does one deal with irrevocable loss? Partly, as we see here and echoed in many other texts, through connecting with the dead, or lost person (the lost 'object', as clinicians like to say), in ways that have aspects of unreality or 'magical thinking', but which may gradually help a person come to terms with grief. For Feinstein, the dead husband reappears and speaks to her in dreams, as in her poem 'A Visit', which begins 'I still remember love like another country' before we learn of her dreaming:

And early this morning you whispered
as if you were lying softly at my side:
Are you still angry with me? And spoke my
name with so much tenderness, I cried.[39]

She tells us that actually she was rarely angry with this man,
even when he gave her cause to be – which, as we shall see,
probably helps in coming to terms with absence. Feinstein's
poems evoke loss with loving clarity, skilfully portraying both
the ghostly presence and the painful absence of her husband:

Last night I wondered where you had found to sleep.
You weren't in bed. There was no-one in your chair.
... I called out miserably: *You will catch cold*
Waking, I let the daytime facts unfold.[40]

The facts, of loss, unfold.

These poems are clearly about coming to terms with sorrow,
as in the opening poem, 'Winter', in which Feinstein writes:
'My thoughts are bleak', before continuing with an imagined conversation in which the husband teases her in his old
way, and she pictures him, lying 'peaceful and curled / like an
embryo under the squelchy ground'.[41] He knew her so well, she
recalls in her poem, 'A Match', that even, 'All our worst faults
we shared: / disorder, absentmindedness, neglect'.[42] Feinstein
makes one final point in her poems that I'll return to:

It's easy to love the dead.
Their voices are mild
they don't argue.
Once in the earth, they belong to us faithfully.[43]

Feinstein appears to be giving us lessons in how to mourn. Here, Freud's classic essay 'Mourning and Melancholia', written in 1917, has remained unusually influential, with almost everyone interested in mourning returning to it again and again. This is despite Freud himself, characteristically, later shifting his analysis a little. In the original essay Freud introduced the notion of 'the work of mourning', believing it took between one and two years. Without going into too much detail, he argued that in normal mourning we deal with grief by psychically prolonging the existence of lost objects, step by step going through all the memories that we have of them, loving, hostile, ambivalent – above all ambivalent – until we eventually manage to accept that they are no longer there in the world for us.[44] Loosening our attachment to the dead, or just as bad, perhaps worse, to people or beliefs we have loved and lost, means being able to find words or images to register the loss, to mark it, and move on, however strongly we may have internalized our memories of what we have lost.

As Freud again pointed out, those attachments will always have included levels of narcissistic identification, with the loss of self-love, as we all probably know, one of the main injuries of losing in love. Sometimes, however, we may not be able to find ways of mourning or dealing with loss or abandonment. In extreme states of melancholia, Freud suggested, a person cannot come to terms with absence but instead incorporates the lost person in ways that can, in a sense, cause part of the person who feels abandoned also to die, crushing whatever sense of self, or ego, they once had. Moreover, in these cases, a sense of anger at being abandoned is turned inwards into a relentless sense of unworthiness and self-rejection, a depression that can lead to suicidal thoughts and deeds. Summarizing his distinction between mourning and melancholia, Freud concluded: 'In mourning it is the world which has become poor and empty; in melancholia it is the ego itself' (246).

Ironically, the more ambivalence and hostility one has felt towards the lost object of desire, or perhaps the stronger the sense that the lost object was something we never truly possessed and hence never really lost, the less one is able to mourn and the greater the self-laceration and inability to recover. Thus Freud wrote: 'If one listens patiently to the melancholic's many and various self-accusations, one cannot in the end avoid the impression that often the most violent of them are hardly at all applicable to the patient himself, but that with insignificant modifications they do fit someone else, someone whom the patient loves or has loved or should love' (248).

Feinstein's poetry seems to exemplify successful mourning, repeatedly registering the loss, and then noting one's own survival. C. S. Lewis' classic reflections on the extreme anguish he felt following the death of his wife in his late middle age, after a short but extremely happy marriage, was similar. *A Grief Observed*, first published under a pseudonym a year after his wife's death in 1961, began with an account of his immediate total disorientation. He became, he said, an embarrassment to everyone he met, and Lewis recorded his sense that his life, even his body, had become totally empty, a 'miserable phantom'.[45] Yet he hoped that somehow writing down his grief, and his memories of all he had lost, might help him 'get a little outside it' (12). By the end of this short memoir he had managed to do this, at least some of the time, again seeming to confirm Freud's idea that successful mourning is a process that enables grievers to struggle through their memories of the dead or lost person, to ensure that they are no longer colonized by their absence.

Thus Lewis wrote: 'It is just at those moments when I feel least sorrow ... that [my wife] rushed upon my mind in her full reality, her otherness ... The less I mourn her, the nearer I seem to her' (44–6).

However, other clinicians turning their attention to loss and grieving have argued that mourning and melancholia are more interwoven than Freud had suggested in his first account.[46] Indeed, in his later text, *The Ego and the Id* (1923), Freud himself agreed that the process of identification remains an enduring aspect of mourning, and is indeed intrinsic to the formation and strengthening of the ego, which can be seen as 'a precipitate of abandoned object-cathexes'.[47] Almost a century later, the Lacanian psychoanalyst Darian Leader returned to mourning and melancholia in his overview, *The New Black*, finding from his research that, surprisingly, analysts themselves have written comparatively little on the psychology of mourning since Freud. In Leader's view this is because unhappiness in general has been swallowed up by the all-encompassing talk of 'depression' and accompanying popular discourses of its supposed opposite, social wellbeing, and by extension, the desire to live agelessly.

Underpinning both of these hopes is the idea of everybody's 'right' to remain 'productive and happy' throughout their lives, indeed their social obligation to do so, as a form of 'mental hygiene'.[48] Others, including the feminist cultural theorist, Sara Ahmed, have similarly criticized the rhetoric of the burgeoning 'happiness industry', with its bizarrely labeled 'hedometers', telling us, for instance, that those who conform most to normative expectations, usually via marriage, jobs and more, score highest on their happiness scales. Within this framework, people's self-reporting of happiness is also thought to tie in with brain mechanisms involving, in particular, serotonin uptake, described as providing 'the chemistry of well-being'.[49]

This science has even come to influence British government policy, as Richard Layard notes in his book *Happiness: Lessons from a New Science*.[50] Reduced to a medical matter, the shortest route to turn around the reported escalating rates of depression globally is therefore seen in terms of the hopefully quick fix of biochemical or behavioural changes, via drugs or cognitive behaviour therapy (CBT). In this diagnosis of depression and its treatment, any details about its background in mourning and loss are largely absent. Another problem with this medical literature on depression is its exclusive focus on the individual. Yet, as others have noticed, mourning was traditionally more of a collective practice, involving extensive rituals that console and comfort the living. These are ceremonies that publicly celebrate the memories of the dead, symbolizing the breaking, and sometimes partial remaking, of the ties between the living and the dead. In one of his late works, the eminent French historian, Philippe Ariès, for instance, argues that Western society has become increasingly afraid and ashamed of death, especially after 1945, since when death has been almost banished from our daily lives, thereby reducing mourning and grief to a personal and specific 'morbid state' to be shortened and erased as fast as possible.[51] This elimination of public ritual, evident in both Protestant and secular traditions, can make dealing with grief and loss all the more difficult, perhaps partially accounting for the prevalence of depression today.

Those most critical of the biochemical and cognitive approaches to happiness and depression, such as Leader and Ahmed, would emphasize the need to understand the complexity of emotions, and their background and context. Joining their number, Stephen Frosh, in his short book, *Feelings*, suggests that happiness scales appear to be measuring primarily forms of complacency and self-satisfaction, in short, the determined refusal to acknowledge that a full life inevitably involves attending to pain and loss.[52] Moreover, exploring actual experiences of loss enables us to see that dealing with the tragic aspects of life has its own forms of creativity and value. 'Unsettledness and dissent', Frosh notes, is a way of refusing to evade the inevitability of loss, pain and political conflict in human relations, and of helping us to face up to our own finitude: 'Perhaps', he concludes, 'we should never be able to answer the question "Are you happy now?" in the affirmative, if we really want to use feelings to construct the good life.'[53]

The creative side of mourning may be less evident in clinical literature today, but it is certainly everywhere visible in the outpouring of literary narratives from every part of the world. 'Could the arts', Leader asks, 'be a vital tool in allowing us to make sense of the inevitable losses in all our lives?'[54] Well, of course. The American poet, Mark Doty, who became one of the main lyricists of the bereavement gay men in particular endured from HIV/AIDS, writes eloquently on this: 'Loss brought with it a species of vision, an inwardness which was the gift of a terrible time – nearly unbearable, but bracingly real.'[55] In a climate that prefers to banish death and mourning from the public realm, it has been the flourishing aesthetic rendition of grief that has provided the main outlet to help us understand, or perhaps try to express (if only to ourselves) the anguish of personal sorrow. There are a multiplicity of ways in which we feel undone and dispossessed when those we have loved are no longer there for us, or when our bond with them has unravelled, as in the memorable words of the philosopher Judith Butler:

'Let's face it. We're undone by each other. And if we're not, we're missing something. If this seems so clearly the case with grief, it is only because it was already the case with desire.'[56]

Some narratives of mourning, however, lack the sense of process and progress that were evident in the reflections of Feinstein and Lewis, which apparently moved smoothly enough beyond the initial hopeless sense of the world as empty and existence as pointless. No one in my experience has managed to capture the repetitive, disjointed thought patterns of an abiding sense of futility, abandonment and suffering following a loss better than Roland Barthes. 'The world depresses me', he noted in a hundred different ways in the two years following the death of his cherished mother. The day after her death, on 25 October 1977, Barthes began making notes, often several times a day, recording his thoughts and feelings on index-sized slips of paper. This mother, Henriette, with whom he had lived for most of his life, was the single, reliably strong presence in his life; the one person who made sense of his existence: 'Only *maman* was strong, because she was intact against all neurosis, all madness.'[57] For almost two years, in the long days and months following her death, Barthes' words conveyed what others have often sought to portray as the puzzling patterns of grieving, its discontinuous but, in his case, never-ending nature, the stubborn sense of the emptiness, stupidity, pointlessness of the world one inhabits, even though, as Barthes wrote, he continued to function in it, apparently perfectly normally: 'Today is a flat, dreary country – virtually without water – and paltry', he wrote a few weeks after his mother's death (53).

On the first anniversary of her death, things had not improved: 'I feel dry, with no supporting inwardness' (208). Barthes found consolation, not in the company of friends, however sympathetic, nor in travelling to beautiful places, however exotic, but only when solitary, in the moments when he was writing, at least when he was writing about his mother, or with his mother in mind. Moreover, despite his grief remaining much the same – 'I am *continually*, all the time, unhappy since *maman's* death' (124) – in composing his notes he felt he was transforming the work of mourning into the work of writing. The urge to evoke his mother, he felt, was a compulsion '*to make* maman *recognized*'.

Barthes had not, he would claim, introjected his mother, not secretly become her; indeed he kept stressing the contrasts between them, suggesting that since her death he had become *less* like her. He knew that the one true object of his love, the one he would always idealize, could not be brought back to life, but he could, and would, continue to pay homage to her, to her 'nobility', 'sweetness' and 'goodness', in his writing. Her virtues are there in the words in his diary, and more publicly elsewhere, in the work he put into his book on photography, *Camera Lucida*, the whole second half of which he spent eulogizing his mother when discussing the impact of finding a photograph of her as a five-year-old child.[58] It was only with her in mind, he said in *Mourning Diary*, that he was able to 'integrate my suffering with my writing' (105), knowing his mother 'is present in everything I have written: in that there is everywhere a notion of the Sovereign Good' (131, 105).

Interestingly, Barthes believed that his mother's death was the one thing in his life that he had not responded to neurotically, since his grief had 'not been hysterical, scarcely visible to others' (128). While he used to live neurotically in fear of losing his mother, now, he said, echoing Winnicott, he suffered '*from the fear of what has happened*'; but despite and because of his constant awareness of his sorrow, he was no longer neurotic: 'I live in my suffering and that makes me happy' (173). He did not want to suppress his mourning, but 'to change it, transform it, to shift it from a static stage ... to a fluid state' (142). There is no evidence that Barthes expected these notes to be published, but near the opening of his diary he wrote: 'Who knows? Maybe something valuable in these notes?' (7). Barthes survived his mother's death by only two and a half years, yet as he probably hoped, his work of mourning may help others not just to find words for the barely effable, but perhaps even to find ways of tolerating the intolerable.

Something seemingly valuable in producing, or taking in, this expanding language of loss and mourning is much in evidence in the huge popularity of other creative works nowadays. This includes the memoir and subsequent stage production of *The Year of Magical Thinking*, by the eminent American literary journalist and novelist, Joan Didion, which she began nine months after the death of her husband, the writer John Gregory Dunne, at seventy-one. He died of a heart attack, in midsentence, as she was preparing his dinner. The 'magical thinking' Didion relates was a persistent form of wishful thinking or cognitive denial in that first year of bereavement. Yes, she knew that this man, with whom her life had been intertwined for almost every hour of almost every day for over forty years, was dead. Yet she acted in ways that she herself soon recognized indicated that she thought that somehow his death might be reversible.

'I needed to be alone so that he could come back', she said of the first night she spent without him: 'This was the beginning of my year of magical thinking.'[59] She also needed to keep his clothes and shoes, and not to allow his organs to be donated, in case he returned. Nor did she read his obituaries. Always the pellucid, rational, concise observer, even as she calmly describes the 'madness of grief', Didion details the sense of fragility and instability she feels, alongside the many tricks she uses in refusing to accept the permanence of loss: 'I did not believe in the resurrection of the body but I still believed that given the right circumstances he would come back', she writes, also knowingly referencing Freud's 'Mourning and Melancholia' (150). The fragility she feels connects with her new sense of being old, recognizing that as she mourns her husband, she is also mourning herself. She now reflects that her marriage had enabled the denial of time: 'For forty years I saw myself through John's eyes. I did not age' (197). Throughout this time her only child, Quintana, was dangerously ill and, despite several apparent recoveries, would soon die (which Didion's readers know starting the book, but she did not until after the memoir was completed, her daughter's death occuring shortly before its publication). As the book closes, a year later, Didion still has trouble seeing herself as a widow, though she feels 'The craziness is receding but no clarity is taking its place' (225). No clarity, except in the writing itself: 'Is it only by dreaming or writing that I could find out what I thought?' (162).

Didion also comments on the paucity of grief literature and the cultural rejection of public mourning, although this book, like others similarly acclaimed over the last two decades, suggests one form of public mourning. The writing, reading and sometimes performing of these texts have become new guides to survival, a way of commemorating the dead and, except in the case of Barthes, of beginning to move on. Two more mourning memoirs have recently appeared from Didion's literary compatriots. More dramatically than any I have mentioned so far, in *A Widow's Story* the prolific novelist Joyce Carol Oates uses her diary jottings as a stream of consciousness to evoke the hysteria, chaos and pain of her grieving for the husband she had lived with for forty-seven years, at times picturing herself as a wounded animal, a dead creature, at others fearing that she is going out of her mind: 'The widow's terror is that, her mind being broken, as her spine is broken, she will break down utterly. She will be carried off by wild careening banshee thoughts like these.'[60] However, after her year of desolate suffering, often experienced as utter madness, wondering if she should pay someone simply to come and be with her, Oates' memoir closes with a determined upbeat message about the ability to survive grief, however devastating: 'Of the widow's countless death duties there is really only one that matters: on the first anniversary of the husband's death, the widow should think *I kept myself alive.*'[61]

Similarly, in *The Long Goodbye*, the far younger Meghan O'Rourke describes her erratic, intense grieving following her mother's death from cancer at only fifty-five: 'I was not prepared for how hard I would find it to reenter the slipstream of contemporary life ... a world ill-suited to reflection and daydreaming.'[62] O'Rourke describes how in her grief nothing seemed important anymore: 'Daily tasks were exhausting. Dishes piled in the sink, knives crusted with strawberry jam ... I felt that I had abruptly arrived at a terrible, insistent truth about the impermanence of the everyday' (11). Over six months later she still wakes up 'exhausted' and 'leaden', reflecting 'I am ashamed of my pain; it seemed abnormal' (195). However, she is now beginning to realize that she is also attached to her grief, rejecting the consoling advice from friends that it was time to let go of sorrow and move on: 'But I didn't want to let go.' She cites cases from China where the living continue to talk to the dead, commenting that 'in fact studies have shown that some mourners hold on to a relationship with the deceased with no notable ill effects' (154). (She does not, however, spell out the cultural context, myths and religious beliefs that would of course bear upon the social acceptance of such practices of grieving in China.)

By now it is becoming clear that such books are written and widely read not just as survival manuals, but also to convey a certain allure attaching to the fearsome landscape of grief, with all its vividness and intensity compared to normal life. As Adam Phillips noted a decade ago in an essay entitled 'Coming to Grief': 'One of the ironies of the so-called mourning process is that it tends to make people even more absorbed than they usually are; in need of accomplices, but baffled by what they want from them', which is why others want the mourning process to come to a reasonably swift end.[63] In the face of bland incitements to happiness today, however, these memoirs point to a contrasting cultural interest in loss and grieving, with greater acknowledgment of the inevitability of life's tragic contours, at least in certain literary circles. Although, in a shallower vein, what we seem to see in the spectacles of public grief after the death of celebrities, most extravagantly in the case of Princess Diana, is surely people's desire to seize the affect, the opportunity to express feelings, without really having to embrace any personal loss.

Pondering the current appeal of grief memoirs thus returns me to Feinstein's comment that it is easy to love the dead, compared to the challenges of loving the living. This is also noted by Adam Phillips in a subsequent essay, 'Time Pieces', where he points out that grief is full of surprises, even at its most desolate. Phillips, like Frosh, suggests that what we most want is the ability to feel and to express desire, and what we are most threatened by is the absence of any form of love or desire. Ironically, death can help us to express longing, and to communicate more smoothly with those we have lost, those whom we are now freer to idealize in ways formerly denied us: 'When people are alive … they can be a barrier to what we feel about them.' Death can sometimes help us jump those hurdles that kept us apart from those who mattered to us: 'It is easy not to notice people when we are in their presence, and far more difficult to hide from them when they are no longer there … And in this sense, the dead leave us stranded with our potential as it once was, intact.'[64]

Also following in the footsteps of Freud, Frosh similarly suggests that it is better to feel sorrow than to feel nothing at all, which perhaps explains why sorrow may be in some sense experienced as 'pleasurable', even sought after. Moreover, he adds, here in line with Barthes' thoughts expressed in *Mourning Diary*: 'The capacity to feel sad, to embrace sorrow and then to articulate it so that something new is made of it, is a fundamental sign of mental health, supplying the basis of being able to relate constructively to the world.'[65] Mark Doty reaches much the same conclusion when he finally comes to accept that he can survive the death of the last of his two dogs, those creatures who seemed to have carried his 'will to live' over the previous sixteen years, during which he watched his lover die of AIDS. Suffering and compassion, he realizes by the close of his book, *Dog Years*, can make you feel more alive, not less so: 'I am grateful to have felt even this sharp sadness … Despair is one note in the range of feeling that will pour through me, but I do not have to be frozen there, locked in the absence of futurity and hope.'[66]

When still at the height of his emotional loss and sorrow, while caring for his beloved partner dying of AIDS, Doty had written in an earlier memoir of 'everything in the world closing down to one little point of dread'.[67]

It therefore becomes less surprising that it is in talking to the dead or other lost objects – those absent presences – that we may sometimes find more ways of working out how to live in the present. Such thoughts can be found in much of the often mournful, nostalgic yet in my view always life-affirming writing of Colm Tóibín. His narrative twists repeatedly present older characters reflecting on parents and lovers, as well as spaces and places, that they have loved and lost, or loved and left. This is the dominant mood of the short stories in a recent collection, *The Empty Family*, many of which contain sharply perceptive sequences that capture autobiographical fragments Tóibín has mentioned elsewhere.

For instance, at the beginning of 'One Minus One', a son is looking at the moon in Texas and mourning his mother six years after her death: 'The moon is my mother.'[68] In his head, he begins confiding his thoughts about his mother to his former lover who was always so exasperated with him because of his obstinate refusal ever to be direct or truthful, always hiding his feelings in small talk and jokes. What he only now feels he can share with this ex-lover, and only in his absence, are his memories of the journey he made from New York to Ireland as his mother lay dying, and of his feelings after her death. In this imaginary way, he also wants, at last, to 'share' his recollections of a much earlier time in childhood when he and his younger brother had been abruptly sent off to live with an aunt in an empty, neglectful and loveless world at the start of his father's illness from which he died a few years later. During these childhood months of silence and sorrow, his mother never once visited her sons or ever later mentioned the episode or its sequel, leaving a perpetual void of 'sad echoes and dim feelings' (7).

Elsewhere, in interviews, Tóibín has referred to a similar event which occurred when he was eight and his younger brother was four, and which he could never discuss with his own mother. In the short story the episode is succinctly summarized as a deep regret that the narrator knows he can never raise while his mother lives: 'there was this double regret – the simple one that I had kept away, and the other one, much harder to fathom, that I had been given no choice, that she had never wanted me very much, and that she was not going to be able to rectify that in the few days that she had left in the world' (12). For the narrator here, as perhaps for the author, one is led to suspect that it will only be in mourning that the son will ever finally come to feel close to the mother he loved, and resembles, but whom he could never touch or confide in while she lived:

> She loved, as I did, books and music and hot weather. As she grew older, she had managed, with her friends and with us, a pure charm, a lightness of tone and touch. But I knew not to trust it, not to come close, and I never did. I managed in turn to exude my own lightness and charm, but you know that too. You don't need me to tell you that either, do you? (9)

Many of Tóibín's other narrators in *The Empty Family* are, like their author, apparently unattached middle-aged gay men who, when not immersed in work, landscape or other aesthetic pleasures, are often regretful and lonely. They know life is about the accumulation of losses, yet it remains exhilarating and laced with desire despite and sometimes because of its solitude, abandonment and regrets, as the protagonist in the story of the book's title reflects after choosing to return, as Tóibín has, to build a house in the place where he was born:

> And all I have … is this house, this light, this freedom, and I will, if I have the courage spend my time watching the sea, noting its changes and the sound it makes, studying the horizon, listening to the wind or relishing the calm when there is no wind. I will not fly even in my deepest dreams too close to the sun or too close to the sea. The chance for all that has passed.[69]

Once again, in this story the narrator's thoughts are addressed to a former lover, but his gaze is outward, watching the waves which seem to mirror the ironies of human existence, and our time in the world: 'all lifted possibility, all complexity and rushing fervour, to end in nothing on a small strand, and go back out to rejoin the empty family from whom we had set out alone with such a burst of brave unknowing energy' (32). And here we find another, somewhat different and gentler meaning of melancholia, one evoked in Dürer's memorable engraving, *Melencolia I*, which depicts an awareness of the inevitable risks of the imaginative spirit and enquiring mind.

What I have gained and tried to convey from reading so much of this literature on mourning and sorrow is a better understanding not just of the inevitability of the tragic in life, but also a sense that loss is not simply an experience to be surmounted but rather an event to live with and, when circumstances and capacity enable it, to share with others. Some of our later life will hopefully be spent evading loss and misery. But some of it will surely entail trying to find more of the right words, rehearsing new and better ways, to engage with and comfort one another for as long as we can, as we experience the anguish each of us at some stage will face and continue to live with, right up to death itself.

Disobedience and Dissent

There are quiet personal ways of reflecting on one's past, feeling one's age and facing the future. There are also noisy collective ways of observing the present, feeling one's age and challenging the social marginalization of the elderly. The two are not necessarily incompatible, though they usually tend to pull us in opposite directions. Finding gratifications in solitude and learning the strengths to be gained from rethinking one's ties to the past, right back to the beginning, might help us when confronting the difficulties and disregard often encountered in old age. It brings to mind once more Walter Benjamin's concept of memory as an ever-changing repertoire of possibilities rather than any faithful registering of events, whether reappraising the significance of history, its losses usually buried in notions of conquest and progress, or simply looking back over any long life.[70]

Nevertheless, whatever our reflective inclinations, the chances for taking risks and courting danger do not always pass with youth, any more than serenity or withdrawal necessarily comes with age. Writing about the history of gossip, the American literary critic Patricia Meyer Spacks points out that over the centuries older women in particular have proved valuable as resisters, feared for their disobedience, anger, outspokenness and general non-conformity, even if they have more often been mocked than appreciated in the role.[71] It is not hard to flesh out images of ageing truculence, but whereas gossip is more likely to be a favourite tool of the relatively powerless, older people's dissidence sometimes emerges from voices that have remained influential over the decades. In her sixties, the scholar and writer Carolyn Heilbrun, for instance, advised women to use any seniority they might have to take risks, make noise and become unpopular.[72]

Her compatriot, Adrienne Rich, who died in 2012, certainly agreed. Born in Baltimore in 1929, Rich was a poet and writer whose early and continuing literary success made her not only widely acclaimed as 'one of America's best poets' but also recognized in old age as an influential dissident voice.[73] To the very end neither her poetic timbre nor its political power ever weakened, but rather expanded and intensified. In her eighties, Rich often spoke of, then occasionally retreated from, her high hopes that poetry might prove a useful tool in struggles for social change. In an interview in 2011, she mentioned again that the words of poetry, which say more than they mean, and mean more than they say, can 'act physically on the reader or hearer', in their 'abruptness, directness and anger'.[74] At her most optimistic Rich felt that 'in a time of frontal assaults both on language and on human solidarity, poetry can remind us all of what we are in danger of losing – disturb us, embolden us out of resignation.'[75] Nevertheless, especially in her late life, Rich's optimism was always balanced by equal amounts of pessimism, fearing that 'some North American ears have trouble with poetry' because of the general 'whirlpool of disinformation and manufactured distraction'.[76] Quite right, and not just in the USA.

Along with other ageing radicals, Rich hated the harsh drift towards what is usually summed up as 'neo-liberalism' in the social and political life of the USA over the last three decades, with its unbroken commitment to private enterprise and its hostility towards welfare spending, as fiercely articulated in her collection from the 1990s, *Dark Fields of the Republic*.[77] Witnessing the inequality accelerating ever since the 'Reaganomics' of the 1980s, Rich reported losing much of her former critical confidence that social movements might manage to push the USA into becoming a more democratic and peaceful country, one able to confront its many oppressive legacies.

Unexpectedly, it led her to read Marx and to rethink some of her earlier visions, noting the uncomfortable fit between the marketing of feminist-sounding solutions to personal problems and a corporate system that mocked collective action as pointless and sterile. Continuously self-critical, Rich noted her own complicity in helping to unleash the 'demon of the personal' in feminist celebrations of women's experience, unaware then of how words of personal liberation could be 'taken hostage' by 'a horribly commoditized version of humanity'.[78]

Interestingly, it was this which enabled Rich to articulate a new role for the older woman, or older activist, as a 'passionate skeptic', someone who could look back through time and help explain the continuities, slides, shifts and inevitable ruptures in radical thought and action across the generations, knowing that 'one period's necessary strategies can mutate into the monsters of another time'.[79] She still sought meaning in the struggles of the past, never wiping out or disowning them, yet was always ready, she said, to start over again, realizing that looking back one could find that intentions can be rearranged 'in a blip / coherence smashed into vestige'.[80] Recalling her involvement in the peace movements and anti-war struggles of the 1960s, for instance, Rich later talked of their limitations, thinking today that being 'against war' was too comfortable and easy, compared to developing a critical language capable of encompassing possession, deprivation, colonial history and, above all, of asking: 'Who creates the rhetoric of "terror" and "democracy"?'[81]

From middle age up to her death, and in diverse ways, Rich thus stressed the need to keep looking backwards, critically, to see the future. Only the older woman can do this, as the title of another poetry collection *Midnight Salvage* (1999) suggests. The long poems it contains are all dedicated to citing the disorders of the present, while also recalling 'the sweetness of life, the memory of traditions of mercy, struggles for justice ... casting memory forward':

> it's the layers of history
> we have to choose, along
> with our own practice: what must be tried again
> over and over and
> what must not be repeated
> and at what depth which layer
> will we meet others
>
> the words barely begin
> to match the desire
>
> and the mouth crammed with dollars doesn't testify[82]

In this political outlook, charting and communicating the constant interchange between past and present helps to impede what is experienced as the acceleration of time from mid-life onwards:

Open the book of tales you knew by heart, begin driving the
old roads again
repeating the old sentences, which have changed
minutely from the wordings you remembered.[83]

Ageing for Rich thus gained significance as a call to action,
if only the action of watching, witnessing and waiting, ready
to respond to calls for justice, equality and compassion from
around the world.

It is possible to criticize a certain passivity and strategic
vagueness in Rich's rhetorical stance of poetic witnessing. Yet
even at the best of times, the space for effective political resistance is a fluctuating and problematic one. It makes those who
remain steadfastly insistent on the need for a radical transformation of structures that systematically impoverish, harm or
humiliate others the most valuable of resources. Pondering
her Jewish heritage, for instance, Rich frequently surveyed the
deadlock of the historical tragedy of Israel–Palestine, as in her
vivid poem 'Turning', capturing 'that country of terrible leav-
ings and returning':

Her subject is occupation, a promised land,
displacement, deracination, two people called Semites,
humiliation, force, women trying to speak with women,
the subject is how to break a mold of discourse,
how little by little minds change
but they do change.[84]

'Breaking the mould of discourse', shifting old ways of
thinking and speaking, was the point, allowing Rich to stress
the uses of the oppositional imagination in exposing the follies

and violence, the wisdom and worries, linking past to present. With her stress on the significance of collectivity and cross-generational social bonding, it was also clear that passionate political commitment worked as a form of self-renewal for this ageing poet. What never changed was the determination to resist. Moreover, it provided a possible way of confronting the physical impediments of ageing, and for Rich in particular of dealing with the appalling pain of the chronic rheumatoid arthritis she endured from her early twenties. From the beginning, Rich had stressed the place of the body, and its cultural meanings, in her politics, always alert to the disparagement, and frequent abuse, of women's bodies. This was first and most memorably articulated in her reflections on motherhood and the maternal body: 'I am really asking whether women cannot begin, at last, to think through the body', to make better use of 'our complicated, pain-enduring, multi-pleasured physicality'.[85]

But Rich never saw women's 'pain-enduring physicality' primarily in terms of personal victimhood, least of all her own. Rather, she was determined to put her pain to use politically. In a series of poems written in her fifties, entitled 'Contradictions: Tracking Poems', Rich asks repeatedly how she can connect her own pain, her own 'damaged body', with the pain and destruction she observes in the world:

> The problem is to connect, without hysteria, the pain
> of any one's body with the pain of the body's world
> filled with creatures filled with dread.[86]

She knows, of course, that personal and political pains are not identical, nevertheless she asks us to consider them together:

the body's pain and the pain on the streets
are not the same   but you can learn
from the edges that blur   O you who love clear edges
more than anything   watch the edges that blur.[87]

As Sylvia Henneberg also points out, Rich put her personal suffering to work, seeing in it political possibilities allowing her to connect with the sufferings of others, which in turn helped her to escape from herself.[88] Or again, as the historian Joanna Bourke notes in a beautiful reminiscence of the significance of Rich in her life, the poet encourages us to see all the unfamiliar contradictions of lived experiences, drawing us 'into solidarity with other tormented bodies … a politics that refused to be overwhelmed by suffering. That refuses the will to amnesia.'[89]

Suffering, and resistance to it, opened up for Rich a concept of 'radical happiness', which she developed from Hannah Arendt's notion of 'public happiness', both terms referring to the shared happiness that can be found in public displays of freedom, or the forging of communities working for better times.[90] This is the happiness that Rich saw flowing from a sense of 'true participation in society', a condition she longed to see extended to everyone.[91] She talked of experiencing such public happiness in Chile, speaking to the 50,000 people attending the huge poetry festival that followed the arrest of Pinochet in 2001. It was a feeling she could sense around her again, she said, travelling that same year to Seattle where the World Trade Organization was meeting, to witness the collective spirit of 'anti-globalization' protest, which had grown even larger since its beginnings in November 1999.[92] This is what she was seeking in her old age, whether in life or in poetry, both in life and in poetry, as she said introducing a general anthology of American poetry in the mid 1990s: 'I was looking for poetry that could rouse me from fatigue, stir me from grief, poetry that was redemptive in the sense of offering a kind of deliverance or rescue of the imagination, and poetry that awoke delight ... pleasure in recognition, pleasure in strangeness.'[93] Over ten years later, her thoughts were much the same. As she wrote in 2009, the year she turned eighty: 'Wherever I turn these days, I'm looking, from the corner of my eye, for a certain kind of poetry whose balance of dread and beauty is equal to the balance of chaotic negations that pursue us ... A complex, dialogic, coherent poetry to dissolve both complacency and despair.'[94]

However, while engagement in the political may offer individuals some form of transcendence of their isolation, or at least a sense of meaning to life beyond the purely personal, it too can let us down, begetting its own forms of anguish. Confronting complacency and dissolving despair was what women's liberation set out to do over forty years ago. The 'personal is political' became a key axiom of the movement in the 1970s, though hardly one that has survived as an unambiguous unifier. At first, it meant the spotlight of political analysis was to be shone on shared confusions, constraints and troubles in women's personal lives. Later it was suborned as an entitlement to individual satisfaction, or mocked in the sale of Liberty lifestyle accessories – whether as the Faveo 'freedom bra', or liberty footwear or belts for women. It is a more challenging question to wonder whether, as Rich hoped, the political can remain a way of guiding one's life to the end, encouraging us as best we can to support struggles for social justice and, in the process, helping us to maintain meaningful ties to others.

The American feminist and full-time activist Carol Hanisch is generally taken to have coined the phrase 'the personal is political' in her 1969 paper of the same name. In fact, as she later pointed out, the phrase was not her own, but the title attached by others to a piece she wrote to defend the significance of 'consciousness raising' in the search for collective solutions to many women's problems: 'Women, like blacks, workers, must stop blaming ourselves for our "failures".'[95] Exactly twenty years later, in 1989, living alone with little professional, social or emotional security, Hanisch wrote to a friend about the personal costs of being an ageing activist in dispiriting times: 'I have had some pretty bad bouts of depression and burnout, and even sometimes when I've had to focus on just getting through to keep from going down all the way ... I know the panic and fear that getting older engenders – especially without money and family.'[96] At other times, she wrote, her political energy and focus would return, especially when new progressive struggles emerged, enabling her 'to present something more than a despairing, beaten down, aging feminist waxing nostalgically for the "good old days"'.[97]

Many other pioneering women's liberationists from the USA expressed similar sentiments at much the same time. Rosalind Baxandall, for instance, shared her disappointment with the political legacies of women's liberation in the 1990s: 'I never imagined twenty years of conservative rule, nor the steady watering down of feminism by professionals, liberals and self-help artists.' Nevertheless, the majority of these radical women, like Baxandall herself, conclude that politics had enlivened their lives and would continue to be 'a large part' of it, however arrested their dreams for change.[98] Moreover, it is still politics that deepens and gives meaning to their lives, whether animating them with desire, or with despair.

In October 2011, a fresh article by Baxandall, now in her

seventies, expressed a surge of delight as she reported back from visits to the 'Occupy Wall Street' protest, camping out in Zuccotti Park in New York. In it she voiced her unexpected hope that a new movement was being born, one educating itself about the causes of the banking crisis, knowing that even as so many North Americans had lost almost everything – their homes, savings, health insurance and jobs – the salaries of bankers and managerial staff simply continued to rise: 'At last the 99 per cent are shaming them', she wrote exuberantly: '*This is not a Recession; It's Robbery*, one sign read in the Occupy Wall Street (OWS) movement.' Suddenly, for many erstwhile rebels, women and men alike, public joy was again being shared. Baxandall captured what she saw as the renewal of her old ideals: 'The Occupiers have dreams and a vision, too: of a just, peaceful, diverse, democratic world, where democracy serves more than global capitalism and the greedy one per cent.'[99]

However flickering it may prove, Baxandall is thus one of a cross-generational multitude of young and old whose dissenting voices are being heard again throughout the USA. Having been influenced by the Arab uprisings in the winter of 2011, and in turn influencing occupations in other cities around the globe, OWS in its opening weeks not only managed to elicit a radical spirit cutting across generational divisions but, surprisingly, as the British journalist Polly Toynbee celebrated, quickly gained support from 54 per cent of Americans aware of the protest, and strong endorsement from a quarter of the population, according to a poll in *Time* magazine.[100]

Commitment to radical politics certainly has its pitfalls, yet it often turns out to be enduring, even when political hopes wax and wane as resistance is crushed and its initial impact dims.

This is confirmed by Margaretta Jolly, the British scholar who specializes in analysing life-stories. She has studied a variety of late-life memoirs, including my own, which suggest how fluid the boundary can be between success in the mainstream, involving consent, and participation in oppositional protest and dissent: 'People's stories show them going back and forth, often working simultaneously on both sides.'[101] Another practitioner of narrative research, the British sociologist Molly Andrews, also reported on the enduring significance of political commitment throughout the course of a lifetime. She looked at the life histories of fifteen men and women she interviewed, aged between seventy and ninety, who had worked for progressive change for half a century or more. With a couple of exceptions, these were not famous people, but ordinary men and women who 'despite, or perhaps because of, their advanced years' remained committed to securing social justice when called upon for support.[102]

All her interviewees had been active in the peace movement and several in the Communist Party of Great Britain. Each explained that, just as it always had, it was politics that still gave meaning to their lives: 'It gives you a motive for going on living. It's very strong. It is survival' (171), confided the peace activist and long-term member of the Communist Party, Eileen Daffern, in her late seventies. Others in their eighties were just as confident that socialism was a goal worth fighting for, fighting over, though knowing they would not see it realized in their lifetime. In the closing pages of the book, Andrews quotes from her interviews with the late Bishop of Stepney, Trevor Huddleston, who had dedicated his life to the anti-Apartheid campaign in South Africa, where he had lived for many years. In his late seventies he reflected: 'I've become more revolutionary every year I've lived. And certainly now, because life is so much shorter' (204).

The lesson that Andrews herself is eager to convey to her readers is that certain people sustain their radical outlook to the very end, whatever the obstacles, and moreover that, just as we saw with Adrienne Rich, it is precisely this fighting spirit that in turn sustains them in old age. Once again we can turn to another poet, storyteller and feminist heroine of mine, Grace Paley, for an eloquent reiteration of the theme. She also always emphasized what she had gained personally from her political commitments, especially the political ties that kept her in touch with a younger generation as she aged. Approaching seventy she reflected that being more than twenty years older than the movers and shakers of women's liberation, the menopause and the movement arrived together in her life, in the late 1960s and early 1970s, enabling her to savour the 'wild, delighted' activities of her many new friends in women's liberation:

> The high anxious but hopeful energy of the time, the general political atmosphere, and the particular female moment had a lot to do with the fact that I can't remember my menopause or, remembering it, haven't thought to write much about it ... I've asked some of my age mates, old friends, and they feel pretty much the same way. We were busy. Life was simply heightened by opposition, and hope was essential ... If I were going through my menopause now, I think I would remember it years later more harshly.[103]

A few years later, introducing an anthology of all her writing to date in 1994, Grace Paley again briefly surveyed her own life and work. The first piece of 'little luck' in her life was, she said, the way in which she managed to get her early stories published, when it turned out that the father of one of her children's friends worked in publishing. However, the 'big luck', as she saw it, had to do with political movements. It was the fact that before too long her writing coincided with and soon contributed to the women's movement, a powerful wave she felt added buoyancy, noise and saltiness to both her life and her work.

Again she stressed that her political writing and activism also meant she continued to meet new young people, on demonstrations and in meetings, little and large, whether in demanding play spaces for children or in coalitions for peace and justice. It meant as well that she continued to meet the same old companions who, whether 'in lively neighbourhood walks against the Gulf War' or 'in harsh confrontations with ourselves and others', managed to remain 'interested and active in literature and the world and are now growing old together'.[104] The collection is dedicated to one of those friends, the writer and fellow peace activist, Sybil Claiborne, whose black humour she had always shared, even as she lay dying of lung cancer in a hospice. This was a woman with whom Paley had talked and talked for nearly forty years. Three days before Sybil died, Paley recalled, 'she said slowly, with the delicacy of an unsatisfied person with only a dozen words left, "Grace, the real question is – how are we to live our lives"'.[105] Even at death's door, the question remains open until that exit finally closes behind us.

What was unusual about the old people Andrews chose to interview was their certainty that one day, however distant, their radical goals would be accomplished. Few of us share such certainties today, whether we incline towards French philosopher Jean-François Lyotard's radical suspicion of any application of universal standards and values, or are more in tune with the

German critical theorist Theodor Adorno's sense of the inevitability of tragedy in human affairs. Faced with the power and tenacity of the forces producing and sustaining continued inequality and oppression today, a certain intellectual pessimism seems hard to avoid. Nevertheless, a refusal to abandon some form of resistance to the brutalities of the present, and the determination to acknowledge the existence of those whose suffering is routinely ignored or denied, will always add a certain significance and meaning to life. Or perhaps, as Judith Butler pondered recently, on receiving the prestigious Adorno Prize in Frankfurt in 2012, it will enable us to wonder, even when nothing is as we would wish it to be: 'Can One Lead a Good Life in a Bad Life?'[106]

For certain, our political hopes may continue to be disappointed or defeated much of the time. Yet here again, in collective endeavours as in personal life, the conscious effort to understand and communicate the near inevitability of a certain tragic residue in the wake of political struggles helps keep us alive to life itself. Amidst much gloom, resistance has for some of us, and certainly for me, its own intrinsic beauty.

6

Affirming Survival

The real question is – how are we to live our lives? Many may feel that, at some point, old age makes that question redundant. I do not agree. It should be posed so long as we are still capable of asking it. The tragedy, however, may be that there is nobody left alive who is really listening to what the old have to say, especially for those without resources, if or when they become increasingly dependent.

For most people there is a considerable contrast between early and advanced old age, with the relative fitness and sociability of 'early' old age nowadays often extending through people's sixties and seventies, even into their early eighties, at least for those with adequate means of support and access to good healthcare. However, increasing debilities and at times comprehensive dependencies become harder to avoid as people move into their mid-eighties.[1] This is what is causing such political concern at present. The determined and continuing shrinking of welfare resources comes up against the needs of an expanding number of very old people. Providing adequately for the fragile elderly, as well as for those who care for them, is one of the most significant welfare battles of the moment.

Repeatedly, scandals reveal how lamentable is the provision

currently on offer, even in the most affluent societies that could choose to deliver vastly better services for the old and vulnerable.[2] In Britain the campaigning journalist and broadcaster, Joan Bakewell, was appointed the Voice of Older People under the last Labour government in 2008. In recent years she has stressed the urgent need for a more powerful post to be created to defend the interests of old people and deal with the 'national disgrace' evident in the continuous revelations of neglect in provision for social care of the elderly.[3]

Another well-informed social commentator, Yvonne Roberts, has taken up the baton, pointing out that 'over-sixty-fives are a net contributor to society at a rate of 30 to 40 billion pounds a year because they pay tax, spend money that creates jobs and are volunteers, carers and significant contributors to charity'.[4] The question any nation must consider is how to push for more comprehensive resources for its ageing population, strengthening provisions for care in the community for vulnerable old people in order to keep them out of hospital for as long as possible. Instead, the current coalition British government, in 2012, proposed to cut spending on adult social care by a further one billion pounds in the coming year alone. It is deplorable, and hardly cost-effective, when lack of adequate facilities to care for the elderly in their homes takes them into hospital sooner. At the same time, in a vicious cycle, NHS cost-cutting has disproportionately impacted upon older people, with more than half of hospital beds cut in 2011 targeting elderly patients, making it more likely that they will be discharged too soon and returned to hospital faster.[5] Meanwhile, those fighting to improve the care and services for the elderly come up against the orchestration of opinion, taking up the worst tunes emanating from the USA, pitting the old against the young and insisting the old have already appropriated a disproportionate share of resources. In reality, the same lack of adequate provision is evident in the USA, where the care of the elderly remains work that is both poorly paid and extremely stigmatized.[6]

There is much to say about improving the care of the very old, and a burgeoning literature addressing the problem.[7] However, in this book I have been mainly concerned with the ways in which conceptions of the elderly impact upon self-perception, sapping confidence and making it harder to feel that we remain in charge of our lives as we age. As we have seen, some of the main apprehensions expressed, especially in older women's writing, concern questions of intimacy and loneliness, although this is something many of us do not even dare to mention for fear of increasing the shame of appearing discarded and worthless. Added to the sense of isolation that can come from the lack of an intimate partner, there is also the narrowing of social horizons, especially after retirement from jobs or other forms of shared activities. We know that older women (sixty-five and over) are more than twice as likely to find themselves living alone compared with older men, while young men (aged twenty-five to forty-four) are twice as likely to be living alone compared with young women.[8]

It is true that being single when facing old age is not something all women lament, indeed for the most part older women cope with living alone far better than men, although many do complain about loneliness.[9] Nevertheless, it is certainly more definitive, irreversible, and can be more precarious than living alone when still young.[10] These days, living on one's own does not necessarily entail the absence of intimate, even erotic, ties.[11] But sustaining such ties into old age when living alone becomes ever more challenging.[12]

It is surely important to see that embracing life is hardly the same thing as avoiding disappointment, pain and sorrow, whatever our age, or gender. Indeed, as we age, it is often the reverse, even though 'happiness' is officially promoted as an all-encompassing goal, infuriatingly by the very same governments who are busy removing the necessities for living well from the poor, sick and disabled. 'Cruel optimism', is how the American cultural theorist Lauren Berlant summarizes the prevalent rhetoric encouraging everyone to remain attached to fantasies of the good life, especially in the USA since the 1980s. Because living well requires economic stability and durable intimacies, people's sense of personal failure can only increase with the growing precariousness of jobs and the shrinking of welfare entitlements, which are themselves rarely culturally acknowledged as sources of personal misery.[13] Indeed, the growing economic and social insecurity faced by so many in our time has been described as a distinctive form of social regulation produced by neo-liberalism, termed 'precarity' by European social justice movements fighting for better lives for all.[14]

Quite apart from economic survival, however, I have also repeatedly wondered how any of us can approach the end of our lives sufficiently open to the world to stay recognizable to ourselves and others as *in some sense* the same person we have always imagined ourselves to be. Ageing is hardly a straightforward affair, when just shifting from one context to another will always have serious implications for our ties to the world. Giles Fraser, for instance, illustrated this when he compared what were briefly his new surroundings in the *Guardian* newsroom in 2012 with his former workplace at St Paul's Cathedral, where he was the cannon chancellor before resigning following his objection to the eviction threats against the Occupy protesters camped on the Cathedral's doorstep. In the rule-bound, peaceful environs of the Cathedral, he reflected, he could develop an acute sensitivity to what he saw going on in the world. As a journalist in a busy newsroom, however, he needed headphones to block out the ceaseless hubbub. It 'would make your head explode' without them, which risks giving one a much narrower vision of the world: 'So the question is', he wrote, 'how to remain porous to its complexities without suffering the overload that closes down the imagination?'[15]

Older people are not likely to find themselves in noisy newsrooms – though they will be found often enough in hectic Accident and Emergency wards. Trying to ease life in line with one's capacities while retaining certain essential continuities becomes harder. Yet while we may be all too aware of the personal changes that come with ageing, we also have some other sense of there being certain abiding qualities that we possess, which can be disconcerting if others no longer acknowledge them, making it increasingly hard for us either to affirm them or even to recognize ourselves.

How to Live?

Just two months before he died in October 2004, at the relatively young age of seventy-four, *Le Monde* published a long interview with one of the most significant – if always controversial – philosophers of recent times, Jacques Derrida. Though suffering from pancreatic cancer and its treatments, he still remained enormously productive, even energetic; indeed, towards the end of his life he was more passionately and politically engaged with the world than ever before. In the interview

Derrida mentions the Socratic wisdom that to accept death is to learn how to live, and vice versa. However, he insisted that he still did not know how best to live, and could never be taught, because he had never learned 'to accept death': 'I remain ineducable [*inéducable*] with respect to the wisdom of learning to die.'[16]

Nevertheless, paradoxically as ever, to his many friends and admirers he had certainly learned how to live, and was still teaching them right up until his last breath, and now well beyond, even though he could not, would not, make his peace with the inevitability of death: 'It's terrible what's going on in the world, and all these things are on my mind, but they exist alongside the terror of my own death.'[17] One thing Derrida taught his many followers, especially in his final decades, was that one must always affirm life, or 'survival', and its unfinished possibilities, whether pleasurable or painful. Indeed, as he explained in the *Le Monde* interview, embracing survival is always as painful as it is pleasurable, suggesting that he was never more haunted by the inevitability of death than in moments of happiness and pleasure, while conversely he had been 'lucky enough to love even the unhappy moments' of his life: 'Taking pleasure and crying in the face of impending death – for me they are the same thing.' Quoting these words, Judith Butler joined the many friends and followers who mourn Derrida, mentioning the inspiration she still draws from him in her own scholarly and political labours. In one obituary she writes that 'without him, with him', what 'is finished and what is left to be affirmed is precisely the equivocation of survival itself'.[18]

It is indeed just this 'equivocation', admitting yet embracing what will often be the increasing challenges and sorrows of our longer lives, that I have hoped to capture in this book and will return to in this closing chapter. Perhaps we can all agree that affirming life is certainly far from the same thing as 'enjoying' it in any straightforward sense, and even less eschewing suffering, whether one's own or that of others. Rather, it is better seen as the capacity to feel and react to life, when sadness, anger or other negative emotions may often be the most appropriate response to what we experience or can comprehend of worldly matters, near and far. Moreover, as I noted in the last chapter when discussing mourning, it is the possibility of feeling *any* strong emotions at all that can often elude us, diminishing our lives as the years begin to flash by – a situation that is not confined to old age. Stephen Frosh notes this when he writes that '*any* feelings' might be sought after as an alternative to feeling nothing at all: 'the more intense and "deep" that feeling is, the more it is experienced as, in an important sense, "pleasurable" ... failure to feel sadness, like the failure to mourn, may be more disturbing than the state of sadness itself'.[19] Indeed, one of the intrinsic paradoxes of human existence, which we usually prefer to ignore, is that the most intense feeling we know, capable of eclipsing all others, is that of pain, beginning with bodily pain (the labour pains of child-birth come readily to my mind).

In a fragment of his as yet unpublished memoir, British literary scholar Jonathan Dollimore writes beautifully about his episodes of clinical depression, which made him reclusive for several years and cost him his academic career. He quickly adds, however, that given the government's denial of funding for the humanities – and the pressure on academics to downplay the importance of teaching in order to work on whatever might prove acceptable for publication in the most prestigious 'peer reviewed journals' – 'maybe I should say it saved me' from the complicities and compromises of professional success. But what he most wants to convey is his sense that the ordeal of depression and the realities of loss can also serve as a means of renewal, offering awareness of 'the many insidious kinds of deadening that life *in time* habituates us to, including professionalism'. Leaving academia in his early fifties, Dollimore started planting trees, and becoming more attentive to his new non-metropolitan surroundings. We are back with sentiments we have heard before from people finding ways of coping with change and loss:

> departure can also sensitise us to a meta-stillness within and beyond loss. There is the noise of life and there is the silence when life is absent. And then there is the deeper silence only to be intimated from within life, but at one remove from it. It's this I'm talking about: I hear it in the winds of March or in the stillness of a foggy November landscape; even in the stillness of the late morning in any season. It opens us to the silence of oblivion, Marvel's 'deserts of vast eternity,' in relation to which desire and individuation are an irrelevance ... We can die just by staying alive; living becoming a dying to life. Which means that if we do survive, we incur an even greater obligation to life as against survival: not just to stay alive but to stay alive to life itself.[20]

The sentiments are about solitude, and the affect of absorption into that 'vast eternity' is strong. But the feelings are clarified only by the words we find to reflect upon and share them, if only with ourselves – whether or not they make their way into any form of text or image, for personal or public use. This is because our ties to the world, and how we feel about them, even when experienced alone, are surely most easily maintained and their significance fully registered when we have opportunities for communicating them. As Hannah Arendt pointed out over fifty years ago, even our most intense experiences 'lead an uncertain and shadowy kind of existence' until they find their way into the public realm, usually through the stories we tell about them, or the ways in which they are registered by others.[21] For some, although I must confess not for me, or not yet, that public realm may simply mean sharing our thoughts with a notepad or diary.

If I am asked to list the things I see as the essential elements of a good life, all the usual comforting clichés immediately surface. Most of them involve the diverse gratifications of close amicable ties to others. At a minimum, a reasonable quality of life must include some form of recognition, respect and concern from those around us; better still, it encompasses moments of shared admiration, inspiration, laughter, joy; ideally, the satisfaction of what we can identify as mutual love, whatever form it takes. These ingredients inevitably sound trite, are never guaranteed, and are certainly always complex, perhaps even contradictory, especially when encompassing tales of love and desire. Many of us, myself included, know we will often have to make do with only remnants or memories of many of those things we have most cherished in the past.

I notice nowadays I have less to say about individual goals, and anyway, as a product of the 1960s, I always shared what was perhaps the conceit of imagining that my main ambitions involved collective struggles for a better life, a better world for all. Nonetheless, of course, personal ambitions remain, tied in with the enduring desire for the validation and approval of others. On the one hand, I know one sorrow that comes with ageing, often mentioned by others such as Beauvoir, is that there will be little if any time to achieve goals one might have hoped to fulfil, especially new ones. Although for me, and I suspect for many, such personal ambition really does seem to become a little less pressing. On the other hand, life is also more than the sum of our relationships to others, whatever their confirmations, joys and disappointments. I too know something about the many things that can, and sometimes must, be enjoyed in solitude, whether they involve intellectual work, sensual pleasure or erotic reverie.

At the most basic level, our sense of wellbeing begins simply with what the anthropologist Daniel Miller sums up as 'the comfort of things'.[22] Material objects play a crucial part in sustaining identities, 'things' have meaning, which is what is so terrifying about exile or destitution, especially in old age, or perhaps just removal into a care home, at least in most of the institutions providing such services. Looking up from my writing, for instance, I see first the colourful felt flowers given to me recently by my friend and colleague, Matt. Winter flowers, I call them, and they make me smile, all the more pleased with their effect as I have placed these cheap and cheerful knitted objects in the middle of a live plant, creating the most incongruously textured floral and live waxy leaf display. When people visit, I like to point out these fake flowers, hoping they will be admired. Our special relationship to things – material objects, sounds, texts, food and much more – can include all the challenges and pleasures available to the senses, whether actively producing or passively absorbed in music, dance, images, writing or whatever most engages us across the whole array of creative pastimes. But the delight we find in them, when we do, surely stems from all the joyful associations they conjure up for us from over a lifetime.

John Berger, that lyrical observer and versatile draftsman, now in his eighties, is still eager to express through text, drawing and photographs the interconnections between objects, places and people. His many books in recent decades, mostly written from his rural retreat in the far South of France, all elucidate how objects, and our attentiveness to the most mundane of experiences, as well as the most awe-inspiring, remain our keys to unlocking the past and its pleasures. They may also serve as triggers for reflection on the present, with its widespread political pessimism, continuing injustices and distance from the world many of us, and certainly I, once hoped for. In the lyrical collection of short stories gathered together in *Here is Where We Meet*, for instance, which is perhaps the nearest Berger has come to the autobiography he says he will never write, his protagonist, a man named John, walks alone through all the cities and villages he has most loved – from urban Lisbon to rural Poland. These stories allow Berger not only to depict places he clearly knows so well in the most vibrant and memorable detail, but also to comment upon their history, transformations and diverse traditions, while conjuring up dead people whom he has loved as they resonate with his latest experiences in each city.

In the exquisite opening story, set in Lisbon, it is a mother who appears. They converse lovingly as Berger depicts her returning, playfully, poignantly to haunt him while he recalls their conversations and quarrels, his own boyhood bravado, guilt and pride, alongside memories of her cooking, his favourite pastries, and her unassuming ways. It is the trams that bring her back, this mother of his who has been dead for fifteen years, and he has her explain: 'The dead don't stay where they are buried.'[23] Berger recalls the tram – number 194 – that he and his mother took every day when he was growing up in Croydon, South London. On and off those trams, now vanished from most British cities, he remembers how he would routinely contradict his mother's certainties, which he feared veiled vulnerabilities, hoping he could thereby goad her into displaying an underlying invincibility. Instead, he now realizes, his perpetual disagreement would leave her 'more frail than she usually was and the two of them would be drawn, helpless, into a maelstrom of perdition and lamentation, silently crying out, he now feels, for an angel to come and save us. On no occasion did an angel come' (6).

I think that angel does finally appear in Lisbon, as John wanders in reverie around the city. It enables him to imagine that he might make some deferred reparation for those wounds he knows he inflicted long ago. 'All my books were about you', he tells his mother. 'Nonsense! Maybe you wrote them so I should be there, keeping you company. And I was', he imagines her replying, but 'I had to wait until now, until you are an old man in Lisboa, for you to be writing this very short story about me' (41). Regrets? Perhaps he has a few, and they can be put to work in his creative labour.

Sometimes it is returning home that triggers the reveries connecting time and place, people and things. Here is Berger again, back in London, in a recent commentary reflecting upon urban life today, following the riots that began in Tottenham in the summer of 2011. He muses that for him, any moment, anywhere, has its joyful resonances. He doubts this could be true for the young rioters, urged everywhere to display their status through the possession of the latest high-tech and other commodities, while living without them, bored and near penniless, in the commercial noise of urban spaces. The free delights of an ageing man in rural France, he points out, could not be further from their horizon:

> The taste of chocolate. The width of her hips. The splashing of water. The length of the daughter's drenched hair. The way he laughed early this morning. The gulls above the boat. The crow's feet by the corners of her eyes. The tattoo he made such a row about. The dog with its tongue hanging out in the heat. The promises in such things operate as passwords: passwords towards a previous expectancy about life. And the holiday-makers on the lakeside collect these passwords, finger them, whisper them, and are wordlessly reminded of that expectancy, which they live again surreptitiously.[24]

Interestingly, Berger himself, like Julian Barnes, has always seemed to show considerable respect, never even a trace of horror, when pondering the process of ageing. Back in the mid 1960s, in his controversial book on Picasso published almost five decades ago when he was not yet forty, he wrote: 'There is not, I think, a single example of a great painter – or sculptor – whose work has not gained in profundity and originality as he grew older.'[25] As if to prove the accuracy of Berger's comment, throughout 2012 London was filled with the work of ageing artists. The year opened with tens of thousands of people going to view the work of the British artist David Hockney at the Royal Academy exhibition entitled 'A Bigger Splash'. The public (if not always the critics) showed near-ecstatic enthusiasm for Hockney's gigantic landscapes. The artist, at seventy-four, had made his way back home to evoke so vividly the Yorkshire he had left behind over forty years earlier.

The following month, at Tate Modern, a six-decade

retrospective of the eighty-three-year-old Japanese artist, Yayoi Kusama, was being summed up by many reviewers as magical and full of surprises, her recent work suggesting that she is today perhaps more in touch with current events than ever before.[26] Around the same time, London's Freud Museum was displaying some of the work of Louise Bourgeois. The most beautiful and memorable piece, 'The Dangerous Obsession', consisted of a blue figure cradling a sphere of blood red glass, made in 2003 when the artist was ninety-two. This was interpreted as the artist's awareness of the damage inflicted by clinging to past torments, while other late work seemed to reveal a shift away from a fixation on her father's bullying and philandering to focus more on memories of her mother's nurturing care.[27] By the summer of 2012, the National Portrait Gallery was exhibiting seven decades of work by the late Lucian Freud, establishing that the extraordinary portraits he continued to produce, right up to his death at eighty-nine, retained the stylistic development and technical virtuosity of his youth.

Looking at artists across the generations, one can find a continuous array of figures from Rembrandt at the opening of the seventeenth century, through Klee, Matisse and Picasso, up to Barbara Hepworth, Frank Auerbach or Paula Rego, closer to home, all working in new ways in their old age. Much the same could be said of various composers, from Bach who was still creating his complex fugues and canons shortly before his death at sixty-five, to Haydn who composed his two great oratorios *The Creation* and *The Seasons* approaching seventy, or Schoenberg, busy composing his difficult and haunting concertos in his seventies. I have looked earlier at the writing of various ageing authors. Any other list of writers might seem unending, but would certainly include William Trevor and Alice Munro, two authors in their eighties I have not discussed, though they are currently writing some of the most lyrical short stories available about the dreams, dilemmas and sorrows of old age.[28] In his eighties, and looking backwards, the masterly Chinua Achebe, who died in 2013, reflected on the traumas and legacy of the Biafran War over four decades ago. Toni Morrison's extraordinary writing, too, remains as vibrant as ever, her last book, *Home*, vividly evoking the strictly segregated world of the fifties America of her youth.[29]

Furthermore, what may be produced or consumed in old age clearly extends well beyond the potential pleasures of high culture, or any delight in surveying the sensual abundance of nature or of erotic encounter. Mass culture today offers infinite possibilities, especially in the virtual arena. In my view, we are lucky to be ageing at a time when there are ever-expanding online communities. In another of his texts on material culture, *Tales from Facebook*, Daniel Miller researches the impact of the global internet and social networking sites on inhabitants in Trinidad. In one of the twelve vignettes in this book, Miller explores the world of a once very active but now housebound man in his sixties. This man maintained his ties with the world and regained much of his former confidence through his communications on Facebook, telling Miller that through it he has been 'gifted his life back'.[30]

Miller suggests that, on the one hand, sometimes it is material possessions that 'can be made to speak more easily and eloquently' of a person's sense of who and what they are, and their relationship to the world, than can interpersonal exchanges. Yet on the other hand, he wants us to think more carefully about the possibilities of virtual communities and exchanges. Nevertheless, despite his keen interest in monitoring material culture and its uses, Miller also reports that in the thirty households he entered on a random street in South London his informants almost all tended 'to equate living alone with failure', whether single themselves or coupled up.[31] This equation of living alone to failure is a combination that is hard to dislodge, despite all we know about the fractures of intimacy inside relationships, which is a theme I explore more fully below.

How Queer Is That?

Most of my adult life I have lived outside the traditional family unit, trying to sustain alternative forms of intimacy. Some of my earliest writing explored and celebrated this new trend, beginning with the first book I edited thirty years ago, *What Is to Be Done about the Family?*, which concluded confidently: 'To call for the return of the traditional family is like calling for the return of the British Empire. Its time has passed.'[32] Some years later I wrote another essay about the family, inspired by Angela Carter's last novel, *Wise Children*, whose bizarre plot illustrated her desire that we could put families together from 'whatever comes to hand'.[33] Here are Carter's words: 'Grandma invented this family. She put it together out of whatever came to hand – a stray pair of orphaned babes, a ragamuffin in a flat cap. She created it by sheer force of personality. It is a characteristic of human beings, one I've often noticed, that if they don't have a family of their own, they will invent one.'[34] Would that it were so!

I was both right and wrong in my predictions about the future of the family, just as Carter's words were both exhilarating and exaggerated. On the one hand, surveys routinely reported in our daily papers tell us that only a small minority in Britain, just 16 per cent indeed, see themselves as part of a traditional family unit, that is, one involving married parents and two or more children; on the other, as I write, our current government's defence of this consecrated unit seems as robust as ever, with David Cameron, the Tory leader, still promising to legislate for tax breaks for married couples.[35] Many have indeed tried to invent alternative modes of lasting intimacy, but how easy has it been to sustain them?

It was an important question for Carter when *Wise Children* was published in 1991, as she had only months to live, and a young son who would need to be raised without his mother. It was an important issue for me too, having lived and raised my son in a collective household where we had shared domestic arrangements for almost two decades. However, attempting to create new and lasting forms of domesticity outside traditional families has never proved easy. Notions of shared housework, childcare and commitments to the wellbeing of all existed in obvious tension with ideas of personal independence, sexual autonomy and flexibility of lifestyle, not to mention the unpredictable dynamics of jealousy, resentment, competitiveness and envy.

As I explored in my last book, *Making Trouble*, and Michèle Roberts addressed in her memoir, *Paper Houses*, in the early years of women's liberation collective living was viewed by many feminists as a lifestyle that was not only more economical, but would also encourage the supportive companionship, domesticity and childcare arrangements that seemed most compatible with the community engagement and other forms of activism many of us pursued.[36] Such households usually tried to embody the type of egalitarian and nurturing communities we wanted to help to build, in what we hoped might prove a long march through all existing institutions to transform them along similar lines. Thus the majority of the young women and men I worked with politically in the 1970s and early 1980s lived in some form of shared housing. For many, including me, it seemed to work; at least this arrangement flourished during those years in which we were still young, and could all feel connected to efforts for promoting change in the world at large. It also lasted for me because I owned the large house I shared with others, and was never planning to leave it. Others lived there for only a few years, as alternative choices became more attractive, or as distressing forms of jealousy emerged between the women who predominated in that household in the 1970s.

However, no living arrangement ever escapes those inchoate needs and deep vulnerabilities emerging from our childhoods and shadowing any form of intimacy, and these are bound to multiply in confusing ways when living in more open and collective households, as new alliances are formed, or friendships fade. Moreover, it is obviously hard to introduce one's own distinct personal and aesthetic style in more collective spaces, except if or when some one person or intensely like-minded clique manages to dominate them.

Fascinatingly, the British historian Matt Cook, researching the complex history of 'queer domesticities' in twentieth-century London, reveals that family life was often far more makeshift, diverse and alternative than is usually assumed. Indeed, long before the legal changes legitimizing same-sex unions and parenting rights, some gay men, for instance, had already managed to negotiate complex household arrangements, involving not just shifting sexual partners but sometimes even informal parenting or other nurturing relationships. Nevertheless, in collecting accounts of the determined political attempts to establish collective living spaces among gay squatters in Brixton in the 1970s, Cook found that most of them were relatively short lived. Decades later, his informants reflected 'on their experiences in the squats with sadness, anger, humour, and sometimes a little embarrassment', even though many of these ex-squatters remained in contact and a few were still sharing homes with other gay men 'in a muted echo of earlier times'.[37]

Lacking the sanctioned expectations and juridical obligations of marriage, alternative living arrangements are intrinsically unstable, unlikely to survive shifting personal relationships or changing times. Like the Brixton squats, most of the collective households I knew declined rapidly in the 1980s. It was not just that careers, and ageing generally, tend to refocus and limit our objectives with the passing years, but also that youthful dreams of community usually encounter increasing obstacles – never more suddenly and dramatically than with the triumph of Thatcher's monetarist regime and the rising inequality of the 1980s. Obstacles, however, seem to come as much from within as from without.

By the close of the 1980s, with my son in his late teens and about to leave home, my shared household folded and I began living in a more tightly bonded heterosexual coupledom from my early forties. Fourteen years later, this cradle of intimacy collapsed, leaving me with the wounding shards of our broken romance. With the deepest expression of pain and regret, my partner of a decade and a half moved on. Being fifteen years younger than I was, he could all too easily imagine life without me, before long creating a brand new existence for himself, settling down and having children in his late forties. In my late fifties I was left aching and grieving for him, and the life we had shared.

For some years I became one of that ever-growing number of middle-aged women facing life 'on our own'. As another, highly successful, acquaintance of mine commented to her women friends soon after the departure of her own long-time partner for a younger woman: 'I went to the theatre the other night and saw in the queue ahead of me so many women I knew, all now single, and I said to myself "this is a group I never wanted to join"'. Definitely, a group she never wanted to join, but one many find it very hard to leave. Only a few older women seem to choose to join this group, but demographics suggest that the odds on most of them coupling up again could hardly be less favourable, despite, and I suspect partly because of, their status, charms and, by all standards other than youth and physical attractiveness. As I have mentioned often enough, many of the cultural stereotypes of old age remain distinct, and more damaging, when the focus is on women as compared with men.[38]

A further twist of the knife for many older women who find themselves abandoned is that it can be hard to stifle a certain sense of shame at their situation. Sharon Olds captures this exquisitely in her poem 'Known to Be Left', from her recent collection *Stag's Leap*, recalling the end of her marriage after her husband of thirty years left her for another woman:

> If I pass a mirror, I turn away,
> I do not want to look at her, and she does not want to be seen.
> Sometimes
> I don't see how I'm going to go on doing this ... I am so
> ashamed

before my friends – to be known to be left
by the one who supposedly knew me best,
each hour is a room of shame, and I am
swimming, swimming, holding my head up,
smiling, joking, ashamed, ashamed,
like being naked with the clothed, or being
a child, having to try to behave
while hating the terms of your life.[39]

Recent surveys of households in twenty-first-century Britain show that the majority, 56 per cent, still consist of married couples. The rest are made up of cohabiting couples and a tiny minority of civil partnerships (legalized in 2005), but it is single people who constitute the second largest and fastest growing domestic unit, with women accounting for 70 per cent of those living alone over the age of sixty-five.[40] There are many reasons why older people, but in vastly greater numbers, older women, and also gay men, live without partners or intimate friends from mid-life onwards.[41] The question is, can they do so without feeling diminished, without that feeling of shame described by Olds, when any sense of lack the single person might experience without another to hold, or to quarrel with, is made all the harder by a sense of failure at being identified as alone?

Shortly before she died Eve Sedgwick described herself as 'an essential, central member of a queer family'.[42] Was she fooling herself? Sedgwick also wrote about what love meant to her, speaking of the sort of intimate connection one can sometimes share with another, without which 'both your soul and your whole world might subsist forever in some desert-like state of ontological impoverishment'.[43] Sedgwick, however, was a much-acclaimed literary scholar and queer theorist, with a large and significant band of admirers, who are still mourning her years after her premature death at fifty-eight. I am sure she was indeed able to feel secure in her deep and distinctive attachments to her closest friends, such as her gay friend Michael Moon, in whose company she delighted, while also retaining the life-long commitment of her husband, Hal. In her middle age she lived in domestic harmony, sharing a house with Michael and his partner, which was only sometimes the space where Hal joined her from his house elsewhere.

However, household demographics tell us that Sedgwick's experience is far from typical, and I fear that forms of 'ontological impoverishment' are exactly what many old people do experience, although they might not put it quite like that. Personally, I do still live with a few other people, often eating together and sharing household tasks. But it is not the collective living of my youth, which is no doubt just as well. Moreover, it is not just my own experience of the insecurities of collective living that tells me it can be very difficult to establish and maintain queer families of choice. Such households rarely last for more than a few years, and barely register in surveys of household forms such as that mentioned above (being a mere 1 per cent of living arrangements in the official statistics on households in the UK over the last decade, 2001–10). The comfort of marriage, or long-term partnerships, in so far as they remain monogamous, is precisely that they usually remove us from the intense jealousies that always shadow desire, even if they inevitably moderate or dramatically decrease desire in the process. Disruption always threatens when other adults enter the space of coupledom, which is indeed a standard plot in domestic fiction.

In her latest book, *The Queer Art of Failure*, the American gender critic Judith (now Jack) Halberstam urges her readers to embrace failure. After all, as she summarizes at the close of her book: 'To live is to fail, to bungle, to disappoint, and ultimately to die, rather than searching for ways around death and disappointment, the queer art of failure involves the acceptance of the finite, the embrace of the absurd, the silly, and the hopelessly goofy.'[44] That sounds promising in relation to reflections on the experiences of ageing, for which Beckett's 'Fail again. Fail better', can often serve as a mantra.[45] In this text, Halberstam explores the magical whimsies of kids' films, teen comedies and other 'queer fairy tales' of and for the young. She uses them to further her well-known probing of the inventive failures at the heart of all gender dissidence (quoting Quentin Crisp's axiom: 'If at first you don't succeed, failure may be your style', not just once, but four times).[46] She also discusses the 'radical passivity' of female masochism, on display in literature, such as Elfriede Jelinek's *The Piano Teacher*, or in performance art, referencing Yoko Ono's classic *Cut Piece*.

Drawing upon the French philosopher Gilles Deleuze, among others, she suggests that the female masochist's apparent obedience here is also a failure to conform, concealing a criticism and provocation of women's situation within and outside language.[47] This is all interesting. However, there is a thunderous silence in Halberstam's celebration of failure, which is the complete absence of any interest in the queer dreams and refusals of the old, especially those who fail most flagrantly to age 'successfully'. This failure might entail the defiant rejection of all blandishments to camouflage or soften signs of old age, on the one hand; or the refusal to dress and behave according to what is considered appropriate for one's age, on the other.

Halberstam could, for instance, have looked at the old age of Brigitte Bardot, who has provoked intense scorn and derision by brazenly ageing 'disgracefully'. She is seen as 'letting herself go', refusing cosmetic surgery, while at the same time retaining the 'sexy' hair-style, make-up, and outspoken insolence of her youth. Irritating almost all of her potential supporters, she is passionately committed to animal welfare, yet so fervently anti-Muslim she voted for the Front National in 2012. In this, Bardot is at odds with the customary political conformity, clandestine face-lifts, and careful cosmetic enhancements of most of her contemporary sex icons, such as Sophia Loren.[48] Halberstam does point out that gay and lesbian groups and queer scholars generally have searched for different ways of relating to and caring for one another outside the 'disciplinary matrix' of the traditional family, yet even here, this does not take her to any thoughts on ageing. Nor does her writing on the uses of forget-fulness, seen as a tool for interfering with the smooth operations of the normal, take her there, despite those most troubled by their increasing forgetfulness being old people.

There has always been a political point in applauding certain forms of 'failure'. It is not so new to attempt to respect the mul-tiple diversities and deficiencies of most people's lives, as the frail but forceful voice of one of Halberstam's earlier compa-triots of the left, Malvina Reynolds, used to sing: 'I don't mind failing in this world ... Somebody else's definition / Isn't going to measure my soul's condition.'[49] Despite certain social mobili-ties at different historical moments, which have never reached most of those at the bottom of entrenched social hierarchies – least of all in recent decades around the world – power, prestige and moral authority, not to mention wealth, have always been stubbornly reserved for the few: or 'the sons of bitches' who succeed by 'stepping on you', as Reynolds referred to them, long before political correctness would have tempered her language.

But objecting to the narrow limits of conventional success is one thing; preventing the destructive impact of 'failure' on those judged as 'losers', especially when considering the sphere of intimacy, is quite another. Halberstam was among the small group drawing up and signing the manifesto *Beyond Same Sex Marriage*, who in 2006 hoped to start a movement calling for visionary, creative and practical alternatives to marriage, whether heterosexual or same-sex. They wanted to see public recognition of *and* state assistance for all existing domestic arrangements offering shared intimacy, social care, and support for dependent people, whatever the form of the household. Included among the alternative households they mention are those of 'senior citizens living together and serving as each other's caregivers'. Importantly also, they stress the need for 'recognition of interdependence as a civic principle'.[50]

Admirable as this manifesto is, however – and with some highly visible public figures such as Gloria Steinem, Barbara Ehrenreich and Cornell West in support of it, alongside numerous well-known scholars of all sexual proclivities – it has yet to have any impact on traditional family rhetoric in the USA. Indeed, it has yet to convince the majority of gays and lesbians eager to sanctify their unions with a marriage ceremony. It is easier for critics to express shock and alarm at the eagerness of many gay and lesbian organizations to enshrine traditional marriage as a priority goal, than it is for them to find any adequate way of creating better facilities for the majority of those in most need of care, whether inside or outside traditional families.[51] Meanwhile, the vast numbers of those living alone, especially among the elderly, may find it hard to locate themselves in this debate, queer or straight.

The lesbian and human rights activist I have mentioned before, Amber Hollibaugh, reflecting on her work for SAGE representing elderly LGBT people in the USA, argues passionately that the actual lives of older people have been 'achingly absent' from queer priorities and agendas. In her view, this makes it almost impossible for them to participate in collective activities: 'the progressive LGBT movement is shaped in part by this silence, this ignorance, and this fear of the old'. She points out that 70 to 80 per cent of LGBT people age alone, while urging that a movement once able to tackle the HIV/ AIDS crisis ought to be able to find innovative ways of fighting for the needs and desires of the ever growing number of older people living outside traditional systems of kinship and community support: 'It will require massive, effective, and powerful advocacy and education regarding the needs and realities of this diverse nation of the elderly.'[52]

First up, however, it requires the queer imagination to try to surmount its own obsession with youth and its deep fear of ageing – usually far greater, it seems to me, than even the fear of death, which it has often been far easier to romanticize.[53] It is clearly hard to form or maintain 'families of choice'. But perhaps it is true, as Matt Cook suggests in his *Queer Domesticities*, that at times the queer imagination may at least keep alive hopes for expanding the places and spaces where alternative forms of community and commitment might be cherished. Such at least was the symbolic weight, the wild hope and partial delusion, of the open, unfenced, alternative space created by Derek Jarman (with the love and support of many friends) in the home and garden he built and tended in Dungeness on the Kent Coast,

Prospect Cottage. This is where, shortly before his death, he was ordained as Queer Saint, one determined to encourage ways of questioning entrenched norms around intimacy and exclusion: 'My garden's boundaries are the horizon', he wrote, which he saw as contrasting with 'the castle of heterosex' and its 'walls of tears and dungeons of sadness'.[54]

The Strengths of Solitude

Images of those dungeons of sadness continue to haunt reflections on ageing alone. 'How terrible to live alone!', Michael Cobb, a gay man in his thirties begins his essay, 'Lonely', in the collection *After Sex*. Challengingly, he is explaining why he *chooses* to be single, now that his 'queer-theoretical self has crept' towards a place that 'others might call or presume to be [that of] the person who is lonely'.[55] He explains that his friends and acquaintances constantly express the desire to see him coupled up, no longer a member of that 'despised minority' of single people. I think he is right to suggest that this common attitude makes it all the harder for single people not to feel suffocated by the apparent pity the coupled up are likely to project onto them. In his view, couples need the safety valve of displacing this 'bad affect' onto singles in order to survive themselves.

However, in the face of what he calls 'the perpetual "*Sex and the City* panic"' over failing to find a mate, Cobb wants to assure his readers that 'The loneliest of us are not necessarily those of us who are alone but rather those of us trying not to be alone.'[56] In his subsequent book, *Singles*, Cobb expands upon his view of the inevitable 'fatality' of 'couple love', which he sees, provocatively, as 'an ideological apprenticeship in loneliness', since it calls for a kind of exclusive intensity that is almost impossible to sustain and hence always vulnerable to failure.[57] Cobb is right, of course, at least in the more limited claim about the possibility of a bleak loneliness that can exist inside marriages or relationships; agony aunts are used to hearing from women telling them: 'I am married but lonely.'[58]

As we have seen before, Cobb's views echo a claim made by many an ageing feminist, sometimes quoting Germaine Greer: 'Loneliness is never more cruel than when it is felt in close propinquity with someone who has ceased to communicate.'[59] Greer wrote this in her most famous text, *The Female Eunuch*, when she was a young woman, although as we have seen she remains publicly insouciant about living alone into old age. Less blithely, from New York, Vivian Gornick wrote of recalling past relationships that had ended because in them she had begun to feel 'more alone than when alone'.[60]

Yet while it is clearly a staple of novels, film, theatre and song, not to mention clinical case studies and family courts, that couples can themselves be lonely, bickering and destructive, it is rather different to ask, as Cobb does, whether it is really possible in societies as we know them to be alone, single, often feeling isolated (especially when older), but *not* lonely.[61] For as Cobb takes pains to illustrate, happy or not, marriage and couples remain '*the foundation* on which society is built – they are society's life support systems'.[62]

His question is, therefore, how or whether the person who rejects the underpinning of intimate bonding, even in its most alternative, open or fluid forms mentioned in 'Beyond Same-Sex Marriage', can be affirmed as genuinely part of the social fabric, whether as celibates, widows, or whatever. What Cobb seeks is 'a comforting, non-menacing, form of isolation', in which the solitary person no longer symbolizes a form of 'terrifying loneliness', and no longer confronts the ubiquitous propaganda – 'It takes two' – suggesting that the single person must inevitably, sooner or later, feel abandoned, deserted and lacking in what is everywhere seen as the only 'significant' connection to others: the couple.

One answer, as Cobb suggests, and we have seen others affirm, is to realize and convince the world of the importance and joys of solitude. He tells his readers of his solitary journey out into the awe-inspiring Arizona desert, to discover, like many others before him, the landscapes of the infinite unknown, thereby gaining what he writes of as a sense of 'the sublime'. It is in such places that the single person, however secular, as Cobb is, 'stares at a vast, oceanic, and religious distance', feeling a sense of immortality. Such images of beauty strike Cobb as in some sense 'divine'. At the same time they assure him that however difficult his life may be as a single person, and he agrees that it is difficult, it can also offer up a type of romance: 'that is not marked for tragedy, fatality, and failure from its beginning'.[63]

Many an intrepid voyager has set off in search of the life-intensifying experiences of solitary adventures, determined to find those spectacular spaces of isolation that can trigger a contemplative, even ecstatic, immersion in landscapes or other combinations of stunning silence, serenity and beauty. Or it may be forms of blissful absorption in music, sounds, or any number of overwhelming experiences that are sought out to delight the senses and, for a while, offer feelings of transcendence quite beyond material concerns. It is even possible, like May Sarton, Rosalind Belben or Jonathan Dollimore, to experience such sublime moments closer to home.

Yet, pondering these ecstatic experiences, it seems to me that even in the midst of life-enhancing solitude one is never really outside the social – though it is certainly the shedding of our awareness of the everyday that allows us to feel most confidently at one with the world. The very sense of being outside of our usual selves takes us back to those early encounters with the world, before we were weighed down by any strong sense of ourselves as separate beings, that is, before our conscious egos were formed, all too soon directing and constraining almost every move we make. Such total absorption is evident in the social explorations of young children, although in fact they are never truly solitary, and could not survive if they were, being as yet barely detached from the other, or others, watching over them. It was again Freud who emphasized the permanent traces of such experiences, prior to the capacity for conscious memory or language, leaving their indelible psychic residue that one way or another could always be encountered anew, as if for the very first time. It is this historical 'truth' of lost pieces of experience that is perhaps what seekers of solitude more easily stumble upon, bringing the return of those unknown intensities of the past.[64]

In a short essay, 'Alone', the much-admired Scottish poet, John Burnside, elegantly expresses some of this. He depicts his own intense love for, and annual treks into, the wild and silent beauty of the Nordic Arctic Circle, a place that seemed to him like 'the edge of the world', and strangely also, a place where he felt completely at home: 'There are places where we can make out the curvature of the earth and I always think I can see it out there.' But what is most compelling for me about his narrative is the wisdom he claims to have learned from a friend he made in the Arctic, with the very same love for the region, one who had actually moved to live there decades earlier. What you have to remember, this friend had taken pains to explain, is that the supposedly solitary existence of romantic isolation is actually the opposite of what it seems: '"Here, it's not about solitude, it's about having a real community. Once you have community, *then* you can be alone ... When you go out to the edge of the world, you have to have something to come back to. You may not come back very often, but you have to know that you can. Otherwise, you're lost".'[65]

I agree, and this returns me to Cobb who, after completing his book, said he had become a more confident advocate for the possible joys of singleness, stating in his acknowledgements: 'If writing this book has taught me anything, it's that a single person doesn't have to be lonely, which matters because sometimes we'll each have to confront the worst heartbreak, in our own solitary way.' Of course we will. Yet, as he continues, when that happens, as it happened to him with the death of his dearest friend, Will Munro, from brain cancer in 2010, 'you're lucky if you can see and embrace the wide world of friendship, interest, work, pleasure, and love that might just help you not collapse'.[66] Quite! What we learn from his acknowledgements is another of the important, if implicit, aspects of his text. With or without occasional oceanic feelings of sublimity, what matters, especially when you live alone, is the support and love of friends, all those friends, he tells us, who were always there, and expressing their concern for him as well as for his companion, as he sat beside his own dying friend. Friends who will always be there when you need them, who are also part of a community to which you belong, are precisely what often becomes harder to find for many as they, as we, age – our oldest friends may depart or die, our elective affinities may reside with communities that have faded away, just when we are most in need of personal support. It is the calamity and cliché of ageing.

The Limits of Friendship

What concerns me here, therefore, is the nature and limits of friendship. Inside the sanctified region of the couple, whatever its joy, misery or extreme fragility, one knows one is allowed to love. This is the case even for the lover who lives only with the fear of perpetual rejection. We might recall the quivering worshiper in Barthes' fragments, *A Lover's Discourse,* where adoration is not only permitted, but inevitable:

> Every contact, for the lover, raises the question of an answer: the skin is asked to reply. (A squeeze of the hand – enormous documentation – a tiny gesture within the palm, a knee which doesn't move away, an arm extended, as if quite naturally, along the back of a sofa and against which the other's head gradually comes to rest – this is the paradisiac realm of subtle clandestine signs: a kind of festival not of the senses but of meaning).[67]

Potential lovers have something resembling rights, it would seem, even if it is only the right to live in anguish with or without the presence of the beloved. Outside the couple, the question of who one is allowed to love, painfully or pleasurably, is far less clear. What claims can be made in the name of friendship? How do we know what expectations are allowed here? It is hard to answer. There are no agreed codes of practice at all.

A friend can always simply take their leave, whatever our needs or expectations. One of the most distressing letters I have ever received was from a new friend, whom I was still getting to know when the letter arrived, having spent much of the previous six months in my friend's company. This friendship had brought a delightful, unexpectedly fresh energy and beauty into my life. But the letter conveyed sharp resentment at my expression of regret at the abrupt nature of the departure when this friend left for an extended period away. On my friend's side my distress sparked sudden anger, being interpreted as unfair accusation and unwarranted entitlement; on my side, there was simply the raw pain of what felt like cold dismissal. Who knows what histories of intrusion and rejection were being played out in that scenario; the point was that there was probably little that could be done by either of us to avert the clash within the shifting understandings of friendship. In most such instances there will be scant knowledge, on either side, of the largely unconscious dynamics in play.

I know that this conundrum over being allowed any 'right to intimacy' can seem a perpetually unresolved one for those living outside the confines of coupledom or close family ties. It creates formidable uncertainties over any form of entitlement. I have noticed that many single people keep their distance from any type of new close friendship to protect themselves from the possibility of any such hurt, whether caused by hoping for too much, or giving too little. Of course, everyone knows that there are so many different kinds of love, but they are perhaps less likely to reflect, as Jeanette Winterson wrote on Valentine's Day in 2012, that all our relationships are based on love of different kinds: 'If we could try to experience love as a quality – like compassion or courage – and focus less on love as an event, something that happens, then love would belong to us, rather than being dependent on us belonging to someone.'[68]

In his conversation, *In Praise of Love*, the philosopher Alain Badiou echoes some of Winterson's thoughts, though reinstating the couple as the site of 'love'. Disdaining what he sees, rather oddly, as the 'risk-free' commercialization of love in internet dating, Badiou affirms the truth of 'love' in the movement from the chance encounter to the challenging commitment of an enduring recognition and acceptance of 'difference' between two people, as each negotiates a shared encounter with the world, no longer 'from the perspective of the One, but from the perspective of the Two'.[69] Love may indeed be best seen as a quality of commitment, acceptance and enduring negotiation, but there is surely a little more to add when Winterson or Badiou, in line with many others, object to the commodification of 'love' today, certified by those flowers and chocolates expressing dedication on Valentine's Day. This is because, even when free from the taint of commercialism, love is surely shadowed by various forms of envy, dread of abandonment, and more, on the one hand; and constraint and fears of suffocation on the other.

This underbelly of love persists, whether we see 'love' as a type of event (the expression of desire, the occurrence of sexual activity, the declaration of strong affection); or alternatively as a quality of lasting attachment and care (trying to be always dependable, supportive, comforting, responsive, in sharing one's life with another). In a very brief meditation on the risks of love, Judith Butler agrees that 'love is not a state, a feeling, a disposition, but an exchange, uneven, fraught with history, with ghosts, with longings that are more or less legible to those who try to see one another with their own faulty vision'.[70] The archetypal bond of love, that of a child for its mother, conveys it all; soon enough the child will be caught between need and flight, even as the mother was perhaps once caught between fear and flight at the initial total dependence of the infant on her ceaseless ministrations. We could all love each other more, even that passing stranger, and the world be a far better, an unrecognizable, place. But who dares ask for love without fear of rejection?

As I see it, it is not just a horror of the pitying smugness of the securely (or insecurely) coupled that single people often experience. More importantly, it is a fear that any expression of love coming from those seen as old, however platonic, will be perceived as inappropriate, especially by new friends or acquaintances. For me, the safety of the couple lies very much in the protection it can offer from this sort of humiliation. The visible partner provides a shield that so many older women live without, however creatively they use their time.

The New York journalist Susan Jacoby recently reported writing an article that none of the magazines who usually gladly accepted her work would publish. It was called 'The Loneliness of the Long-Distance Woman', and concluded: 'Loneliness is considered somewhat shameful – one of the last social taboos in a country where people are willing to appear on television and talk about nearly every other form of intimate unhappiness.' In the subway and later in a farmers' market, she describes watching and subsequently chatting to a seventy-seven-year-old woman, whose husband had died three years earlier, whose children lived hundreds of miles away, and whose friends had moved to Florida or Arizona after retirement. This woman's loneliness was so profound that in attempting conversation with strangers she 'was willing to risk one small rejection after another for even the briefest moment of human contact'.[71] Solitude can be wonderful, so long as we have some sort of community that will welcome our return.

Fears of Dependency

We all need some sort of community to return to, if only because old age sooner or later increases the likelihood of new forms of dependence, even if only on the doctors or hospitals who monitor the functioning of our well-worn vital organs. As I indicated in my opening chapter, forms of dependency are a part of the human condition, and we only gain any sense of ourselves through our ties to others. Yet it is just those ties of dependence that we tend to repudiate entering adulthood in cultures such as ours, where what we are taught to value is the notion of autonomy and self-sufficiency above all else. Indeed, more than ever in these neo-liberal times, the idea of dependency has mutated into notions of psychological inadequacy, incapacity or ill health.

My friend Sarah Benton grimly confirms the shameful outcome. She was once deputy editor of the *New Statesman*, but due to multiple sclerosis has been largely denied paid work since her mid-forties, twenty years ago. She is sharp as a whistle and clear as a bell, pointing out that when you are seen as 'dependent' you are always in danger of being ignored, patronized or pitied, seen as having no secrets – this last, having secrets, being a rather essential quality of selfhood. A keen etymologist, she points out that the origins of the word 'selfhood' are 'to separate, divide off', to be an 'independent person', which is the clue to those ties between secrets and individuation, and the valid fear of loss of individuality if seen as dependent: parents / teachers / tyrants allow no secrets. As Bob Dylan once sang harshly: 'You're invisible now, you got no secrets to conceal'.[72]

It is this noxious slide between old age, dependency, inadequacy and invisibility that is surely one of the reasons why old people so forcefully insist that they 'do not feel old', making 'old age' something to be disavowed whatever our age. Yet the idea that 'dependence' may be a collaborative process is rarely mentioned. Nor do we often hear that it is quite possible for old people who require care, much like young dependent people, to give back as much as they receive, a situation best seen as interdependence. However, it is true that the process of role reversal – as the daughter or son who was once cared for must switch, usually in middle age, to become themselves the carer of an aged parent – can trigger complicated and troubling feelings. These will be all the more challenging if the earlier relationship with the parent was tense or ambivalent, as is quite often the case.

For those in need of care, there are often deep levels of shame, guilt and resentment if they find themselves in situations of extreme dependence on partners or children, when they may feel simply a burden on those very people whose wellbeing was always dearest to them. 'She is still young, healthy and at the peak of her career; she doesn't want to be looking after an old man of "ninety"', an ageing friend of mine (in his early eighties) laments. He is someone who has always been and remains hugely loved by those around him, a man of extraordinary charm, authority and charisma, but being at times barely able to walk of late, he can be moved to tears as he speaks of his dependence on the ministrations of his much younger, caring wife.

Challenging, even distressing, as these domestic situations can be, including the tough decision of deciding if and when home-based care can no longer be provided, the borders usually maintained between 'dependency', 'care' and 'autonomy' remain extremely porous. It may indeed sometimes be hard to see what recipients of care might give back to their carers, although very often the situation is more complex. As was evident at the close of Chapter 4, rewards may lie in unsuspected places in such relations. This was manifest, for instance, in Elinor Fuchs' *Making an Exit*, where she describes the final years of caring for her mother with Alzheimer's disease as the best years they had spent together; just as Ruth Ray suggested that her few years with her very old, incapacitated lover with Parkinson's disease provided the best loving she had known. Two leading social scientists studying the work of caring, Michael Fine and Caroline Glendinning, discuss these complexities in their essay, 'Dependence, Independence or Inter-dependence?'[73] As they and others before them have commented, politicians determined to make welfare cuts since the Thatcher and Reagan years have done much to extend and amplify the pathologization of notions of dependency, as well as the anxieties of those in need of care. In Britain, John Moore, Secretary of State for Social Security at the height of the Thatcherite drive against state dependency in the late 1980s, exemplified the move: 'A climate of dependence can in time corrupt the human spirit. Everyone knows the sullen apathy of dependence and can compare it with the sheer delight of personal achievement.'[74]

Such is the pervasive, pejorative rhetoric around dependency that some men – it has usually been men – have found a market-friendly audience in publicizing narratives of old people's remorseless decline into second childhood. We see this in a book by the American legal scholar, Bill Miller, simply entitled *Losing It*, which brusquely dismisses any and all possible affirmations of old age. Although himself generally fit, still at the peak of his university career, exercising regularly and often visiting his astute and relatively healthy mother, in her nineties,

Miller noticed that he is more easily distracted by ambient noise, and more forgetful, on reaching the age of sixty-five. Like Larkin, Roth, Amis, and other men before him, this leads Miller to insist on the unmitigated disaster of ageing. He labels those who mention any possibility of greater wisdom, contentment or wellbeing in old age as either 'culpably moronic' or purveyors of 'swindle'. One of the chief causes of Miller's lamentation is that ageing turns men into women, or at the very least 'neuters them': 'which is what old, even middle, age effectively does to males anyway'.[75] The 'culpably moronic' whom Miller names are almost all women who, like Laura Carstensen, are determined to 'pretend' that there can be a certain positivity in old age. They refuse to acknowledge the realities of 'demented' oldies with their 'sagging, rotting bodies', or to accept that to become old is to become 'dimwitted'. The merely moronic are those 'deluded souls' who reported in Carstensen's surveys that they had shifted from 'the learning of new things' to activities with others that 'deepen existing relationships' and enable them 'to savor life'.[76]

For Miller and his kind, the culpably moronic would include all those humanistic gerontologists whom I have mentioned in this book, men and women alike. They are all equally guilty of trying to 'delude' us in their concern with issues of wellbeing in old age, failing to insist upon the inexorable miseries of cognitive and bodily decline that so agitates these men. In particular, it would include his compatriot, the feminist scholar Toni Calasanti, who reflected a few years ago on her own career as a sociologist and gerontologist. Always self-reflexive, she pointed out that she had not only had to keep battling against ageism in society and in her own two disciplines, but has even had to combat it in herself. When first teaching a course on 'The

Sociology of Aging', she later reflected, she had avoided using the word 'old', encouraging her students to see 'older people' as just like themselves. She only later realized that she had constantly emphasized sameness rather than differences between the old and the young, reminiscent of the once familiar way of 'praising' a woman for being 'just like a man'. It seemed as if the only way to overcome ageism was to suggest that old people were not 'really old', but could be seen in some sense as 'still young'. In contrast with her previous practices, Calasanti now argues that such deliberate 'age-blindness' is itself a more subtle expression of age prejudice.[77]

In Calasanti's initial formulation – a reflexive way of siding with the elderly – we are all basically the same, and that sameness means we must all 'really' be young. Unwittingly, this is seen as the only means of avoiding the stigma of 'demented oldies' that others unashamedly broadcast. The British sociologist Molly Andrews, whose interviews with ageing political activists we looked at in the last chapter, had earlier made the same point even more forcefully in her article 'The Seductiveness of Agelessness'. Researchers on ageing, she argues, must resist the temptation of agelessness, suggesting that this denial of difference 'strips the old of their history and leaves them with nothing to offer but a mimicry of their youth … pitting body and soul against each other as if they were not part of one whole'.[78] Surveying the difference ageing makes will mean accepting that new forms of dependence are increasingly likely, without this necessitating the dread men have proclaimed, echoing Larkin's howl in his poem, 'The Old Fools': 'why aren't they screaming?'

Yet, for all the differences we need to acknowledge, denying agelessness should not mean downplaying the continuities, alongside the changes. This is elegantly illustrated in the

beautiful poem by Stanley Kunitz, 'The Layers', that I mentioned earlier. It was written when he was in his seventies:

> I have walked through many lives,
> some of them my own,
> and I am not who I was,
> though some principle of being
> abides, from which I struggle
> not to stray.

The poem concluded with the thought:

> 'Live in the layers,
> not on the litter.'
> Though I lack the art
> To decipher it,
> No doubt the next chapter
> In my book of transformations
> Is already written
> I am not done with my changes.[79]

Interestingly, Kunitz was a poet who had thought about old age
all his life, claiming that even in youth he always saw 'death and
life as inextricably bound to each other'.[80] Indeed, in his thirties,
Kunitz had written the extraordinary poem, 'I Dreamed That I
Was Old':

> I dreamed that I was old: in stale declension
> Fallen from my prime, when company
> Was mine, cat-nimbleness, and green invention,
> Before time took my leafy hours away.

This poem concluded with the stanza:

> I wept for my youth, sweet passionate young thought,
> And cozy women dead that by my side
> Once lay: I wept with bitter longing, not
> Remembering how in my youth I cried.[81]

At the end of his long life, we know this old man did, in fact, remember, at least some of both the continuities and the changes of his journey.

Most people are inclined to think of ageing in terms of the loss of power, or ways of shoring up impending loss. But things are not quite so simple, especially when confronting that devious coupling, age and power. It is from literature that we might learn that even in old age, even with extreme forms of bodily decay and facing death – indeed, beyond death itself – the old may still continue to exert power over those who have loved, feared, or cared for them. The maddened and dethroned King Lear is not the only patriarch in literature, and his fate required extreme and grotesque departures from normal patterns of familial interdependence.

Deliberately turning Lear's fate on its head, Mexico's best-known writer, Carlos Fuentes, one of the most revered authors in the Spanish-speaking world (who died shortly after I wrote this), published the powerful short story 'Eternal Father' in the collection he ironically entitled *Happy Families*, written in his late seventies. In this compelling narrative, middle-aged daughters, although all successful and financially independent in their different professions, have continued to abide by their father's characteristically tyrannical wishes right up to and now long after their father's death, agreeing to meet up once a year as their father had ordered them to do in his will, in order to gain their inheritance. None of them wishes to do this, nor do they need his money, yet they cannot escape his legacy, or envisage him as other than he was in his powerful prime. As Augusta, the sister who considers herself his true heir, reflects after the latest annual gathering is over: 'Let them run from their father. As if they could get away from him ... What an idea.'[82] The hold of the old on the young is not always easily shaken, although hopefully, as in Barthes' love for his mother, their enduring, perhaps even posthumous, power is not always so tyrannical.

Youth may be a cherished state many mourn, the object of unrequited desire, the image some wish to hold on to at almost any cost, as the leisure and cosmetic industries grow fat from our yearnings to appear forever fit and beautiful. Yet, compared with many of the young who currently face joblessness and other constraints as a result of the economic downturn, a significant minority in Western contexts have gained greater access to financial power and other benefits with the passage of time, and negotiated continued social standing in old age.

As we have seen before, it is thus the gulf between old people themselves that is so evident today, should we care to look for it. On the one had, 20 per cent of Britain's ageing population are living in poverty, suffering from all the related humiliations that amplify with ageing, with the recession thought to have had a particularly devastating impact on men over fifty-five, whose suicide rate has risen by 12 per cent over the past decade, according to the latest data from the British Office for National Statistics, while the rate among young men has fallen.[83] On the other hand, 25 per cent of people over fifty-five can be found in the top fifth of the population's income groups, many of them with access to the levels of control over their lives that money can buy and experience assist, whatever their needs.[84] The old are very far from all being in the same situation in their need for physical and emotional attention. Those in greatest need of care certainly include, but are far from confined to, the elderly. However, for those of us wanting to confront the most damaging clichés of ageing, we can at least begin by querying the cultural obsession with notions of 'independence' in favour of acknowledging the value of our life-long mutual dependence. This is the human condition. Recognizing it might help us to see that those most disparaged in the circuit of human interdependence, or worse, largely abandoned within it, call into question the humanity of all of us.

Saving the Moment

I have frequently expressed suspicion of claims that old people are no longer at the mercy of desire, especially sexual desire. It is a claim made far more often about, and indeed by, older women. However, the fact that it also reflects the drastic curtailing of choice open to older women, above all in forming new heterosexual relationships, accompanied by a clear cultural disdain for their physicality, suggested to me the likelihood of many women's self-protective renunciation of sexual desire in old age. Here, among other sources, I have dared to draw upon the evidence of my own experience, as in my late sixties I find that desire for the admiring attention and tender touch of another has shown little sign of abating. I also still often mourn the physical presence of the last person I loved and lost. Such thoughts come to me, especially, when I retire at night or wake in the morning. Indeed, I can tell when some new person fascinates me in the present, for then such thoughts disappear, and are replaced by others. I have been lucky enough to love and be loved anew in my sixties, in a relationship that continues to this day, although we live apart. As a few other women have found in old age, they have not only been able to love again, but to love differently, experiencing, as I have, new sources of erotic pleasure and satisfaction. A poem by the Black American writer, Alice Walker, now in her late sixties, posted in her blog in 2011, asks the question 'What Do I Get for Getting Old? A Picture Story for the Curious! (You supply the pictures!)'. These are some of her thoughts:

> I get to meditate
> In a chair!
> Or against the wall
> with my legs
> stretched out
> …
> I get to spend time with myself
> whenever I want!
> …
> I get to snuggle all
> morning
> with my snuggler
> of choice:
> counting the hours
> by how many times
> we get up
> to pee!
> I get to spend time with myself
> whenever I want!

...
I get to see
& feel
the suffering
of the whole
world
& to take
a nap
when I feel
like it
anyway!

I get to spend time with myself
whenever I want!

I get to feel
more love
than I ever thought
existed!
...
I feel this
especially for You! Though I may not remember
exactly which You
you are!
How cool is this!

Still, I get to spend time with myself
whenever I want!

And that is just a taste
As the old people used to say

down in Georgia
when I was a child
of what you get
for getting old.[85]

Interestingly, Walker's poems today could hardly be in sharper contrast with the sense of rage, anger, disappointment and betrayal that she once described as the experiences of so many young black women in her early writing. Back then, she wrote of women who were often caught up in the civil rights movement, as Walker herself was in the 1960s, and who suffered not just from the poisons of American racism, but from the intense sexism of the very men they tried hardest to love. Suicidal despair pervades this early writing. In the short story 'Her Sweet Jerome', the woman protagonist can never please the schoolteacher she married. As the husband reads his books, excludes her from his meetings, and beats her, she decides to destroy the thing that enslaves her by burning herself to death: 'she screamed against the roaring fire, backing enraged and trembling into a darkened corner of the room, not near the open door'.[86]

In her interviews over the last decade and more, Walker still passionately laments the injustice, racism and violence in the world, and remains an active protester, but the mood she conveys is very different. She spelt this out when preparing to sail to Gaza in July 2011 to breach the Israeli blockade and bring messages of hope to its besieged people: 'I am in my sixty-seventh year, having lived already a long and fruitful life, one with which I am content. It seems to me that during this period of eldering it is good to reap the harvest of one's understanding of what is important, and to share this, especially with the young.'[87] Walker knows something about the layers of deter-mined self-invention that boost her contentment nowadays, and so we hear nothing from her about the inevitable losses of ageing. Whatever these might be, Walker presents herself enjoying solitude, still engaged with the world, while occasion-ally able to spend time with her 'snuggler of choice'.

Clearly, affirming any sort of desire, sexual or otherwise, can prove a volatile, fragile thing, so I would always distrust any generalizations about it. Perhaps also I employ a more open and fluid notion of desire than others. I have little problem agree-ing, at least partially, that we may desire somewhat differently, maybe even less urgently, as we dwell in old age, especially if the focus is exclusively upon genital penetration, with all its symbolic excess. This could be why many older women, includ-ing some of my own friends, insist that they feel a new freedom from the turbulent sexual desires of their youth. In a letter to Freud written in 1927, Lou Andreas-Salomé commented on her own experience of old age, at sixty-six:

> I had feared that old age might set in too late (because speak-ing physiologically it had only set in at sixty) and that in this way I might be cheated of what old age specifically has to offer. Fortunately, I was able to capture something of it. And certainly, it did bring happiness – indeed, if I had to choose between the two phases of life, I am truly not sure on which my choice would fall. For when one leaves erotic experience in the narrower sense, one is at the same time leaving a cul-de-sac, however marvelous it may be, where there is only room for two abreast; and one now enters upon a vast expanse – the expanse of which childhood too was a part and which for only a while we were bound to forget.[88]

That letter was a response to an earlier letter from Freud mentioned before, in which, although only five years her senior, and responding to 'his dear indomitable' friend's birthday congratulations on his reaching seventy-one, Freud drew upon his love of Shakespeare to announce: 'with me crabbed old age has arrived – a state of total disillusionment, whose sterility is comparable to a lunar landscape, an inner ice age'.[89] In stark contrast, Salomé's description of the joys of old age, 'after leaving erotic experience in the narrower sense', and returning to some of the joys of childhood, but with greater independence, is certainly appealing. Salomé's own case, however, was surely unusual. In old age she grew closer to the husband she had married four decades earlier, in a relationship that was never apparently sexually consummated. Only after her midthirties did Salomé abandon her chaste but passionate intellectual friendships with men for a series of younger male lovers, first and most famously her two-and-a-half-year affair with the poet Rainer Maria Rilke.[90] These relationships, which were always begun and ended on her own terms, made Salomé an exceptionally confident and independent woman for her time, or perhaps for any time, as she dismissed the physical depredations of ageing for the delights that could arrive in ways that were 'new and unexpected': 'It is true that in all this the body, which in youth helped to build the bridges of love, grows constantly more troublesome, and remains so to the end, as an alien part of ourselves – confound it!'[91]

Such sentiments are very much in keeping with the *zeitgeist* for 'ageing well', evident, for instance, in the mood portrayed by one of Britain's iconic figures for acceptable old age, Joan Bakewell. Yet the contradictions remain. Launching her weekly column, 'Just 70', which ran for a few years in the *Guardian* as the twenty-first century kicked off, Bakewell asserted that, whatever your age, you are no older than you feel: 'which', she quickly announced, 'is young'.[92] Somehow, calmly accepting one's age mutates again into barely ageing at all. The same light, ironic, self-mocking tone pervades the very successful magazine *The Oldie*, in which, for instance, one typical cartoon portrays a young woman introducing her boyfriend to an old man flaunting Mickey Mouse ears and absurd teenage clothing: 'This is grandpa, he's having a late mid-life crisis.'[93]

As I have said often enough, any source of optimism in old age requires a platform of economic security and wellbeing, one that in the foreseeable future will never be the preserve of all in old age, even less so as cut-backs in care facilities and threats to pension rights continue to undermine its possibility. Meanwhile, and more chillingly, the main way in which longevity is increasingly culturally registered, when it is not being airbrushed away as some enduring spirit of youthfulness, is coupled with disability. In a survey of the representation of old age in cinema in the twenty-first century, but especially that of old women, Sally Chivers argues that older people must be presented as disabled to be legible at all as 'old': 'in the public imagination, disability exists separately from old age, but old age does not ever escape the stigma and restraints imposed upon disability'.[94] Looking at a number of recent films, including *Iris* (2001), *A Song for Martin* (2001), and *Away from Her* (2006), Chivers suggests that in all of them the cognitively disabled body comes to represent 'normative aging'.[95] We can now add *The Iron Lady* (2011) to this list, in which Meryl Streep represented the old age of Margaret Thatcher.

There is thus clearly a very fine line to tread, and one I find hard to tread even at the close of this book, in trying to

acknowledge the actual vicissitudes of old age while also affirming its dignity and, at times, grace or even joyfulness. As I have
mentioned, Beauvoir's extensive research on the topic led her
to conclude that the only way to age thoughtfully was to try
to hold on to those things that have given life its meaning –
friendships, group affinities, as well as former political, intellectual and creative endeavours or interests. This is a challenging
task, at times impossible. Friends may die; political contexts
change; creative challenges overwhelm us. However, Beauvoir
is on firmer ground when she continues: 'One's life has value
so long as one attributes value to the life of others, by means of
love, friendship, indignation, compassion.'[96]

Here, at least, I feel I can gain some foothold. Another of
my old mentors, Stuart Hall, addressing a rapt audience at the
celebration of his eightieth birthday, closed with some of his
thoughts on ageing. Since they summed up many of my own
meditations on the subject, I later interviewed him. He began
by saying that 'everyone expects us to become wiser as we
age, but that's not the case'. However, he continued with the
thought that he did often wonder what it might be that he could
pass on to anyone, knowing that the overall lesson of ageing is
that, contrary to everything we are taught, 'life isn't primarily
a self-project':

> The first thing is, as I've got older I believe less and less in the
> language of the independent self, personal achievement, the
> autonomy of the individual ... [In every sense] we are never
> self-sustaining but constituted by others who are different
> from us ... Another aspect of this is that I've lived between
> 'home', but where I don't feel at home, where I can't be home,
> and that place I 'feel at home' but which will never be quite

home. So I've learned not to mourn but to embrace displacement as a strategy of survival ... Secondly, I'm less and less
impressed by the singularity of my own contribution but
value more the many collective occasions when I've worked
together with others, whether in intellectual or political activities. I could hardly list all the ways these communal enterprises
have mattered, and how much I've appreciated the opportunity
to work in this way with other people. So, thirdly, I've come
to see how completely we are 'dependent' on others ... My
favourite example is Robinson Crusoe, a very early example
of the capacity of the individual to survive on his own ... In
fact, Crusoe could not have survived for a moment without
all the things made by others he scavenged from the boat. He
barricaded himself against The Other, especially after he saw
that footprint in the sand. But when finally he encountered
The Other he felt obliged to make some relationship with
him, though of course, good colonialist that he was, he also
had to subjugate him. Human life is dialogic – something that
happens between people.

Human life is about other people, both the contexts and the
ways in which they leave their mark on us. Hall's fourth and
final thought about ageing, though, concerns the continuities
that sustain us through time. For him, these have been and
remain those political aspirations that have guided him through
life, which, even in politically bleak times such as these, suggest
that change is always possible:

Finally, for someone who is committed to political and social
change, I am astonished, looking back, to find how consistent
I remain. I still believe that the poor should inherit the earth,

that capitalism is a barbarous way of organizing social life, that despite all its political complexities that social, sexual and racial justice is possible and worth fighting for. I think that while sometimes the situation looks extremely bleak – as it does at the moment – there are always what Raymond Williams calls 'emergent forces and ideas', which cannot be contained within the existing structure of settlements and compromises which constitute the dominant social order. Other wishes, desires, ideas and interests cannot be indefinitely contained. They will always break through in ways you cannot anticipate or predict.

Hall's words reprise my own conclusions about ageing, and I can see that I sometimes involuntarily echo him. Whatever our losses or regrets, whatever our continuing sources of satisfaction, pleasure or occasional delight, we can always try to retain and express compassion for the lives of others. In so doing, we will be reaffirming, as best we can, the political and ethical outlooks that have most often helped us make sense of the world, and that keep us close to those remaining friends and companions who share our concerns, in whatever form they appear and change across the decades. So long as our ethical imagination survives, we remain attached to the world, although where, how, and with what consequence we communicate our views will surely shift with the passing years. These are my thoughts as I end this book, still looking out for others, of whatever age, who wonder whether some of their transformative visions of the past, looked at critically anew, just might be put to use to help them imagine different futures from the ominous one that seems most likely at present.

For both personal and political reasons, in old age we are unlikely to retain the confidence of those youthful dreams we might have had of leaving our collective mark on the future. Apart from all the obstacles we have encountered, with age we usually become more aware of, and prepared to admit, just how much we fail to understand the complexities of power bearing down on any who challenge its manifest operations, not to mention its largely hidden ones. We will no longer be significant catalysts for envisioning the future, if indeed we ever were. Yet we can still feel our lives have meaning in so far as we are collecting up, contemplating and perhaps even communicating something about the past, and the aspirations we once shared. One way or another, ageing should encourage us to live more in the moment, salvaging what we can from where we have been. The quality of affirming the moment is perhaps what the Italian philosopher Giorgio Agamben alludes to when he writes of 'the time of the now' in his book *The Time That Remains*.[97] For Agamben, attending to the time of the now means seeing that which is itself outside of chronological time, a form of politics that means attending to the possibilities of life itself, 'a life for which what is at stake in its way of living is living itself'.[98] Agamben's messianic reflections on the possibilities of 'life itself', however, hardly tell us what it is about living we might most want to savour, politically or otherwise.

Here I can only speak personally. Part of my life's ambition, or at least the better part of it, has been dedicated to trying to work for greater equality overall and increased democratic accountability, seeing feminism as a key player in the process. Today, I can see the significant changes that feminism helped to introduce in making the world a less harsh, less confusing, and more fulfilling place for many women, raising people's awareness of sexual oppression, domestic violence and the exclusion of women as significant players in cultural, political and economic life. I see also what has worsened. At the vulnerable end of old class, ethnic and geographical hierarchies, both women and men have crashed to the bottom of that deepening chasm between rich and poor, while unfettered market forces have been allowed, even encouraged or forced, to erode workers' rights, and been given greater leverage in the public sector. I can register as well the connection between what we have won, and what we have lost.

Failing to see any rainbow on the horizon, and knowing the brutal forces protecting every pot of gold, how do we nurture any hope for better times? In another of his recent books, *Bento's Sketchbook*, John Berger contemplates the futility of words, or even actions, now that 'democracy and the free market have fused into a single predatory organism with a thin constricted imagination that revolves almost entirely around the idea of maximizing profit'. In this situation, he suggests, the first thing to do is to accept that our actions may indeed be 'inconsequential' in altering the shape of the future, certainly in producing a future that is truly close to our heart's desire.

Nevertheless, Berger also sums up my own thoughts nicely when he writes: 'One protests because not to protest would be too humiliating, too diminishing, too deadly. One protests ... in order to *save the present moment*, whatever the future holds.'[99] This is why living in the present is best seen as also living within or staying in some sense connected to our pasts, remaining true to their trampled hopes, whatever the current terrain. It returns me again to the thought that there can be beauty in the tragic, at least when loss arrives without malice, brutality or personal fallibility, whatever the suffering. I see this in the poetry of Denise Riley, mourning the sudden and unexpected death of her son Jacob, at thirty-seven. With his death, she says, time stopped in its flow: 'For I don't experience him as in the least dead, but simply as away … Perhaps only through forgetting the dead could one allow them to become dead. To finally be dead.' 'Meanwhile', she writes, 'I'll try to incorporate J's best qualities of easy friendliness….' Nevertheless, she does wonder, 'By what means are we ever to become reattached to the world?'[100]

Perhaps we cannot anticipate what will reattach us to the world. Any account of coming to terms with age will be a very personal one, with endless stories that could be told and which, maybe today, are just a little more likely to be heard. Attempting to review my own experience so far seems like tempting fate, if not hubristic. It is bound to be partial and somewhat fragile or fleeting. In what still feels like early old age I know I am lucky in so many ways, free from financial hardship and able to keep doing things I enjoy. Occasionally I still receive requests that, surprisingly, seem to point me along slightly different tracks, leading off from ones I have followed in the past. Thus, I know that at least for now I am fortunate enough to remain one of the older generation with what I like to hope is the extraordinary privilege of still having some time in which to think, write and act, in ways that can take me once more out into the world, to listen and to learn about what is happening in places I have long cared about. This also enables me to keep dreaming of opening doors to encourage more communication across the generations, which is more than enough sustenance, for now.

Notes

Chapter 1. How Old Am I?

1 See 'The Ageing Population', Briefing Paper, available at www. parliament.uk.

2 National Institute on Aging (NIA), *Older Amercians: 2012*, available at www.agingstats.gov.

3 Conal Urquhart, 'Archbishop of Canterbury criticises contempt and abuse of elderly people', *Observer*, 15 December 2012.

4 Martin Knapp and Martin Prince, *Dementia UK*, London, Alzheimer's Society, 2007. Interestingly, some of those afflicted have even begun speaking for themselves, including the American author Thomas DeBaggio, in *Losing My Mind: An Intimate Look at Life with Alzheimer's*, New York and London, The Free Press, 2003.

5 D. W. Winnicott, *Home is Where we Start From: Essays by a Psychoanalyst*, Harmondsworth, Penguin, 1986.

6 Stanley Kunitz, 'The Layers', in *The Poems of Stanley Kunitz: 1928–1978*, Boston, Little Brown and Co., 1979, p. 36.

7 Virginia Woolf, *The Diary of Virginia Woolf, Vol.4, 1931–35*, Harmondsworth, Penguin, 1983, p. 63.

8 Paul Thompson, Catherine Itzin and Michele Abendstern, *I Don't Feel Old: The Experience of Later Life*, Oxford, Oxford University Press, 1990.

9   Ronald Blythe, *The View in Winter: Reflections on Old Age*, Norwich, Canterbury Press, 2005, pp. 226, 228.

10   Lewis Wolpert, *You're Looking Very Well: The Surprising Nature of Getting Old*, London, Faber and Faber, 2011, p. 1.

11   Simone de Beauvoir, *Force of Circumstance*, Harmondsworth, Penguin, 1968, p. 672.

12   Ibid., p. 673.

13   Alison Lurie, 'The day I threw away fashion' *Guardian*, 15 April 2009.

14   Beauvoir, *Force of Circumstance*, p. 673.

15   Simone de Beauvoir, 'Today I've changed – I've really become a feminist', *Seven Days*, 8 March 1972, p. 3.

16   Simone de Beauvoir, *La Vieillesse*, Paris, Gallimard, 1970, first translated into English as *The Coming of Age*.

17   Simone de Beauvoir, *The Coming of Age*, trans. Patrick O'Brian, New York, Putnam, 1972, p. 5.

18   Beauvoir, *Force of Circumstance*, p. 656.

19   Simone de Beauvoir, *The Second Sex*, trans. H. M. Parshley, Picador, London, 1988, p. 295.

20   Beauvoir, *All Said and Done*, New York, Paragon House, 1993, pp. 63–4.

21   See Sheila Rowbotham's chapter, 'The 1970s', in her *A Century of Women*, London, Viking, 1997, p. 402.

22   Sue O'Sullivan, 'Menopause Waltz', in *I Used to be a Nice Girl*, London, Cassell, 1996, p. 62.

23   Vivian Sobchack, 'Cinema, Surgery, and Special Effects', in *Carnal Thoughts: Embodiment and Moving Image Culture*, Berkeley, CA, University of California Press, 2004, p. 38.

24   William Burroughs, *Ghost of Chance*, London, Serpent's Tail, 2002, p. 17.

25   Sidonie-Gabrielle Colette, *Chéri*, London, Vintage, 2001 [1920], p. 88.

26   Susan Sontag, 'The Double Standard of Aging', *Saturday Review*, September 1972, p. 37.

27   Meg Stacey, 'Older Women and Feminism: A note about my experience of the WLM', *Feminist Review* 31 (1989), pp. 140–2.
28   Barbara MacDonald, from her 1985 speech, 'Outside the Sisterhood: Ageism in Women's Studies', in Thomas Cole and Mary Winkler, eds, *The Oxford Book of Aging: Reflections on the Journey of Life*, Oxford and New York, Oxford University Press, 1994, pp. 118–20. See also Barbara Macdonald and Cynthia Rich, *Look Me in the Eye: Old Women, Aging and Ageism*, San Francisco, CA, Spinsters Ink, 1983.
29   Margaret Morganroth Gullette, *Declining to Decline: Cultural Combat and the Politics of Midlife*, London, University of Press of Virginia, 1997.
30   Margaret Morganroth Gullette, *Aged by Culture*, Chicago and London, University of Chicago Press, 2004, p. 137.
31   Gullette, *Declining to Decline*, pp. 6–7.
32   Kathleen Woodward, 'Introduction', in Kathleen Woodward, ed., *Figuring Age: Women, Bodies, Generations*, Bloomington, IN, Indiana University Press, 1999, p. xi.
33   Gullette, *Aged by Culture*, p. 111.
34   See, for instance, James Banks et al., *Living in the 21st Century: Older People in England*, English Longitudinal Study of Ageing (Wave 3), London, Institute for Fiscal Studies, 2008.
35   Stephen Katz, 'Growing Older Without Aging? Positive aging, anti-ageism and anti-aging', *Generations*, Winter 2001–2, pp. 27–32.
36   Some of those exceptions include Elliott Jaques, 'Death and the Mid-Life Crisis', *International Journal of Psychoanalysis*. 46 (1965), pp. 502, 514; Pearl King, 'The Life Cycle as Indicated by the Nature of the Transference in the Psychoanalysis of the Middle-Aged and Elderly', *International Journal of Psychoanalysis* 61 (1980), pp. 153–60; George Pollock, 'Aging or Aged: Development or Psychopathology', in *The Course of Life: Psychoanalytic Contributions Toward Understanding Personality Development*, Vol. III, ed. Stanley Greenspan and

George Pollock, Washington, DC, US Government Printing Office, pp. 529–85, as well as Hannah Segal's one-off case study 'Fear of Death: Notes on the analysis of an old man', *International Journal of Psychoanalysis* 39 (1958), pp. 178–81.

37   Sigmund Freud, 'On Psycho-therapy', in Vol. 7 of *The Standard Edition of the Complete Psychological Works of Sigmund Freud*, ed. and trans. James Strachey, London, Hogarth, 1953–74, p. 262.

38   Sigmund Freud and Lou Andreas-Salomé, *Letters*, ed. Ernst Pfeiffer, trans. William and Elaine Robson Scott, New York and London, Norton, 1972, pp. 165–6.

39   Hilda Doolittle, *Tribute to Freud*, New York, New Direction Books, 1984, p. 16.

40   Sigmund Freud, 'The "Uncanny"', in Vol. 17 of *The Standard Edition of the Complete Psychological Works of Sigmund Freud*, p. 241.

41   Ibid., p. 248, n. 1.

42   Stephen Frosh, *Hauntings: Psychoanalysis and Ghostly Transmissions*, London, Palgrave, 2013, Chapter 2, 'Facing the Truth about Ourselves'.

43   Freud, 'The "Uncanny"', p. 242.

44   Avery Gordon, *Ghostly Matters: Haunting and the Sociological Imagination*, Minneapolis, MN, University of Minnesota Press, 2008, p. 55.

45   Ibid., p. 57.

46   Mark Doty, 'The Embrace', available at www.poets.org.

47   See King, 'The Life Cycle'; Kurt Eissler, 'On Possible Effects of Aging on the Practice of Psychoanalysis: An essay', *Psychoanalytic Inquiry* 13 (1993), pp. 316–32. See also, Frieda Plotkin, 'Treatment of the Older Adult: The impact on the psychoanalyst', *Journal of the American Psychoanalytic Association* (2000), pp. 1591–1616.

48   Christopher Bollas, *Being a Character: Psychoanalysis and Self-Experience*, London, Routledge, 1993, pp. 59, 61.

49   Eva Hoffman, *Time*, London, Profile Press, p. 110.

50 Murray Schwartz, 'Introduction', in Kathleen Woodward and Murray Schwartz, eds, *Memory and Desire: Aging – Literature – Psychoanalysis*, Bloomington, IN, Indiana University Press, 1986, p. 5.

51 Jacques Lacan, 'The Mirror Stage as Formative of the Function of the I as Revealed in Psychoanalytic Experience', in *Écrits: A Selection*, trans. Alan Sheridan, London, Tavistock, 1977, p. 2.

52 Jacques Lacan, *The Language of the Self: The Function of Language in Psychoanalysis*, trans. Anthony Wilden, Baltimore, MD, Johns Hopkins University Press, 1968, see especially the discussion by Wilden, pp. xv–xvii.

53 Schwartz, 'Introduction', *Memory and Desire*, p. 3.

54 Herbert Blau, 'The Makeup of Memory in the Winter of our Discontent', in Woodward and Schwartz, eds, *Memory and Desire*, p. 25.

55 Alliance for Aging Research, 'Centenarians – the Ultimate Survivors!', Spring 2002, available at www.agingresearch.org.

56 See Nancy Lutkehaus, *Margaret Mead: The Making of an American Icon*, Princeton, Princeton University Press, 2008, p. 73.

57 Jane Miller, *Crazy Age*, London, Virago, 2010, p. 1.

58 Helene Moglen, 'Aging and Trans-aging: Trans-generational hauntings of the self', *Studies in Gender and Sexuality* 9:4 (2008), pp. 297–312.

59 Sarah Pearlman, 'Late Mid-life Astonishment: Disruptions to Identity and Self-esteem', in Nancy D. Davis et al., eds, *Faces of Women and Aging*, Binghampton, The Haworth Press, 1993, pp. 1–12.

60 Helene Moglen and Sheila Namir, 'Leaving Analysis and Moving Beyond Pain', *Women and Therapy* 32: 2–3 (2009), pp. 223, 229.

61 Penelope Lively, 'A Life in Books: Penelope Lively', interview with Penelope Lively by Sarah Crown, *Guardian*, 25 July 2009.

62 Penelope Lively, *Moon Tiger*, London, Andre Deutsch, 1987, p. 2.

63 Penelope Lively, 'A Life in Books'.

64 Diana Athill, *Somewhere Towards the End*, London, Granta, 2008, p. 179.

65 Doris Lessing in *The Sunday Times*, Books Section, London, May 1992.

66 Edward Said, *On Late Style: Music and Literature Against the Grain*, London, Bloomsbury, 2006.

67 Maev Kennedy et al., 'Gaza Freedom Flotilla Carried World-renowned Names and Veteran Activists', *Guardian*, 31 May 2010.

68 Temma Kaplan, *Crazy for Democracy: Women in Grassroots Movements*, New York and London, Routledge, 1996.

69 Anne Sexton, 'Old', available at www.allpoetry.com.

70 Anca Cristofovici, 'Touching Surfaces: Photography, Aging, and an Aesthetics of Change', in Kathleen Woodward, ed., *Figuring Age*, Bloomington, IN, Indiana University Press, 1999, pp. 268–96.

71 Alan Connor, 'Dead Popular', BBC News, 3 October 2006, available at www.bbc.co.uk. Thanks again to Sarah Benton, for so many things, but here specifically for drawing this survey to my attention.

72 See, for example, Chapter 6 of Stephen Frosh's *Psychoanalysis Outside the Clinic: Interventions in Psychosocial Studies*, London, Palgrave, 2010.

73 Thompson et al., *I Don't Feel Old: The Experience of Later Life*, p. 228.

74 Paul Taylor et al. 'Growing Old in America: Expectations vs. Reality', Pew Research Center, 29 June 2009, available at www.pewsocialtrends.org.

75 A contemptuous insistence on the unmitigated horror of ageing is evident, for instance, in the latest scholarly polemic of Michigan Law professor, Bill Miller. See William Ian Miller, *Losing It*, New Haven and London, Yale University Press, 2011.

76 'Five Minutes With: Juliet Stevenson', available at www.bbc.co.uk

Chapter 2. Generational Warfare

1   David Willetts, *The Pinch: How the Baby-Boomers Took Their Children's Future – and Why They Should Give It Back*, London, Atlantic Books, 2010.
2   Margaret Morganroth Gullette, *Agewise: Fighting the New Ageism in America*, Chicago, IL, University of Chicago Press, 2011, pp. 165, 182.
3   Pat Thane, 'The History of Aging and Old Age in "Western" Cultures', in Thomas Cole, Ruth Ray and Robert Kastenbaum, eds, *A Guide to Humanistic Studies in Aging: What Does It Mean to Grow Old?*, Baltimore, Johns Hopkins University Press, 2010.
4   See, for example, Robert Garland, *The Greek Way of Life*, Ithaca, NY, Cornell University Press, 1990; Sarah Pomeroy et al. *Ancient Greece: A Political, Social and Cultural History*, New York, Oxford University Press, 1999; Helen Small, *The Long Life*, Oxford, Oxford University Press, 2007.
5   Aristophanes, as quoted in Chris Gilleard, 'Old Age in Ancient Greece: Narratives of desire, narratives of disgust', *Journal of Aging Studies* 21: 1 (2007), p. 85; see also Barry Strauss, *Fathers and Sons in Athens: Ideology and Society in the Era of the Peloponnesian War*, Princeton, Princeton University Press, 1993.
6   Thomas Falkner, *The Poetics of Old Age in Greek Epic, Lyric and Tragedy*, Norman, University of Oklahoma Press, 1995.
7   William Shakespeare, *As You Like It*, Act II, Scene VII, lines 165–6.
8   See, for example, many of the essays in Pat Thane, ed., *The Long History of Old Age*, London, Thames & Hudson, 2005.
9   See Christa Grössinger, *Picturing Women in Late Medieval and Renaissance Art*, Manchester, Manchester University Press, 1997, p. 136.
10 Brian Levack, *The Witch-Hunt in Early Modern Europe*, New York and London: Longman, 1995, p. 129.

11 Deborah Willis, *Malevolent Nurture: Witch-Hunting and Maternal Power in Early Modern England*, Ithaca, Cornell University Press, 1995, p. 65.

12 Robin Briggs, *Witches and Neighbours: The Social and Cultural Context of European Witchcraft*, London, Harper Collins, 1996, pp. 260–1.

13 Susan Hayward, *Cinema Studies: The Key Concepts*, London, Taylor and Francis, 2006, p. 331; see also Richard Dyer, *Heavenly Bodies: Film Stars and Society*, London, British Film Institute, 1986; Christine Gledhill, ed., *Stardom: Industry of Desire*, London, Routledge, 1991.

14 Thomas Cole, *The Journey of Life: A Cultural History of Aging in America*, Cambridge, Cambridge University Press, 1992, p. 234.

15 See Gullette, *Aged by Culture*, pp. 44–6.

16 Mark Hunter, '*Work, Work, Work, Work!*', *Modern Maturity*, May–June 1999.

17 Mark Hunter, Margaret Morganroth Gullette, '"XERS" VS. "BOOMERS"', *American Scholar*, 22 June 2000.

18 Suneel Ratan, 'Generational Tension in the Office: Why Busters Hate Boomers.' *Fortune* 4 October 1993, pp. 56–70; Michael Grunwald, 'Trial by Media', *Boston Globe*, 10 October 1994, p. 31. Bruce Farris, 'All They Wanna Do Is Have Some Fun', *Fresco Bee*, 9 March 1995, p. 4.

19 Gilbert Dennis, *American Class Structure in an Age of Growing Inequality*, Los Angeles: Sage, 2002; Leonard Beeghley, *The Structure of Social Stratification in the United States*, Boston: Pearson, Allyn & Bacon; Daniel Weinberg, 'A Brief Look at Postwar US Income Inequality', *Household Economic Studies: Current Population Reports*, available at www.census.gov.

20 Brendan O'Neill, 'Baby boom … bust', BBC News magazine, 17 August 2006, available at www.bbc.co.uk.

21 Anatole Kaletsky, 'Crisis? Blame the baby-boomers, not the bankers', July 2010, available at www.business.timesonline.co.uk.

22 Neil Boorman, 'Did the over-45s Ruin Life for the Rest of Us?', BBC News magazine, 29 March 2010, available at www.news.bbc.co.uk.

23 Philip Larkin, 'This Be The Verse', available at www.artofeurope.com.

24 Phillip Inman, 'Baby Boomers are Britain's Secret Millionaires', *Guardian*, 28 February 2011; Christina Odone, 'Baby Boomers Made Sacrifice a Dirty Word – but the young are fighting back', 18 March 2010, available at blogs.telegraph.co.uk.

25 Robin Blackburn, 'A Global Pension Plan', *New Left Review* 47 September–October 2007.

26 Willetts, *The Pinch*.

27 Neil Boorman, *It's All Their Fault*, London, The Friday Project, 2010, product description on Amazon website.

28 Francis Beckett, *What Did the Baby Boomers Ever Do For Us?: How the Children of the Sixties Lived the Dream and Failed the Future*, London, Biteback Publishing, 2010.

29 See Sheila Rowbotham's *Promise of A Dream*, London, Penguin, 2000.

30 Beckett, *What Did the Baby Boomers Ever Do For Us?*, p. 6.

31 Will Hutton, 'The Baby Boomers and the Price of Personal Freedom', *Observer*, 22 August 2010.

32 These comments were all gathered together in response to Hutton's commentary, in 'Talkin' 'bout my Generation: Politicians and writers share their memories of growing up as part the baby boomer generation', *Observer*, 22 August 2010.

33 Marina Warner, quoted in Ian Sinclair, *Hackney, that Red Rose Empire: A Confidential Report*, London, Penguin, pp. 280, 278.

34 Ibid., p. 288.

35 Walter Benjamin, 'Theses on the Philosophy of History', in *Illuminations*, New York, Schocken Books, 1969, p. 255.

36 Pat Thane, 'The "Scandal" of Women's Pensions in Britain: How did it come about?', March 2006, available at www.historyandpolicy.org.

37 Beatrix Campbell, 'Don't Blame the Baby Boomers', *Observer*, 21 February 2010.
38 Larry Elliot, 'Right-wing Dogma has had its Day', *Guardian*, 6 September 2010.
39 Richard Wilkinson and Kate Pickett, *The Spirit Level: Why More Equal Societies Almost Always Do Better*, London, Allen Lane, 2009.
40 Marina Warner, 'The Baby Boomers and the Price of Personal Freedom', *Observer*, 22 August 2010.
41 Small, *The Long Life*, p. 272.
42 Thomas Cole and Ruth Ray, 'The Humanistic Study of Aging Past and Present, or Why Gerontology Still Needs Interpretive Inquiry', in Cole, Ray and Kastenbaum, eds, *A Guide to Humanistic Studies in Aging*.
43 Barbara Frey Waxman, *To Live in the Center of the Moment*, Charlottesville, University Press of Virginia, 1997, p. 2.
44 Miller, *Crazy Age*, p. 1.
45 Ibid., p. 7.
46 Penelope Lively, 'Shop till you Drop', *The Spectator*, 18 September 2010.
47 Ibid.
48 Harry Blatterer and Julia Glahn, eds, *Times of Our Lives: Making Sense of Growing Up and Growing Old*, Oxford, Inter-Disciplinary Press, 2009.
49 Giuliana Di Biase, 'Wisdom and Old Age', in ibid., p. 345; John-Raphael Staude, 'Last Works: The Late Life Creativity of Thomas Mann and Hermann Hesse', in ibid.
50 Elizabeth Wilson, *Only Halfway to Paradise: Women in Postwar Britain 1945–1968*, London, Tavistock, 1980; see Lynne Segal, *Making Trouble: Life and Politics*, London, Serpent's Tail, 2007, Chapter 3.
51 Adrienne Rich, *Of Woman Born: Motherhood as Experience and Institution*, New York, Norton, 1976.
52 See, for example, E. Ann Kaplan, 'Motherhood and

Representation: From Postwar Freudian Figurations to Postmodernism', in E. Ann Kaplan, ed., *Psychoanalysis and the Cinema*, New York, Routledge, 1990, pp. 129–42; Amber Jacobs, *On Matricide: Myth, Psychoanalysis, and the Law of the Mother*, New York, Columbia University Press, 2007.

53 Lisa Baraitser, *Maternal Encounters: The Ethics of Interruption*, London and New York, Routledge, 2009.

54 Kathleen Woodward, 'Inventing Generational Models: Psychoanalysis, Feminism, Literature', in Woodward, ed., *Figuring Age*, p. 149.

55 Barbara Mycrhoff, quoted in ibid., p. 166.

56 Mary Russo, 'Aging and the Scandal of Anachronism', in Woodward, ed., *Figuring Age*, p. 28.

57 Rose, quoted in ibid., p. 29.

58 Rosi Braidotti, *Nomadic Subjects: Embodiment and Sexual Difference in Contemporary Feminist Theory*, New York, Columbia University Press, 1994, p. 207.

59 Dana Heller, 'The Anxiety of Affluence: Movements, Markets, and Lesbian Feminist Generation(s)', in Devoney Looser and E. Ann Kaplan, eds, *Generations: Academic Feminists in Dialogue*, Minneapolis, University of Minnesota Press, 1997, p. 310.

60 See the essays in Looser and Kaplan, eds, *Generations*, ibid.

61 Carolyn Heilbrun, *The Last Gift of Time: Life Beyond Sixty*, New York, The Dial Press, 1977, p. 39.

62 Susan Faludi, 'American Electra: Feminism's ritual matricide', *Harper's Magazine*, 16 October 2010.

63 W. H. Auden, from his dedication to Valerie Eliot in *City Without Walls and Other Poems*, London, Faber, 1969.

64 Miller, *Crazy Age*, p. 99.

65 Robert Frost, 'Provide, Provide', in *Literature and Aging: An Anthology*, ed. Martin Kohn, Carol Donley and Delese Wear, Kent, OH, The Kent State University Press, 1992, p. 38.

Chapter 3. The Perils of Desire

1 Adam Phillips, 'Time Pieces', in *Side Effects*, London, Hamish Hamilton, p. 104.

2 Katharine Whitehorn, 'This Lopsided Mirror to Life', *Guardian*, 6 November 2010, p. 35.

3 Elizabeth Markson and Carol Taylor, 'The Mirror Has Two Faces', *Ageing and Society* 20: 2 (2000), p. 137; see also Sarah Grogan, *Body Image: Understanding Body Dissatisfaction in Men, Women and Children*, London, Routledge, 2008.

4 Simone de Beauvoir, *The Coming of Age*, 1972, p. 542. Further page references are given in the text.

5 Jaques, 'Death and the Mid-life Crisis', *International Journal of Psychoanalysis*, (1965), 46, pp. 502–13.

6 See Lynne Segal, *Slow Motion, Changing Masculinities, Changing Men*, London, Palgrave, 2007; Anthony Clare, *On Men: The Crisis of Masculinity*, London, Chatto & Windus, 2000; World Health Organization, *What About Boys? A Literature Review on the Health and Development of Adolescent Boys*. WHO, Geneva, Switzerland, 2000; The Men's Health Forum, *Getting It Sorted: A New Policy for Men's Health, A Consultative Document*, available at www.menshealthforum.org.uk, June 2002.

7 Stephen Frosh et al., *Young Masculinities*, London, Palgrave, 2001.

8 Susan Faludi, *Stiffed: The Betrayal of the American Man*, London, Harper Perrenial, 2000.

9 Gullette, *Aged by Culture*, pp. 82–7.

10 Gregory Gross and Robert Blundo, 'Viagra: Medical Technology Constructing Aging Masculinity', *Journal of Sociology and Social Welfare* 32: I (2005).

11 David Blanchflower and Andrew Oswald, 'Is Well-being U-shaped Over the Life Cycle?', *Social Science and Medicine* 66:8 (2008), pp. 1733–49.

12 S. Coren and P. L. Hewitt, 'Sex Differences in Elderly Suicide

Rates: Some Predictive Factors', *Aging and Mental Health* 3:2 (1999), pp. 112–18; Department of Health and Human Services, *The Surgeon General's Call to Action to Prevent Suicide*, Washington DC, 1999.

13   Christine Moutier, Julie Wetherell and Sidney Zisook, 'Combined Psychotherapy and Pharmacotherapy for Late-life Depression', *Geriatric Times* 4:5 (2003), pp. 14–15.

14   Lenard Kaye and Jennifer Crittenden, 'Principles of Clinical practice with Older Men', *Journal of Sociology and Social Welfare*, March, 2005, 32: 1, pp. 99-124.

15   Leslie Fiedler, 'More Images of Eros and Old Age: The Damnation of Faust and the Fountain of Youth', in *Memory and Desire: Aging—Literature—Psychoanalysis*, Woodward and Schwartz, eds, 1986.

16   Philip Roth, *Exit Ghost*, Boston, Houghton Mifflin Harcourt, 2007, p. 103.

17   Ibid., pp. 109–10.

18   Philip Roth, *Everyman*, London, Jonathan Cape, 2006, p. 130.

19   'Philip Roth', documentary for French television series *Writers of the Century*, 1997, quoted in Debra Shostak, 'Roth and Gender', in Timothy Parrish, ed., *The Cambridge Companion to Philip Roth*, Cambridge, Cambridge University Press, p. 111.

20   William Butler Yeats, 'Sailing to Byzantium', available at www. online-literature.

21   Roth, *Everyman*, p. 156.

22   Updike has his ageing protagonist, Ben Turnball, reflect: 'ferocious female nagging is the price men pay for our much lamented prerogatives, the power and mobility of the penis', in *Toward the End of Time*, London, Penguin, 1997, p. 13.

23   John Updike in conversation with Joanna Cole, 'Sex, Age and Underpants', *Mail and Guardian Online*, 9 April 1998, available at www.mg.co.za.

24   Updike, *Toward the End of Time*, p. 268.

25   Andrew Anthony, 'Martin Amis: The wunderkind comes of age', *Observer*, 10 January 2010.

26   Joe Brooker, 'The Middle Years of Martin Amis', in R. Mengham and P. Tew, eds, *British Fiction Today*, London, Continuum, pp. 3–14.

27   Martin Amis, *The Information*, London, Harper Collins, 1996, p. 62.

28   Martin Amis, *Experience*, London, Vintage, 2001, p. 64.

29   Martin Amis *The Pregnant Widow*, London, Vintage, 2009, pp. 3, 462.

30   Edmund White, *Chaos*, London, Bloomsbury, 2010, pp. 19, 20, 21.

31   Jeremy Laurance, 'Four in 10 Men Over 75 Say They are Still Having Sex (But Only Two in 10 Women)', *Independent*, 10 March 2010; Stacy Tessler Lindau et al., 'A Study of Sexuality and Health Among Older Adults in the United States', *New England Journal of Medicine* 357 (2007), pp. 762–74.

32   Linn Sandberg, *Getting Intimate: A Feminist Analysis of Old Age, Masculinity and Sexuality*, Linkoping, Linkoping University, 2011, p. 258.

33   Margaret Cruickshank, *Fierce with Reality*, Minneapolis, North Star Press, 1995.

34   Germaine Greer, *The Change: Women, Ageing and the Menopause*, London, Hamish Hamilton, 1991, pp. 2–4, 61–2, 433–5, 440.

35   Ibid., p. 435.

36   Gloria Steinhem, *Doing Sixty and Seventy*, San Francisco, Elders Academy Press, 2006.

37   Heilbrun, *The Last Gift of Time*, p. 50.

38   Barbara Ehrenreich, *Smile or Die*: *How Positive Thinking Fooled America and the World*, London, Granta, 2010.

39   Virginia Ironside, *The Virginia Monologues*, London, Penguin, 2009, pp. 74–5.

40   Ibid., p. 73.

41 Irma Kurtz, *About Time: Growing Old Disgracefully*, London, John Murray, 2009.

42 Eva Figes, 'Coming to Terms', in Joanna Goldsworthy, ed., *A Certain Age: Reflecting on the Menopause*, London, Virago, 1993, p. 145.

43 Karen Peterson, 'Till Viagra do us part?', *USA Today*, 21 March 2001, available at usatoday30.usatoday.com.

44 See William Masters and Virginia Johnson, *The Human Sexual Response*, Philadelphia, Lippincott Williams and Wilkins, 1966.

45 See Richard Lewontin, 'Sex, Lies, and Social Science', *New York Review of Books*, 20 April 1995.

46 Frida Kerner Furman, *Facing the Mirror: Older Women and Beauty Shop Culture*, Routledge, New York and London, 1997; Laura Hurd, 'Older Women's Perceptions of Ideal Body Weight: The tensions between health and appearance motivations for weight loss', *Ageing and Society* 22 (2002), pp. 751–7.

47 Tiina Vares, 'Reading the "Sexy Oldie": Age(ing) and Embodiment', *Sexualities: Studies in Culture and Society* 12: 4 (2009), pp. 503–24.

48 See Sally-Marie Bamford, report for The International Longevity Centre – UK, *The Last Taboo: A guide to dementia, sexuality, intimacy and sexual behaviour in care homes*, June 2011, available at ilcuk.org.uk; Alzheimer's Society, *Sex and Dementia*, available at www.alzheimers.org.uk.

49 Sara Maitland, 'Role Models for the Menopausal Woman', in Goldsworthy, ed., *A Certain Age*, p. 208.

50 Lisa Appignanesi, *Losing the Dead: A Family Memoir*, London, Chatto & Windus, 1999, p. 223.

51 Simone de Beauvoir, *The Ethics of Ambiguity*, New York: Citadel Press, 1996 (first published, Paris, Gallimard, 1947). As the feminist scholar Anne McClintock notes, Beauvoir always hoped to convey 'the perpetual dance of nuance and ambiguity' as well as the 'preposterous unpredictability in human lives'; see

Anne McClintock, 'Simone (Lucie Ernestine Marie Bertrand) de Beauvoir (1908–1986)', in George Stade, ed., *European Writers: The Twentieth Century*, Vol. 12, New York, Charles Scribner's Sons, 1990.

52 Beauvoir, *The Coming of Age*, pp. 290; 316; 319; 349.

53 Beauvoir, *Force of Circumstance*, p. 672; *The Coming of Age*, p. 5.

54 Beauvoir, *Force of Circumstance*, p. 297.

55 Ibid., p. 657.

56 Simone de Beauvoir, *The Woman Destroyed*, translated by Patrick O'Brian, New York, Putnam, 1968.

57 Reported in Deirdre Bair, *Simone de Beauvoir: A Biography*, New York, Summit Books, 1990, pp. 528; 509.

58 In ibid., p. 510.

59 Beauvoir, *The Coming of Age*, p. 348.

60 Alison Huang et al., 'Sexual Function and Aging in Racially and Ethnically Diverse Women', *Journal of the American Geriatrics Society* 57: 8 (2009), pp. 1362–8.

61 Doris Lessing, *Walking in the Shade: Volume Two of My Autobiography – 1949–1962*, London, Flamingo, 1997, p. 314; Natasha Walter, 'Doris Lessing: An Unusual Feminist', *Independent*, 18 August 2001.

62 Lessing's autobiographies are *Under My Skin* and *Walking in the Shade*; the novels addressing women and ageing include *The Summer Before the Dark*, *The Diary of a Good Neighbor*, *If The Old Could* (the last two first published under the pseudonym Jane Somers) and, most memorably, *Love, Again*, as well as in *Alfred and Emily*. See also a characteristic short story, 'Two Old Women and a Young One', in *London Observed: Stories and Sketches*, London, Harper Collins, 1992.

63 Doris Lessing, *Under My Skin: Volume One of My Autobiography, to 1949*, London, Flamingo, pp. 302–3.

64 Lessing, *Walking in the Shade*, p. 262.

65 Ibid.

66 Sigmund Freud, 'On Narcissism: An Introduction', in *On*

Metapsychology: The Theory of Psychoanalysis, The Pelican Freud Library, Vol. 11, Harmondsworth, Penguin, 1985, p. 95.

67 Ibid., pp. 82–3.

68 Lessing, *Under My Skin*, p. 205.

69 Lessing, *Walking in the Shade*, p. 130.

70 Doris Lessing, *Love, Again*, London, Flamingo, 1997. Further page references are given in the text.

71 Will Self, 'Young in all But Age', Review of Lewis Wolpert's *You're Looking Very Well*, *Guardian*, Review section, 30 April 2011, p. 9.

72 Billy Gray, 'Lucky the Culture Where the Old Can Talk to the Young and the Young Can Talk to the Old: In Conversation with Doris Lessing', in Mana Vidal Grau and Nuria Casado Gual, eds, *The Polemics of Ageing*, Lleida (Spain), University of Lleida, 2004, p. 88.

73 Ibid., p. 97.

74 Lessing, *Under My* Skin, p. 205.

75 Doris Lessing 'On Sufism and Idries Shah's *The Commanding Self* (1994)' available at www.ishk.net/sufis/lessing_commanding self.html.

76 Miller, *Crazy Age*, p. 28.

77 Paul Johnson and Pat Thane, eds, *Old Age from Antiquity to Post-Modernity*, London, Routledge, 1998; Edurne Garrido Anes, ' "Aware too late," said Beauty as she passed." The *Expiry Date* to be Liked and to Love: Some Medieval Views on Old Age and Sexuality', in Brian Worsfold, ed., *The Art of Ageing: Textualising the Phases of Life*, Lleida, University of Lleida, 2005.

78 Lindau et al., 'A Study of Sexuality and Health Among Older Adults in the United States'.

79 A. Nicolosi et al., 'Sexual Behavior and Sexual Dysfunctions After Age 40: The global study of sexual attitudes and behaviors', *Urology* 64 (2004), pp. 991–7.

80   Laumann, quoted in 'Old Age "No Barrier" to Sex Life', BBC News online, 23 August 2007.

81   Nicolosi et al., 'Sexual Behavior', p. 994.

82   Lewontin, 'Sex, Lies, and Social Science'.

83   Lillian Faderman, *Odd Girls and Twilight Lovers: A History of Lesbian Life in the Twentieth Century*, New York, Columbia University Press, 1991.

84   Maureen Duffy, 'That time of year thou mayst in me behold …', quoted in 'Older and Wiser: Carol Ann Duffy introduces poems of aging', *Guardian*, 13 March 2010.

85   Carol Ann Duffy, 'Medusa', *The World's Wife*, London, Picador, 1999, p. 40.

86   Lisa Diamond, *Sexual Fluidity: Understanding Women's Love and Desire*, Cambridge, MA, Harvard University Press, 2008, pp. 22, 161.

87   Ibid., p. 50.

88   Adam Phillips, 'Who'd Want to Be a Man?', *London Review of Books*, 19 June 2008, p. 29.

89   Amber Hollibaugh, '2, 4, 6, 8: Who Says that Your Grandmother's Straight: Enhancing the Lives of LGBTQ Older Adults in the Twenty-First Century', in Joseph N. Defilippis et al., eds, 'A New Queer Agenda', *The Scholar and Feminist Online* 10.1–10.2 (2011/2012), Barnard Center for Research on Women, available at www.sfonline.barnard.edu.

90   Joan Nestle, 'Sixty and Sexy', interview by Angeline Acain and Susan Eisenberg available at www.joannestle.com.

91   Joan Nestle, *A Fragile Union*, San Francisco, Cleis Press, 1998, p.10.

92   Nestle, 'Sixty and Sexy'.

93   Joan Nestle, 'Desire Perfected: Sex after Fifty', in Lee Lynch and Akia Woods, eds, *Off the Rag: Lesbians Writing on Menopause*, Norwich, VT, New Victoria Publishers, 1996, p. 81.

94   June Arnold, *Sister Gin*, Plainfield, Vermont, Daughter's Inc., 1975, pp. 70, 129.

95 Ibid., p. 189.

96 See, for instance, Adrienne Rich, 'And Now', *Dark Fields of the Republic: Poems, 1991–1995*, New York, Norton, 1995.

97 Adrienne Rich, 'Memorize This', available at www.aprweb.org.

98 Seamus Heaney, *The Human Chain*, London, Faber and Faber, 2011, p.12.

99 Hortense Calisher, *Age: A Love Story*, New York, London, Marion Boyars, 1996, pp. 7, 8.

100 Ibid., p. 128.

101 Stanley Fish, *Is There a Text in This Class?: The Authority of Interpretive Communities*, Cambridge, MA, Harvard University Press, 1980.

102 Grace Paley, 'Goodbye and Good Luck', in *The Little Disturbances of Man*, New York, New American Library, 1973, p. 9.

103 Ibid., p. 18.

104 Grace Paley, in Grace Paley and Robert Nichols, 'Here', *Here and Somewhere Else: Stories and Poems*, New York, *The Feminist* Press, 2007, p. 46.

105 Diana Athill, *Somewhere Towards the End*, London, Granta, 2008, p. 35.

106 Ibid., pp. 31, 84–5.

Chapter 4. The Ties That Bind

1 Lisa Baraitser, *Maternal Encounters: The Ethics of Interruption*, London, Routledge, 2008, p. 66.

2 Mark Doty, *Dog Years*, London, Jonathan Cape, 2008.

3 May Sarton, *The House by the Sea: A Journal*, New York, Norton, 1977.

4 May Sarton, *Journal of a Solitude*, New York, Norton, 1973, p. 6.

5   Sarton, *House by the Sea*, p. 221.

6   May Sarton, quoted in Silvia Henneberg, *The Creative Crone: Aging and the Poetry of May Sarton and Adrienne Rich*, Columbia, University of Missouri Press, 2010, p. 9.

7   May Sarton, *As We Are Now*, London, The Women's Press, 1983.

8   Kathleen Woodward, 'May Sarton and Fictions of Old Age' in Janet Todd, ed. *Gender and Literary Voice*, pp. 108-27. New York, Holmes & Meier, 1980; Anne Wyatt-Brown, 'Another Model of the Aging Writer: Sarton's Politics of Old Age', in Anne Wyatt-Brown and Janice Rossen, eds, *Aging and Gender in Literature: Studies in Creativity*, Charlottesville and London, University Press of Virginia, 1993, pp. 49–60; Barbara Frey Waxman, *To Live in the Center of the Moment: Literary Autobiographies of Aging*, Charlottesville and London, University Press of Virginia, 1997; and Henneberg, *The Creative Crone*.

9   May Sarton, interview by Janet Todd, in Janet Todd, ed., *Women Writers Talk*, New York, Homes and Meier, 1983, p. 14.

10 May Sarton, *Collected Poems: 1930–1993*, New York, Norton, 1993, p. 369.

11 Henneberg, *The Creative Crone*, p. 36.

12 May Sarton, *Plant Dreaming Deep*, New York, Norton, 1968, p. 183.

13 May Sarton, *At Seventy*, New York, Norton, 1993, pp. 9–10, 37, 217–18.

14 Heilbrun, *The Last Gift of Time*, pp. 75–6.

15 Sarton, *Plant Dreaming Deep*, p. 183.

16 Sarton, *Journal of a Solitude*, p. 13.

17 *World of Light: A Portrait of May Sarton*, documentary film, dir. Marita Simpson and Martha Wheelock, New York, Ishtar Films, 1979.

18 Alix Kates Shulman, *Drinking the Rain: A Memoir*, London, Bloomsbury, 1995.

19 May Sarton, *At Eighty-Two*, London, The Women's Press, 1996, pp. 41, 84.

20 Sheila Rowbotham, *Women's Consciousness; Man's World*, Harmondsworth, Penguin, 1973. For a reassessment of these arguments see Segal, *Making Trouble*.

21 Michèle Barrett and Mary McIntosh, *The Anti-Social Family*, London, Verso, 1982, p. 80.

22 Robyn Stone et al., 'Caregivers of the Frail Elderly: A National Profile', *The Gerontologist* 27: 5 (1987), pp. 616–26; Martha Bruce et al., 'Major Depression in Elderly Home Health Care Patients', *American Journal of Psychiatry* 159 (2002), pp. 1367–74.

23 Alix Kates Shulman, *Burning Questions*, New York, Knopf, 1978.

24 See Alix Kates Shulman, 'A Marriage Disagreement, or Marriage by Other Means', in Rachel Blau DuPlessis and Ann Snitow, eds, *The Feminist Memoir Project: Voices from Women's Liberation*, New Brunswick, Rutgers University Press, 2007, pp. 284–303; Alix Kates Shulman, *To Love What Is: A Marriage Transformed*, New York, Farrar, Straus & Giroux, 2008.

25 Shulman, *To Love What Is*, p. 157. Further page references are given in the text.

26 Alix Kates Shulman, 'Caring for an Ill Spouse, and for Other Caregivers', *New York Times*, 9 May 2011.

27 John Bayley, *Iris: A Memoir of Iris Murdoch*, London, Harper Collins, 1999, p. 62.

28 Genelle Weule, 'Male Carers Need Care Too', *The Pulse*, 11 February 2010.

29 Elizabeth Bishop, 'One Art', in *Elizabeth Bishop: Poems, Prose, and Letters*, New York, Library of America, 2008, p.166.

30 Jane Rule, *Memory Board*, New York, Naiad Press, 1987, p. 37. Further page references are given in the text.

31 Elinor Fuchs, *Making an Exit: A Mother-Daughter Drama with Machine Tools, Alzheimer's, and Laughter*, Waterville, ME, Thorndike Press, 2005, p. 283.

32   Ibid., pp. 283, 285.

33   Judith Levine, *Do You Remember Me?: A Father, A Daughter and a Search for Self*, Waterville, ME, Thorndike Press, 2004, p. 195. Further page references given in the text.

34   David Rothschild, 'The Practical Value of Research in the Psychoses of Later Life', *Diseases of the Nervous System* 8 (1947), pp. 125–8; Tom Kitwood, *Dementia Reconsidered: The Person Comes First*, Buckingham, Open University Press, 1997.

35   Joanne Koenig Coste, *Learning to Speak Alzheimer's: A Groundbreaking Approach for Everyone Dealing with the Disease*, New York, Mariner Books, 2004.

36   Andrea Gillies, *Keeper: A Book About Memory, Identity, Isolation, Wordsworth and Cake*, London, Short Books, 2010, pp. 289–90.

37   Ibid., p. 357.

38   Ruth Ray, *Endnotes*, New York, Columbia University Press, 2008. Further page references given in the text.

39   Margaret Gullette, 'Leaping Across the Abysses of Ageism', *Journal of Aging, Humanities, and the Arts* 3: 4 (2009), p. 305.

40   Ibid., p. 307.

41   Eve Sedgwick, *A Dialogue on Love*, New York, Beacon, 2000, p. 175.

42   Eve Sedgwick, *Touching Feeling*, Durham, NC, Duke University Press, 2003, p. 24–5.

43   Ibid., p. 24

44   Doty, *Dog Years*, pp. 3, 214–15.

45   Donna Haraway, *Companion Species Manifesto: Dogs, People and Significant Otherness*, Chicago, IL, University of Chicago Press, 2003 p. 16.

46   Angela Carter, *Wise Children*, London, Chatto & Windus, 1991, p. 232.

47   Martin Amis, quoted in Caroline Davies, 'Martin Amis in New Row Over "Euthanasia Booths"', *Guardian*, 24 January 2010.

48   Quentin Crisp, *The Naked Civil Servant*, London, Flamingo, 1968, p. 211.

49 Philip Roth, *Patrimony: A True Story*, New York: Simon & Schuster, 1991, p. 99–100. Further page references given in the text.

50 Roth, *Everyman*, pp. 160, 128–9.

51 Richard Adelman, 'John Updike Packing', *Journal of Aging, Humanities, and the Arts* 4 (2010), p. 68.

52 Philip Larkin, 'The Old Fools', available at www.poetry connection.net.

53 John Updike, *Self-Consciousness*, New York, Alfred A. Knopf, 1989, p. 238.

54 John Updike, 'The Full Glass', in *My Father's Tears and Other Stories*, London, Penguin, 2009, p. 276.

55 Ibid., p. 281.

56 Suburban adultery is one of the main themes of Updike's famous 'Rabbit' series, beginning with *Rabbit, Run*, New York, Knopf, 1960.

57 Updike, 'The Full Glass', pp. 291–2.

58 John Updike, *Endpoint and Other Poems*, New York, Alfred A. Knopf, 2009, p. 24. Further page references are given in the text.

59 Updike, *Self-Consciousness*, p. 211.

60 Updike, 'The Accelerating Expansion of the Universe', in *My Father's Tears*, p.148.

61 Updike, 'Free', in ibid, p.36.

62 Updike, 'The Full Glass', p.283.

63 Updike, *Self-Consciousness*, p. 217.

64 Beauvoir, *The Coming of Age*, p. 540.

65 Ibid., p. 542.

66 Julian Barnes, *Nothing To Be Frightened Of*, London, Vintage Books, p. 23. Further page references given in text.

67 Quoted by D. J. Taylor, reviewing *Pulse* by Julian Barnes, *Financial Times*, 23 December 2010.

68 See Sigmund Freud, 'The Ego and the Id', in Vol. 19 of *The Standard Edition of the Complete Psychological Works of Sigmund Freud*.

69   Julian Barnes, 'Knowing French', in *The Lemon Table*, London, Cape, 2004, p. 151.
70   Julian Barnes, 'Marriage Lines', in *Pulse*, London, Jonathan Cape, 2011, p. 120.
71   Julian Barnes, *Staring at the Sun*, London, Cape, 1986, Further page references are given in the text.
72   Stan Smith, *The Cambridge Companion to W. H. Auden*, Cambridge, Cambridge University Press, 2004, p. 235.
73   André Gorz, *Letter to D: A Love Story*, trans. Julie Rose, Cambridge, Polity Press, 2009, p. 105–6.
74   Kenneth Vail et al., 'When Death is Good for Life: Considering the Positive Trajectories of Terror Management', *Personality and Social Psychology Review*, 16:4 (2012), pp. 304–29.

Chapter 5. Flags of Resistance

1   Sarton, *As We Are Now*, p. 17.
2   Margaret Cruickshank provides just such a description of old age in giving an account on the back cover of her collection, *Fierce with Reality*.
3   See www.songfacts.com.
4   Christopher Bollas, *Cracking Up: The Work of Unconscious Experience*, London, Routledge, 1995, p. 119.
5   Thomas von Zglinicki, ed., *Aging at the Molecular Level*, New York, Springer, 2003.
6   Mike Featherstone, 'The Body in Consumer Culture', in Mike Featherstone, Mike Hepworth and Bryan Turner, eds, *The Body: Social Process and Cultural Theory*, London, Sage, 1991, p. 183.
7   Andrew Blaikie, *Ageing and Popular Culture*, Cambridge, Cambridge University Press, 1999, pp. 73–4.
8   Hanif Kureishi, 'The Body', in *The Body*, London, Faber and Faber, 2002, p. 29.

9   Fiona Macrae, 'The Forever Young Drug: Scientists make sick and ageing cells healthy again', *Daily Mail*, 30 June 2011.

10 Fiona Macrae, 'Forever Young: The pill that will keep you youthful by preventing the ills of old age', *Daily Mail*, 11 June 2011.

11 Catherine Mayer, *Amortality: The Pleasures and Perils of Living Agelessly*, London, Vermilion, 2011, p. 6. Further page references are given in the text.

12 Sigmund Freud, *Jokes and Their Relation to the Unconscious*, trans. James Strachey, Harmondsworth, Penguin, 1991, p. 135.

13 See Keith Cushman, '*Letters to Felice* by Franz Kafka', *Chicago Review* 26: 3 (1974), p. 188.

14 Sara Maitland, *A Book of Silence*, London, Granta, 2008, p. 286.

15 Ruth Ray, *Endnotes: An Intimate Look at the End of Life*, New York, Columbia University Press, p. 115.

16 Sedgwick, *Touching Feeling*, p. 160.

17 Peter Osborne, *The Politics of Time: Modernity and Avant-Garde*, London, Verso, 1995, p. 137.

18 Ibid., p. 104.

19 See, for instance, Douwe Draaisma, *Why Life Speeds Up As You Get Older: How Memory Shapes our Past*, Cambridge, Cambridge University Press, 2006.

20 World Health Organisation, *Gender in Mental Health Research*, Geneva, WHO, 2004; Office of National Statistics, *Mental Health of Older People*, London, The Stationery Office, 2003.

21 Heather Lacey, Dylan Smith and Peter Ubel, 'Hope I Die Before I Get Old: Mispredicting happiness across the adult lifespan', *Journal of Happiness Studies* 7: 2 (2006), pp. 167–82; Blanchflower and Oswald, 'Is Well-Being U-Shaped over the Life Cycle?', *Social Science and Medicine*; Arthur Stone et al., 'A Snapshot of the Age Distribution of Psychological Well-being in the United States', June 2010, Research Paper available at www.princeton.edu.

22 Denise Riley, ' "What I Want Back Is What I Was": Consolations

Retrospect', in *Impersonal Passion: Language as Affect*, Durham, NC, Duke University Press, 2005, p. 30.

23 Ibid.

24 Lessing, *Under My Skin*, p. 205.

25 Ruth Fainlight, 'Friends' Photos', in *New and Collected Poems*, London, Bloodaxe Books, 2010, p. 380.

26 Penelope Lively, *Spiderweb*, London, Penguin, 1999, p. 85.

27 William Shakespeare, Sonnet 63, quoted by Denise Riley, ' "What I Want Back" ', p. 36.

28 Ruth Fainlight, 'The Wedding Chapel', in *New and Collected Poems*, p. 33.

29 Penelope Lively, 'Party', in *Singing in Tune with Time: Stories and Poems about Ageing*, Elizabeth Cairns, ed., London, Virago, 1993, p. 14.

30 Tove Jansson, *The Summer Book*, trans. Thomas Teal, London, Sort Of Books, 2003, Foreword by Esther Freud.

31 Joy Goodfellow and Joyce Laverty, *Grandcaring: Insights into Grandparents' Experiences as Regular Child Care Providers*, Canberra: Early Childhood Australia, 2003; Lihda Nicholson Grinstead et al., 'Review of Research on the Health of Caregiving Grandparents', *Journal of Advanced Nursing* 44:3 (2003), pp. 318–26; Gay Ochiltree, *Grandparents, Grandchildren and the Generation in Between*, Victoria, Australian Council Educational Research, 2006.

32 'Grandparents "Exploited" over Childcare', BBC News, 28 April 1999, available at www.news.bbc.co.uk.

33 Epictetus, quoted in Simon Critchley, *The Book of Dead Philosophers*, London, Verso, p. 71.

34 Marcus Aurelius, quoted in ibid., p. 73.

35 Rosalind Belben, *Dreaming of Dead People*, London, Serpent's Tail, 1979, pp. 7–9 (italics in the original text). Further page references are given in the text.

36 Elaine Feinstein, 'Long Life', in *Cities*, Manchester, Carcanet Press, 2010, p. 57.

37   Anne Hunsaker Hawkins, *Reconstructing Illness: Studies in Pathography*, West Lafayette, IN, Purdue University Press, 1993.

38   Elaine Feinstein, 'Unsent Email', in *Talking to the Dead*, Manchester, Carcanet Press, 2007, p. 15.

39   Feinstein, 'A Visit', in ibid., p. 12.

40   Feinstein, 'Beds', in ibid., p. 14.

41   Feinstein, 'Winter', in ibid., p. 9.

42   Feinstein, 'A Match', in ibid., p. 23.

43   Feinstein, 'A Pebble on Your Grave', in ibid., p. 27.

44   Sigmund Freud, 'Mourning and Melancholia', in Vol. 14 of *The Standard Edition of the Complete Psychological Works of Sigmund Freud*, p. 253. Further page references are given in the text.

45   C. S. Lewis, *A Grief Observed*, London, Faber and Faber, p. 18. Further page references are given in the text.

46   Nicolas Abrahams and Maria Torok, for example, saw mourning and melancholia as always intermixed, insisting plausibly that the internalization of the lost other in the work of mourning is never abandoned. Instead they distinguish two forms of internalization: 'introjection', which is enduring but closer to Freud's normal work of mourning; and 'incorporation', which resembles Freud's account of the 'internalization' in melancholia, in that it involves a form of identification that cannot be worked through because it accompanies a type of denial of the loss of the other, through a secret 'encryption' that remains alive in the body. See Nicolas Abrahams and Maria Torok, *The Shell and the Kernel: Renewals of Psychoanalysis*, Vol. 1, trans. Nicholas Rand, Chicago, University of Chicago Press, 1994, p. 129.

47   Freud, 'The Ego and the Id', p. 53.

48   Darian Leader, *The New Black: Mourning, Melancholia and Depression*, London, Penguin, 2009, p. 2.

49   Sara Ahmed, 'The Happiness Turn', *New Formations* 63 (2007–8), p. 9; see also Sara Ahmed, *The Promise of Happiness*, Durham, NC, Duke University Press, 2010.

50   Richard Layard, *Happiness: Lessons from a New Science*, London, Penguin, 2005.

51   Philippe Ariès, *Western Attitudes Toward Death: From the Middle Ages to the Present*, Baltimore, Johns Hopkins University Press, 1974, p. 100.

52   Stephen Frosh, *Feelings*, London, Routledge, pp. 46–56.

53   Ibid., p. 56.

54   Leader, *The New Black*, p. 6.

55   Mark Doty, *Heaven's Coast*, London, Jonathan Cape, 1996, p. ix.

56   Judith Butler, *Undoing Gender*, London, Routledge, 2004, p. 19.

57   Roland Barthes, *Mourning Diary*, trans. Richard Howard, New York, Hill and Wang, 2010, p. 216. Further page references are given in the text.

58   Roland Barthes, *Camera Lucida: Reflections on Photography*, New York, Farrar, Straus and Giroux, 1981.

59   Joan Didion, *The Year of Magical Thinking*, New York, Harper Perennial, 2006, p. 33. Further page references are given in the text.

60   Joyce Carol Oates, *A Widow's Story: A Memoir*, London, Fourth Estate, 2011, p. 88.

61   Ibid., p. 416.

62   Meghan O'Rourke, *The Long Goodbye: A Memoir*, London, Virago, 2011, p. 13. Further page references are given in the text.

63   Adam Phillips, 'Coming to Grief', in *Promises, Promises: Essays on Literature and Psychoanalysis*, London, Faber and Faber, 2002, p. 257.

64   Phillips, 'Time Pieces', p. 105.

65   Frosh, *Feelings*, p. 5.

66   Doty, *Dog Years*, p. 197.

67   Doty, *Heaven's Coast*, p. ix.

68   Colm Tóibín, 'One Minus One', *The Empty Family*, London, Penguin, 2010, p. 1. Further page references are given in the text.

69   Tóibín, 'The Empty Family', in ibid., p. 35.

70 Walter Benjamin, 'Theses on the Philosophy of History' (1940), in Richard Kearney and Maria Rainwater, eds, *The Continental Philosophy Reader*, London, Routledge, 1996, pp. 215–23.

71 Patricia Meyer Spacks, *Gossip*, New York: Knopf, 1985.

72 Carolyn Heilbrun, *Writing a Woman's Life*, New York, Ballantine Books, 1989, p. 131.

73 See, for instance, Margaret Atwood, *Second Works: Selected Critical Prose*, Toronto, House of Anansi Press, 1982, p. 254.

74 Kate Waldman, 'Adrienne Rich on "Tonight No Poetry Will Serve"', *The Paris Review*, 2 March 2011.

75 Ruth Prince, 'The Possibilities of an Engaged Art: An Interview with Adrienne Rich', *Radcliffe Quarterly* (Fall 1998).

76 Waldman, 'Adrienne Rich on "Tonight No Poetry Will Serve"'.

77 See especially, Rich, 'And Now', *Dark Fields of the Republic*, p. 31.

78 Adrienne Rich interviewed by Michael Klein, 'A Rich Life: Adrienne Rich on Poetry, Politics, and Personal Revelation', *Boston Phoenix*, June 1999, available at www.bostonphoenix. com

79 Adrienne Rich, *Arts of the Possible*, New York and London, Norton, 2001, p. 2.

80 Adrienne Rich, 'Tendril', *The School Among the Ruins: Poems 2000-2004*, New York, Norton, 2006, p.110.

81 Waldman, 'Adrienne Rich on "Tonight No Poetry Will Serve"'.

82 Adrienne Rich, excerpt from *Midnight Salvage: Poems 1995–1998*, New York and London, Norton, 1999, pp. 64–5.

83 Adrienne Rich, *Time's Power: Poems, 1985–1988*, New York and London, Norton, 1989, p. 46.

84 Rich, 'Turning', in ibid., p. 54.

85 Adrienne Rich, *Of Woman Born*, New York, Norton, 1976, p. 284.

86 Adrienne Rich, 'Contradictions: Tracking Poems', in *Your Native Land. Your Life*, New York, Norton, 1986.

87 Ibid., p. 111.

88 Henneberg, *The Creative Crone*, p. 126; Adrienne Rich, 'Collaborations', in *The School Among the Ruins: Poems, 2000–2004*, New York, Norton, 2004, p. 55.

89 Joanna Bourke, 'Pain and Poetics: Forty Years of Adrienne Rich', in *Virago is 40: A Celebration*, London, Virago, 2013 available at www.virago.co.uk/virago-ebook.

90 Hannah Arendt, 'The Pursuit of Happiness', *On Revolution*, New York, The Viking Press, 1963, Chapter 3.

91 Michael Klein, 'A Rich Life: Adrienne Rich on Poetry, Politics, and Personal Revelation', *Boston Phoenix*, June 1999, available at www.poets.org.

92 Adrienne Rich, 'Standing at the InterReal', *Real Change News*, 19 April 2001.

93 Adrienne Rich, quoted in Henneberg, *The Creative Crone*, p. 138.

94 Ibid., p. 139.

95 Carol Hanisch, 'The Personal Is Political', originally published in *Notes from the Second Year: Women's Liberation*, 1970, available at www.carolhanisch.org.

96 Carol Hanisch, 'Paying the Pied Piper: Did I Blow my Life?', in Blau DuPlessis and Snitow, eds, *The Feminist Memoir Project*, pp. 202, 204.

97 Ibid., p. 205.

98 Rosalind Fraad Baxandall, 'Catching the Fire', in Blau DuPlessis and Snitow, eds, *The Feminist Memoir Project*, pp. 223–4.

99 Rosalind Fraad Baxandall, 'The Populist Movement Reborn, At Last, In Occupy Wall Street', *On The Issues Magazine*, 14 October 2011, available at www.ontheissuesmagazine.com.

100 Polly Toynbee, 'In the City and Wall Street, Protest has Occupied the Mainstream', *Guardian*, 17 October 2011, p. 33.

101 Margaretta Jolly, 'Consenting Voices? Activist Life Stories and Complex Dissent', in *Life Writing*, in press.

102 Molly Andrews, *Lifetimes of Commitment*, Cambridge, Cambridge University Press, 1991, p. 1. Future page references are given in the text.

103 Grace Paley, 'How Come', collected in *Just as I Thought*, Farrar Straus & Giroux, 1998, p. 285.

104 Grace Paley, 'Two Ears, Three Lucks', in *Grace Paley: The Collected Works*, New York, Noonday Press, 1994, p. xi.

105 Ibid.

106 Judith Butler, 'Can One Lead a Good Life in a Bad Life?', paper delivered in Frankfurt, on accepting the Adorno Prize, 11 September 2012.

Chapter 6. *Affirming Survival*

1 David Cutler and David Wise, eds, *Health at Older Ages: The Causes and Consequences of Declining Disability Among the Elderly*, Chicago, University of Chicago Press, 2009.

2 See, for instance, on care in the UK, Denis Campbell and James Meikle, 'Half of NHS Hospitals Failing to Care for Elderly', *Guardian*, 13 October 2011.

3 Joan Bakewell, 'We Need a Commissioner for Older People', *Guardian*, 15 February 2012.

4 Yvonne Roberts, 'One Hundred Not Out: Resilience and Active Ageing', *Observer*, 20 February 2012.

5 Donna Bowater and Sarah Rainey, 'NHS Cost-cutting Drives Disproportionately Impacting on Older People', *Telegraph*, 9 January 2012.

6 Robyn Stone and Joshua Wiener, *Who Will Care for Us? Addressing the Long-Term Care Workforce Crisis*, Washington, The Urban Institute, 2001.

7 See, for instance, Charles Patmore, 'Morale and Quality of Life Among Frail Older Users of Community Care: Key issues

for success of community care', *Quality in Ageing* 3: 2 (2002), pp. 30–8; Alistair Hewison et al., 'Delivering Gold Standards in End-of-Life Care in Care Homes: A question of teamwork?', *Journal of Clinical Nursing* 18: 12 (2009), pp. 1756–65; José-Luis Fernandez and Julien Forder, 'Equity, Efficiency, and Financial Risk of Alternative Arrangements for Funding Long-Term Care Systems in an Ageing Society', *Oxford Review of Economic Policy* 26: 4 (2011), pp. 713–33.

8 Adam Smith, Fran Wasoff and Lynn Jamieson, *Solo Living Across the Adult Lifecourse*, Edinburgh, Centre for Research on Families and Relationships, 2005, available at www.crfr.ac.uk.

9 Harriet Young and Emily Grundy, *Living Arrangements, Health and Well-being: A European Perspective*, available at www.eurekalert.org.

10 Elaine Eshbaugh, 'Perceptions of Living Alone Among Older Adult Women', *Journal of Community Health Nursing* 25: 3 (2008), pp. 125–37.

11 S. Roseneil, 'On Not Living with a Partner: Unpicking coupledom and cohabitation', *Sociological Research Online* 11: 3 (2006); Simon Duncan and Miranda Phillips, 'People Who Live Apart Together (LATs) – How different are they?', *The Sociological Review* 58: 1 (2010), pp. 112–34.

12 John Haskey and Jane Lewis, 'Living-Apart-Together in Britain: Context and meaning', *International Journal of Law in Context* 2:1 (2006), pp. 37–48.

13 Lauren Berlant, *Cruel Optimism*, Durham, NC, Duke University Press, 2011.

14 'Precarity' as a product of neo-liberal times has been explored by many, including the economist Guy Standing, *The Precariat: The New Dangerous Class*, London, Bloomsbury, 2011; and Judith Butler, *Precarious Life: The Powers of Mourning and Violence*, London and New York, Verso, 2004.

15 Giles Fraser, 'This Newspaper is Muddling my Mind', *Guardian*, G2, 30 January 2012, p. 2.

16 See Anne Tomiche, 'Derrida's Legacy for Comparative Literature' *Comparative Critical Studies*, 7:2-3 (2010), pp. 335-346.

17 Derrida quoted in Critchley, *The Book of Dead Philosophers*, p. 274.

18 Judith Butler, 'Affirm the Survival', *Radical Philosophy* 129 (2005), p. 25.

19 Frosh, *Feelings*, p. 4.

20 Jonathan Dollimore, 'On Leaving', in John Schad and Oliver Tearle, eds, *Crrritic!*, Brighton, Sussex University Press, 2011, p. 205.

21 Hannah Arendt, *The Human Condition* (1958), Chicago, University of Chicago Press, 1998, p. 50.

22 Daniel Miller, *The Comfort of Things*, Cambridge, Polity Press, 2008.

23 John Berger, *Here is Where we Meet*, London, Bloomsbury, 2005, p. 6. Further page references are given in the text.

24 John Berger, 'The Time We Live', *OpenDemocracy.net*, 23 August 2011.

25 John Berger, *The Success and Failure of Picasso*, Harmondsworth, Penguin, 1965, p.128

26 'Cosmic Queen: Yayoi Kusama is painting more intensely than ever, as can be seen in a major travelling retrospective of six decades of her work', *Economist*, 4 February 2012.

27 Rhiannon Starr, 'Louise Bourgeois: The return of the repressed at London's Freud Museum', *Culture 24*, 12 March 2012.

28 William Trevor, *Cheating at Canasta*, New York, Viking, 2007; Alice Munro, *Dear Life*, New York, Knopf, 2012

29 Chinua Achebe, There Was a Country: A Personal History of Biafra, London, Allen Lane, 2012; Toni Morrison, *Home*, London, Chatto & Windus, 2012.

30 Daniel Miller, *Tales from Facebook*, Cambridge, Polity Press, 2011, p. 28.

31 Ibid., pp. 286–7.

32 Lynne Segal, ed., *What Is to Be Done about the Family?*, Harmondsworth, Penguin, 1983, p. 230.

33 Lynne Segal, 'Making Families from Whatever Comes to Hand', in Gil McNeil, *Soul Providers: Writings by Single Parents*, London, Virago, 1994.

34 Carter, *Wise Children*, p. 35.

35 Liz Fraser, 'Helping to Understand the Modern British Family', Centre for the Modern Family/Scottish Widows, 2011, available at www.centreformodernfamily.com.

36 See Lynne Segal, *Making Trouble*, Chapter 3, for an extended version of my own and others' experience of collective living in the 1970s; see also Michèle Roberts, *Paper Houses: A Memoir of the '70s and Beyond*, London, Virago, 2007.

37 Matt Cook, *Queer Domesticities: Homosexuality and Home Life in Twentieth-Century London*, London, Palgrave, forthcoming.

38 Editing one of the earlier feminist collections on gender and ageism from the USA, Evelyn Rosenthal summed up the essays she had assembled by suggesting they 'contribute to a picture of aging women as unproductive, dependent, rigid, weak, defenceless, morally old-fashioned, timid, ugly, senile and lonely' (*Women, Aging and Ageism*, London, Routledge, 1990, p. 6). Today the template seems even more cruel and absurd when surveying the lives of older women, but the skewed statistics on women living alone suggest that too little has shifted in cultural perceptions of older women.

39 Sharon Olds, 'Known To Be Left', *Stag's Leap*, London, Jonathan Cape, 2012.

40 Office for National Statistics, *Families and Households in the UK, 2001–2010*, April 2011, available at www.ons.gov.uk.

41 Christina Victor, 'The Prevalence of, and Risk Factors for, Loneliness in Later Life: A survey of older people in Great Britain', *Ageing and Society* 25 (2005), pp. 357–75.

42 Taken from Nancy Miller, 'Reviewing Eve …', in Stephen Barber and David Clark, eds, *Regarding Sedgwick: Essays*

on Queer Culture and Critical Theory, New York, London, Routledge, 2000, p. 219.

43 Ibid.

44 Judith Halberstam, *The Queer Art of Failure*, Durham, NC, Duke University Press, 2011, p. 187.

45 Samuel Beckett, *Westward Ho*, New York, Grove Press, p. 7.

46 Halberstam, *The Queer Art of Failure*, pp. 3, 87, 96, 110.

47 Ibid., p. 137.

48 See, for instance, Ginette Vincendeau, *Brigitte Bardot*, London, Palgrave Macmillan, 2013.

49 Malvina Reynolds, 'I Don't Mind Failing in this World', available at www.youtube.com.

50 See www.beyondmarriage.org.

51 See, for one, Lisa Duggan, 'Beyond Same-Sex Marriage', *Studies in Gender and Sexuality* 9: 2 (2008), pp. 155–8.

52 Hollibaugh, '2, 4, 6, 8: Who Says that Your Grandmother's Straight?: Enhancing the Lives of LGBTQ Older Adults in the Twenty-First Century', *The Scholar and Feminist Online*, 10.1–10.2, Fall 2011/Spring 2012.

53 Oscar Moore, *A Matter of Life and Death*, London, Penguin, 1994; Jonathan Dollimore, *Death, Desire and Loss in Western Culture*, London, Penguin, 1994.

54 From Cook, *Queer Domesticities*, in press.

55 Michael Cobb, 'Lonely', in Janet Halley and Andrew Parker, eds, *After Sex? Writing Since Queer Theory*, South Atlantic Quarterly 106: 3 (2007), p. 445.

56 Ibid., p. 449.

57 Michael Cobb, *Singles*, New York and London, New York University Press, p. 53. Further pages references are given in the text.

58 'I Am Married But Lonely. Marriage = Loneliness = Divorce?' available from www.experienceproject.com

59 Germaine Greer, *The Female Eunuch* (1970), New York, Farrar, Straus & Giroux, 2002, p. 274.

60 Vivian Gornick, *Approaching Eye Level*, Boston, Beacon Press, 1996, p. 140.

61 As my friend Sarah Benton points out, etymologically, it is very interesting to note how sometime during the industrial revolution the word 'one' commuted into lone and alone – all neutral – and then produced the adjective 'lonely' which now has *only* a miserable meaning.

62 Cobb, 'Lonely', p. 452, italics in the original.

63 Ibid., p. 213.

64 Sigmund Freud, 'Moses and Monotheism: Three Essays', in Vol. 23 of *The Standard Edition of the Complete Psychological Works of Sigmund Freud*, p. 130.

65 John Burnside, 'Alone', *London Review of Books*, 9 February 2012, p. 24.

66 Cobb, *Singles*, p. ix.

67 Roland Barthes, *A Lover's Discourse*, London, Penguin, p. 67.

68 Jeanette Winterson, 'The Money has Gone, so Make Love our Alternative Currency', *Guardian*, 14 February 2012, p. 1.

69 Alain Badiou, *In Praise of Love*, trans. Nicolas Truong, London, Serpent's Tail, 2012, p. 29.

70 Judith Butler, 'On Doubting Love', in James Harmon, ed., *Take My Advice: Letters to the Next Generation*, New York, Simon and Schuster, 2002, p. 65.

71 Susan Jacoby, *Never Say Die: The Myth and Marketing of the New Old Age*, New York, Pantheon Books, 2011, p. 137.

72 Bob Dylan, 'Like a Rolling Stone', available at www.lyricsfreak.com.

73 Michael Fine and Caroline Glendinning, 'Dependence, Independence or Inter-dependence? Revisiting the concepts of "care" and "dependency"', *Ageing and Society* 25 (2005), pp. 601–21.

74 Quoted in Paul Cloke, 'Rural Poverty and the Welfare State: A discursive transformation in Britain and the USA', *Environment and Planning A* 27: 6 (1995), p. 1001.

75 William Ian Miller, *Losing It*, New Haven and London, Yale University Press, 2011, p. 3.

76 Ibid., pp. 34–6.

77 Toni Calasanti, 'A Feminist Confronts Ageism', *Journal of Aging Studies* 22: 2 (2008), pp. 152–3.

78 Molly Andrews, 'The Seductiveness of Agelessness', *Ageing and Society* 19 (1999), p. 317.

79 Stanley Kunitz, 'The Layers', in *The Poems of Stanley Kunitz: 1928–1978*, Boston, Little Brown and Co., 1979, p. 36.

80 Stanley Kunitz, quoted in 'Au Revoir, Stanley Kunitz', *Living Poetry*, May 19, 2006, available at www.livingpoetry.blogspot.co.uk/2006/05/au-revoir-stanley-kunitz.html.

81 Kunitz, 'I Dreamed That I Was Old', *The Poems of Stanley Kunitz: 1928-1978*, p.220.

82 Carlos Fuentes, 'Eternal Father', in *Happy Families*, London, Bloomsbury, 2008, p. 331.

83 Helen Nugent, 'Suicide on the Rise Among Older Men', *Guardian*, 15 July 2012.

84 Jessica Allen, *Older People and Wellbeing*, Institute for Public Policy Research, July 2008, available at www.vhscotland.org.uk.

85 Alice Walker, 'What Do I Get For Getting Old? A Picture Story for the Curious!' available at www.alicewalkersgarden.com. This poem was sent to me by one of my students, Marai Larasi.

86 Alice Walker, 'Her Sweet Jerome', *In Love and Trouble: Stories of Black Women*, New York, Harcourt, 1973, p. 34.

87 Alice Walker, 'Why I'm Joining the Freedom Flotilla to Gaza', *Guardian*, 25 June 2011.

88 Freud and Andreas-Salomé, *Letters*, pp. 165–6.

89 Ibid., p. 165.

90 See, for instance, Angela Livingstone, *Lou Andreas Salomé: Her Life and Work*, London, Gordon Fraser, 1984; Julia Vickers, *Lou von Salomé: A Biography of the Woman Who Inspired Freud, Nietzsche and Rilke*, Jefferson, McFarland, 2008.

91 Freud and Andreas-Salomé, *Letters*, p. 165.

92 Joan Bakewell, 'At 70', *Guardian*, 3 October 2003.

93 *The Oldie, Cartoons, reviews and sanctuary from the celebrity obsessed media and culture!*, available at www.the.oldie.magazine.co.uk.

94 Sally Chivers, *The Silvering Screen: Old Age and Disability in Cinema*, Toronto, University of Toronto Press, 2011, p. 8.

95 Ibid., p. 62.

96 Beauvoir, *The Coming of Age*, p. 601.

97 Giorgio Agamben, *The Time That Remains: A Commentary on the Letter to the Romans*, trans. Patricia Dailey, Stanford, Stanford University Press, 2005.

98 Giorgio Agamben, *Means Without Ends: Notes on Politics*, trans. Cesare Casarino and Vincenzo Binetti, Minneapolis, University of Minnesota Press, 2000, p. 4.

99 John Berger, *Bento's Sketchbook*, London, Verso, 2011, pp. 80, 79, emphasis in original.

100 Denise Riley, *Time Lived, Without Its Flow*, Capsule Editions, London, 2012, p. 45–46, p. 22, p. 48.

Index

319

On the Typeface

Out of Time is set in Monotype Fournier, a typeface based on the designs of the eighteenth-century printer and typefounder Pierre Simon Fournier. He in turn was influenced by the constructed type designs of the Romain du Roi, commissioned by Louis XIV in 1692, which eschewed the calligraphic influence of prior type-faces in favour of scientific precision and adherence to a grid.

With its vertical axis, pronounced contrast and unbracketed serifs, the Fournier face is an archetype of the 'transitional' style in the evolution of Latin printing types – situated between the 'old style' fonts such as Bembo and Garamond and the 'modern' faces of Bodoni and Didot. Other distinguishing features include the proportionally low height of the capitals and the lowercase 'f', with its tapered and declining crossbar.

The italics, which were designed independently, have an exaggerated slope with sharp terminals that retain the squared serifs in the descenders.

The Fournier design was commissioned as part of the Monotype Corporation's type revival programme under the supervision of Stanley Morison in the 1920s. Two designs were cut based on the 'St Augustin Ordinaire' design shown in Fournier's *Manuel Typographique*. In Morison's absence, the wrong design was approved, resulting in the typeface now known as Fournier.